Cities of Belgium – A Travel Guide of Art and History

A comprehensive guide to the historic cathedrals, churches and art galleries of Bruges, Ghent, Brussels and Antwerp

Maxime Jensens

© Maxime Jansens 2016

All rights reserved. No text of this publication may be reproduced, distributed, or transmitted in any form or by any means, including photocopying, recording, or other electronic or mechanical methods, without the prior written permission of the publisher, except in the case of brief quotations embodied in critical reviews and certain other non-commercial uses permitted by copyright law.

This book features the work of several independent, private photographers and artists. Where appropriate, they have been attributed for their work. Images used under any Creative Commons and GNU free license remain under their respective licenses. No copyright or trademark infringement is intended by the imagery displayed within this book.

Acknowledgments

I would chiefly like to thank my tutor and friend Pierre Durand for fostering my interest and knowledge in the representation of history in civic buildings. The many tour guides, tourism bureau clerks, and individuals I have encountered during my tours of the country I am proud to call my home also deserve due credit for their illuminating advice. Finally, I appreciate the help rendered by administrators of both Antwerp and Brussels respective fine art museums, whose clarifications were invaluable in the completion of this guide.

About the Author

Growing up in Brussels, Maxime Jensens developed a keen interest and sense of the historic legacies which underpin the towns of his nation. As a child, he beheld the many stunning achievements in architecture and art, whether they be on the parts of institutions such as the Christian church or individually prolific artists, sculptors or architects. Noting how these beautiful attributes seldom fail to awe visitors with their uniqueness, Jensens ambitiously aimed to make a career from their depiction, accurately relaying of the past which so underpins his home nation.

Formerly a student of art history, Jensens today acts as a lecturer and blogger studying the old cities of both Belgium and France. Fluent in both French and English, his stated aim is to increase the awareness, appreciation and regard for his country's art. It is to this end that this guide was published, for the benefit of visitors eager to plunge into the cultural bulwarks Belgium has to offer.

Introduction

The object and plan of these city guides is somewhat different from that of any other guides presently available. They do not compete or clash with such existing works; they are rather intended to supplement than to supplant them. My purpose is not to direct the stranger through the streets and squares of a Flemish town towards the buildings or sights which he may desire to visit; still less is it my intention to give him practical information about hotels, taxi fares, trains, tramways, and other every-day visiting conveniences. For such details, the traveller must still have recourse to the trusty pages of other, more general and utilitarian guides.

My desire rather is to supply the tourist who wishes to use his travel as a means of culture with such historical and antiquarian information as will enable him to understand, and therefore enjoy the architecture, sculpture, painting, and minor arts of the towns he visits. In one word, it is my object to give the reader in a very compendious form the result of all those inquiries which have naturally suggested themselves to my own mind during thirty-five years of foreign travel, the solution of which has cost myself a good deal of research, thought, and labour, beyond the facts which I could find in the everyday tour guide handbooks.

For several years past I have devoted myself to collecting and arranging material for a set of books to embody the idea I had thus entertained. I earnestly hope they may meet a want on the part of tourists, especially Americans, who, so far as my experience goes, usually come to Europe with an honest and reverent desire to learn from the Old World whatever of value it has to teach them, and who are prepared to take an amount of pains in turning their trip to good account which is both rare and praiseworthy. For such readers I shall call attention at times to other sources of information.

Brussels - Saints Michel et Gudule cathedral spires - Image: Ally Crockford

This guide book will deal more particularly with the four Belgian Great Towns where heritage architecture, objects of art and other antiquities are numerous. In every one of them, the general plan pursued will be somewhat as follows. First will come the inquiry why a town ever gathered together at all at that particular spot—what induced the aggregation of human beings rather there than elsewhere. Next, we shall consider why that town grew to social or political importance and what the stages were by which it assumed its present shape. Thirdly, we shall ask why it gave rise to that higher form of handicraft which we know as Art, and towards what particular arts it especially gravitated. After that, we shall take in detail the various strata of its growth or development, examining the buildings and works of art which they contain in historical order, and, as far as possible, tracing the causes which led to their evolution. In particular, we shall lay stress upon the origin and meaning of each structure as an organic whole, and upon the allusions or symbols which its fabric embodies.

Royal Museum of Fine Arts - Main Hall

A single instance will show the method upon which I intend to proceed better than any amount of general description. A church, as a rule, is built over the body or relics of a particular saint, in whose special honour it was originally erected. That saint was usually one of great local importance at the moment of its erection, or was peculiarly implored against plague, foreign enemies, or some other pressing and dreaded misfortune. In dealing with such a church I endeavour to show what the circumstances were which led to its construction, and what memorials of these circumstances it still retains. In other cases it may derive its origin from some special monastic body—Benedictine, Dominican, Franciscan—and may therefore be full of the peculiar symbolism and historical allusion of the order who founded it. Wherever I have to deal with such a church, I try as far as possible to exhibit the effect which its origin had upon its architecture and decoration; to trace the image of the patron saint in sculpture or stained glass throughout the fabric; and to set forth the connection of the whole design with time and place, with order and purpose. In short, instead of looking upon monuments of the sort mainly as the product of this or that architect, I look upon them rather as material embodiments of the spirit of the age—crystallizations, as it were, in stone and bronze, in form and colour, of great popular enthusiasms.

By thus concentrating attention on what is essential and important in a town, I hope to give in a comparatively short space, though with inevitable conciseness, a fuller account than is usually given of the chief architectural and monumental works of the principal art-cities.

As regards the character of the information given, it will be mainly historical, antiquarian, and, above all, explanatory. I am not a connoisseur—an adept in the difficult modern science of distinguishing the handicraft of various masters, in painting or sculpture, by minute signs and delicate inferential processes. In such matters, I shall be well content to follow the lead of the most authoritative experts. Nor am I an art-critic—a student versed in the technique of the studios and the dialect of the modeling-room. In such matters, again, I shall attempt little more than to accept the general opinion of the most discriminative judges. What I aim at rather is to expound the history and meaning of each work—to put the intelligent reader in such a position that he may judge for himself of the aesthetic beauty and success of the object before him. To recognise the fact that this is a Perseus and Andromeda, that a St. Barbara enthroned, the other an obscure episode in the legend of St. Philip, is not art-criticism, but it is often an almost indispensable prelude to the formation of a right and sound judgment. We must know what the artist was trying to represent before we can feel sure what measure of success he has attained in his representation.

For the general study of Christian art, alike in architecture, sculpture, and painting, no treatises are more useful for the tourist to carry with him for constant reference than Mrs. Jameson's Sacred and Legendary Art, and Legends of the Madonna (London, Longmans). For works of Italian art, both in Italy and elsewhere, Kugler's Italian Schools of Painting is an invaluable vade-mecum. These books should be carried about by everybody everywhere. Other works of special and local importance will occasionally be noticed under each particular city, church, or museum.

I cannot venture to hope that handbooks containing such a mass of facts as these will be wholly free from errors and misstatements, above all in early editions. I can only beg those who may detect any such to point them out, without unnecessary harshness, to the author, care of the publisher, and if possible to assign reasons for any dissentient opinion.

Table of Contents

Acknowledgments 3
About the Author 4
Introduction 5
How to Use this Guidebook 13
Origins of the Belgian Towns 15
Order of the Tour 24

Bruges 26
Origins of Bruges 27
The Heart of Bruges 33
    Old St. John's Hospital 51
Walks through Bruges 69
    First Walk 69
    Second Walk 72
    Third Walk 74
    Fourth Walk 75
The Churches 77
    St. Salvator 77
    Church of Our Lady 86
    The Church of Saint Jacob / Sint-Jakobsberk 96

Ghent 112
Origins of Ghent 113
The Core of Ghent 119

- Saint Bavo's Cathedral 134
  - Lower Tier 144
  - Upper Tier 148
- The City and Outskirts of Ghent 155
  - Ghent Museum of Fine Arts 165

Brussels 170
- Origins of Brussels 171
- The Heart of Brussels 174
- Royal Museums of Fine Arts of Belgium 188
  - Room I - Hall of the Old Flemish Masters 191
  - Room II 213
  - Room III 221
  - Room IV 223
  - Room V 226
  - Room VI 229
  - Room VII 232
  - Room VIII 234
- Cathedral of St. Michael and St. Gudula 235
- The Upper Town and Churches 248
- Places of Interest near Brussels 267
  - Laeken 267
  - Leuven / Louvain 268

Antwerp 279
- The Origins of Antwerp 281

- Cathedral of Our Lady 288
- Royal Museum of Fine Arts - Antwerp 303
  - Room C - Hall of the Ancient Masters 308
  - Room A 322
  - Room B 325
  - Room D 327
  - Room E 329
  - Room F 329
  - Room H 330
  - Room I 332
  - Room J 340
  - Room G 341
  - Room K 343
- The Town of Antwerp 345
  - St. James Church 354
  - St. Paul's Church 361
- Historical Notes on Belgium 365

How to Use this Guidebook

As noted already, the guidance within this book does not profess to supply practical information in aid of transport, dining, accommodation, guided tours or general sightseeing, but rather is intended to enlighten the visitor about the old town and interesting items of culture, history and art said locale harbours. As such, it is best suited as a companion to a more general guidebook, enhancing and conferring depth in matters artistic and cultural.

You can happily read this book at leisure at home prior to your journey. The sections upon specific art galleries or cathedrals however are best read while you explore and view each respective building and its contents. Individual artworks and artifacts are described, while descriptions upon their creators also feature.

Portions relating to each principal objects of art should be quietly read and digested before a visit, and referred to again afterwards. The portion to be read on the spot is made as brief as possible. For eBook readers it is advised to read with a large font size so as to be easily read in the dim light of churches, chapels, and galleries. Those with editions in print may benefit from reasonably sized, 12 point fonts. Where objects are numbered, the numbers used are always those of the latest official catalogues.

Individual works of merit are distinguished by an asterisk (*); those of very exceptional interest and merit have two asterisks. Undistinguished art of little notability is omitted, so that the tourist may appreciate works of renown.

As for touring advice, you should little at a time, and see it thoroughly. Never attempt to "do" any place or any monument in a quick, whirlwind tour characterized by brief milling around. By following strictly the order in which objects are noticed in this book, you will gain a conception of the historical evolution of the town which you cannot obtain if you go about looking at churches and palaces haphazardly.

This book does not profess to be an exhaustive account of the art and architecture present in Belgian cities. Its focus is mainly on the ancient heritage art and architecture of the medieval, renaissance and baroque periods, which together span epochs between the 12th and 18th century. These fruitful centuries birthed much of the best and most beautiful Belgian art and architecture, the styles of which remain with ease the most associated with the country and each of its significant cities.

Clearer memories, enjoyment and appreciation of the architecture and art of Belgium's principle art galleries and churches is what this book intends to convey, in contrast to ordinary guides which lack focus and depth upon the important historical and cultural characteristics of the cities they focus upon. Where they merely brush over art of supreme importance, as if ticking boxes off a list – this book aims to interest the artistic tourist with due description and intensity.

In aid of this aim parts relating directly to the old town, galleries, church and cathedral interiors, this book acts as a walking tour. Concise descriptions and instructions are made, enlightening you as to when to stop and observe specific items of significance.

Origins of the Belgian Towns

The somewhat heterogeneous country which we now call Belgium formed part of Gaul under the Roman Empire. But though rich and commercial even then, it seems to have been relatively little Romanised; and in the beginning of the 5th century it was overrun by the Salic Franks, on their way towards Laon, Soissons, and Paris. When civilization began to creep northward again in the 9th century through the districts barbarised by the Teutonic invasion, it was the Frankish Charlemagne (Karl the Great) who introduced Roman arts afresh into the Upper and Lower Rhinelands.

The Rhine from Basle to Cologne was naturally the region most influenced by this new Roman revival; but as Charlemagne had his chief seat at Aix-la-Chapelle (Aachen), near the modern Belgian frontier, the western Frankish provinces were also included in the sphere of his improvements. When the kingdom of the Franks began to divide more or less definitely into the Empire and France, the Flemish region formed nominally part of the Neustrian and, later, of the French dominions. From a very early date, however, it was practically almost independent, and it became so even in name during its later stages. But Brabant (with Brussels) remained a portion of the Empire.

The Rhine constituted the great central waterway of mediæval Europe; the Flemish towns were its ports and its manufacturing centres. They filled in the 13th and 14th centuries much the same place that Liverpool, Glasgow, Manchester, and Birmingham fill in the 20th. Many causes contributed to this result. Flanders, half independent under its own Counts, occupied a middle position, geographically and politically, between France and the Empire; it was comparatively free from the disastrous wars which desolated both these countries, and in particular (see under Ghent) it largely escaped the long smouldering quarrel between French and English which so long retarded the development of the former. Its commercial towns, again, were not exposed on the open sea to the attacks of pirates or hostile fleets, but were safely ensconced in inland flats, reached by rivers or canals, almost inaccessible to maritime enemies. Similar conditions elsewhere early ensured peace and prosperity for Venice.

An ancient canal running through rural Belgium - Image: Arctic-Cycler

The canal system of Holland and Belgium began to be developed as early as the 12th century (at first for drainage), and was one leading cause of the commercial importance of the Flemish cities in the 14th. In so flat a country, locks are all but unnecessary. The two towns which earliest rose to greatness in the Belgian area were thus Bruges and Ghent; they possessed in the highest degree the combined advantages of easy access to the sea and comparative inland security. Bruges, in particular, was one of the chief stations of the Hanseatic League, which formed an essentially commercial alliance for the mutual protection of the northern trading centres. By the 14th century Bruges had thus become in the north what Venice was in the south, the capital of commerce. Trading companies from all the surrounding countries had their "factories" in the town, and every European king or prince of importance kept a resident minister accredited to the merchant Republic.

Some comprehension of the mercantile condition of Europe in general during the Middle Ages is necessary in order to understand the early importance and wealth of the Flemish cities. Southern Europe, and in particular Italy, was then still the seat of all higher civilization, more especially of the trade in manufactured articles and objects of luxury. Florence, Venice, and Genoa ranked as the polished and learned cities of the world. Further east, again, Constantinople still remained in the hands of the Greek emperors, or, during the Crusades, of their Latin rivals. A brisk trade existed viâ the Mediterranean between Europe and India or the nearer East. This double stream of traffic ran along two main routes—one, by the Rhine, from Lombardy and Rome; the other, by sea, from Venice, Genoa, Florence, Constantinople, the Levant, and India.

On the other hand, France was still but a half civilized country, with few manufactures and little external trade; while England was an exporter of raw produce, chiefly wool. The Hanseatic merchants of Cologne held the trade of London; those of Wisby and Lübeck governed that of the Baltic; Bruges, as head of the Hansa, was in close connection with all of these, as well as with

Hull, York, Novgorod, and Bergen. The position of the Flemish towns in the 14th century was thus not wholly unlike that of New York, Philadelphia, and Boston at the present day; they stood as intermediaries between the older civilized countries, like Italy or the Greek empire, and the newer producers of raw material, like England, North Germany, and the Baltic towns.

The Hunt of Maximilian tapestry

The local manufactures of Flanders consisted chiefly of woolen goods and linens; the imports included Italian luxuries, Spanish figs and raisins, Egyptian dates, Oriental silks, English wool, cattle, and metals, Rhenish wines, and Baltic furs, skins, and walrus tusks.

In the early 16th century, when navigation had assumed new conditions, and trade was largely diverted to the Atlantic, Antwerp, the port of the Schelde, superseded the towns on the inland network. As Venice sank, Antwerp rose.

The art that grew up in the Flemish cities during their epoch of continuous commercial development bears on its very face the visible impress of its mercantile origin. France is essentially a monarchical country, and it is centralized in Paris; everything in old French art is therefore regal and lordly. The Italian towns were oligarchies of nobles; so the principal buildings of Florence and Venice are the castles or palaces of the princely families, while their pictures represent the type of art that belongs in its nature to a cultivated aristocracy.

But in Flanders, everything is in essence commercial. The architecture consists mainly, not of private palaces, but of guilds, town halls, exchanges, belfries: the pictures are the portraits of solid and successful merchants, or the devotional works which a merchant donor presented to the patron saint of his town or business. They are almost overloaded with details of fur, brocade, jewelry, lace, gold, silver, polished brass, glasswork, Oriental carpets, and richly carved furniture. In order to understand Flemish art, therefore, it is necessary to bear in mind at every step that it is the art of a purely commercial people.

Another point which differentiates Flemish painting from the painting of Italy during the same period is the complete absence of any opportunity for the display of frescoes. In the Italian churches, where the walls serve largely for support, and the full southern light makes the size of the windows of less importance, great surfaces were left bare in the nave and aisles, or in the lower part of the choir, crying aloud for decoration at the hands of the fresco-painter. But in the northern Gothic, which aimed above all things at height and the soaring effect, and which almost annihilated the wall, by making its churches consist of rows of vast windows with intervening piers or buttresses, the opportunity for mural decoration occurred but seldom.

The climate also destroyed frescoes. Hence the works of pictorial art in Flemish buildings are almost confined to altar-pieces and votive tablets. Again, the great school of painting in early Italy (from Giotto to Perugino) was a school of fresco-painters; but in Flanders no high type of art arose till the discovery of oil-painting. Pictures were usually imported from the Rhine towns. Hence, pictorial art in the Low Countries seems to spring almost full-fledged, instead of being traceable through gradual stages of evolution as in Italy. Most of the best early paintings are small and highly finished; it was only at a comparatively late date, when Antwerp became the leading town, that Italian influence began to produce the larger and coarser canvases of Rubens and his followers.

Very early Flemish art greatly resembles the art of the School of Cologne. Only with Hubert and Jan van Eyck (about 1360-1440)

does the distinctively Flemish taste begin to show itself—the taste for delicate and minute workmanship, linked with a peculiar realistic idealism, more dainty than German work, more literal than Italian. It is an art that bases itself upon truth of imitation and perfection of finish: its chief æsthetic beauty is its jewel-like colour and its wealth of decorative adjuncts. The subsequent development of Flemish painting—the painting that pleased a clique of opulent commercial patrons—we shall trace in detail in the various cities.

Whoever wishes to gain a deeper insight into Flemish painting should take in his portmanteau Sir Martin Conway's "Early Flemish Artists," a brilliant and masterly work of the first importance, to which this Guide is deeply indebted.

The political history of the country during this flourishing period of the Middle Ages has also stamped itself, though somewhat less deeply, on the character of the towns and of the art evolved in them. The Counts of Flanders, originally mere lords of Bruges and its district, held their dominions of the Kings of France. Their territory included, not only Arras (at first the capital, now included in France) with Bruges, Ghent, Courtrai, Tournay, and Ypres, but also the towns and districts of Valenciennes, Lille, and St. Omer, which are now French. From the time of Baldwin VIII. (1191), however, Arras became a part of France, and Ghent was erected into the capital of Flanders. In the beginning of the 13th century, two women sovereigns ruled in succession; under them, and during the absence of the elective Counts on crusades, the towns rose to be practically burgher republics. Bruges, Ypres, Ghent, and Lille were said to possess each 40,000 looms; and though this is certainly a mediæval exaggeration, yet the Flemish cities at this epoch were at any rate the chief manufacturing and trading centres of northern Europe, while London was still a mere local emporium.

A statue of Jacob van Artevelde - Image: Demeester

In the 14th century, the cities acquired still greater freedom. The citizens had always claimed the right to elect their Count; and the people of Ghent now made treaties without him on their own account with Edward III. of England. To this age belongs the heroic period of the Van Arteveldes at Ghent, when the burghers became the real rulers of Flanders, as will be more fully described hereafter. In 1384 however, Count Louis III died, leaving an only daughter, who was married to Philip the Bold of Burgundy; and the wealthy Flemish towns thus passed under the sway of the powerful princes of Dijon. Brabant fell later by inheritance to Philip the Good. It was under the Burgundian dynasty, who often held their court at Ghent, that the arts of the Netherlands attained their first great development. Philip the Good (1419-1467) employed Jan van Eyck as his court painter; and during his reign or just after it the chief works of Flemish art were produced in Bruges, Ghent, Brussels, and Tournai.

Charles the Bold, the last Duke of Burgundy, left one daughter, Mary, who was married to Maximilian, afterwards Emperor. From that date forward the history of the Flemish towns is practically merged in that of the dynasty of Charles V., and finally becomes the story of an unwilling and ever justly rebellious Spanish province. The subsequent vicissitudes of Belgium as an Austrian appanage, a part of Holland, and an independent kingdom, belong to the domain of European history. For the visitor, it is the period of the Burgundian supremacy that really counts in the cities of Belgium.

Yet the one great point for the tourist to bear in mind is really this—that the art of the Flemish towns is essentially the art of a group of burgher communities. It is frankly commercial, neither royal nor aristocratic. In its beginnings it develops a strictly municipal architecture, with a school of painters who aimed at portraiture and sacred panel pictures. After the Reformation had destroyed sacred art in Holland, painting in that part of the Netherlands confined itself to portraits and to somewhat vulgar popular scenes: while in Belgium it was Italianised, or rather Titianised and Veronesed, by Rubens and his followers. But in its best days it was national, local, and sacred or personal.

Take Conway's "Early Flemish Artists" with you in your portmanteau, and read over in the evening his account of the works you have seen during the day.

Order of the Tour

If possible, visit the cities of Belgium in the order in which they are treated in this Guide:—Bruges first; then Ghent, Brussels, and finally Antwerp. For this order you will find very good reasons. Bruges is the most antique in tone and the least spoiled of all the Flemish towns; it best exhibits the local peculiarities we have here specially to consider; and it leads up naturally to the other cities.

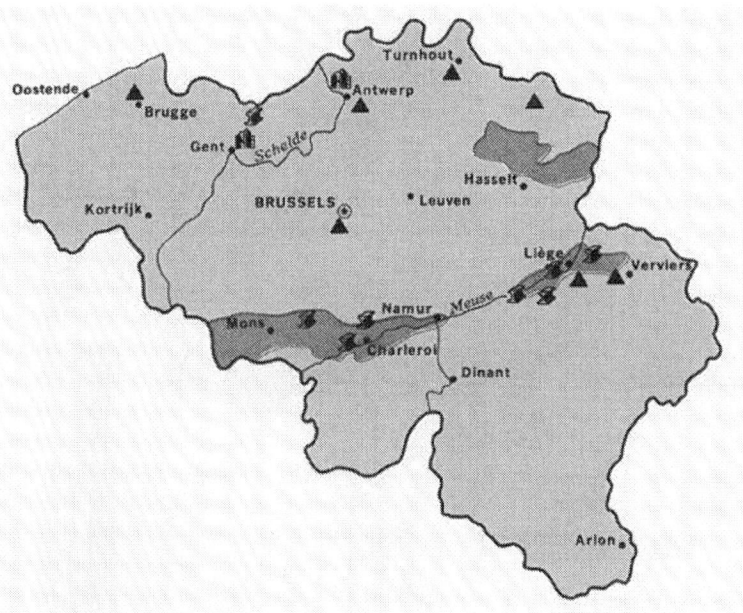

It is true, Memling, the great painter whom we have chiefly to study at Bruges, is later in date than Jan van Eyck, whose principal work (with that of his brother Hubert) is to be seen at Ghent. But historical sequence in this minor matter is somewhat less important than a due apprehension of the general air of an old Flemish town such as those in which the art of the Van Eycks arose; and besides, there is at least one characteristic Van Eyck at Bruges, while there are many Memlings for comparison in other cities.

As a rule, too little time is given by tourists to Bruges and Ghent, and too much to Brussels. I should advise three or four days each to the first-named towns, and a week to the capital. If you are condensing your stay in Belgium to a fortnight or a week, adjust proportionally your touring agenda.

Those who intend to combine a visit to Holland in the same tour should certainly see Belgium in the order here given first, and then proceed to Rotterdam, the Hague, Haarlem, and Amsterdam. For such a sequence, which is geographically the easiest, is also chronologically natural. Bruges is the most medieval of all the towns, and has for its principal great artist Memling. Ghent comes next, with the Van Eycks and a few later painters. Brussels represents the end of the Middle Ages, and contains a general metropolitan collection of early and middle Flemish art. Antwerp gives us in particular Quentin Matsys and his contemporaries, as well as Rubens and Van Dyck. And the Dutch towns lead us on through Van Dyck and the later transitionals to Rembrandt, Van der Helst, Frans Hals, and the other mighty masters of Holland. I may add that as the arrangement of this Guide is roughly chronological, the tourist will use it best if he follows its order.

The Ostend route takes the towns naturally in the sequence I suggest. Visitors arriving by Harwich or Calais should not stop first at Antwerp or Brussels, but go straight to Bruges, and then double back again.

Bruges

Panorama of Bruges' canals at Spiegelrei and Langerei – Image: Mark D. Hammond

The capital of West Flanders, Bruges situation in the Belgian northwest place it in proximity to the capital, with public transport well-developed. The centre, or *Groenerei*, is renowned for its beautiful canals and architectural marvels which span the centuries defining Gothic and Medieval styles. Many of the buildings lining the canals remain as they have for several centuries, and were granted the status of UNESCO World Heritage Site in 2000.

Given its undeniable beauty and juxtaposition of ancient history with the majesty of fine architecture, Bruges has become one of Belgium's most visited cities. For lovers of artwork and culture its beautiful streets, religious and monastic structures offer a wondrous opportunity to soak up a defining history and centuries of artistic talent whose results manifest impressively.

The city has enjoyed popularity, featured in such films as *In Bruges*, and *The Monuments Men*. Its presence in literary works and in documentaries of the wider European continent further serves to elevate its profile, with resultant rises in visitor numbers providing prosperity to the town and its people.

Origins of Bruges

In a lost corner of the great lowland flat of Flanders, defended from the sea by an artificial dyke, and at the point of intersection of an intricate network of canals and waterways, there arose in the early Middle Ages a trading town, known in Flemish as Brugge, in French as Bruges (that is to say, The Bridge), from a primitive structure that here crossed the river. (A number of bridges now span the sluggish streams. All of them open in the middle to admit the passage of shipping.) Bruges stood originally on a little river, the Reye, once navigable, now swallowed by canals: and the Reye flowed into the Zwin, long silted up, but then the safest harbour in the Low Countries.

Bruge and its belfry - Image: Hans Hillewaert

At first the capital of a petty Count, this land-locked internal harbour grew in time to be the Venice of the North, and to gather round its quays, or at its haven of Damme, the ships and merchandise of all neighbouring peoples. Already in 1200 it ranked as the central mart of the Hanseatic League. It was the port of entry for English wool and Russian furs: the port of departure for Flemish broadcloths, laces, tapestries, and linens. Canals soon connected it with Ghent, Dunkirk, Sluys, Furnes, and Ypres. Its nucleus lay in a little knot of buildings about the Grand' Place and the Hôtel de Ville, stretching out to the Cathedral and the Dyver; thence it spread on all sides till in 1362 it filled the whole space within the existing ramparts, now largely abandoned or given over to fields and gardens. It was the wealthiest town of Europe, outside Italy. In the 14th century, Bruges was frequently the residence of the Counts of Flanders; and in the 15th it became the seat of the brilliant court of the Dukes of Burgundy. Under their rule, the opulent burghers and foreign merchants began to employ a group of famous artists who have made the city a place of pilgrimage for Europe and America, and to adorn the town with most of those buildings which now beautify its decay.

The foreign traders in Bruges lived in "factories" or guilds, resembling monasteries or colleges, and were governed by their own commercial laws. The Bardi of Florence were among its famous merchants: the Medici had agents here: so had the millionaire Fuggers of Augsburg.

Bruges is the best place in which to make a first acquaintance with the towns and art of Flanders, because here almost all the principal buildings are mediæval, and comparatively little that is modern comes in to mar the completeness of the picture. We see in it the architecture and the painting of Flanders, in the midst of the houses, the land, and the folk that gave them origin. Brussels is largely modernised, and even Ghent has great living manufactures; but Bruges is a fossil of the 15th century. It was the first to flourish and the first to decay of the towns of Belgium.

Bruges canals and parkland - Image: Rodrigo Menezes

The decline of the town was due partly to the break-up of the Hanseatic system; partly to the rise of English ports and manufacturing towns; but still more (and especially as compared with other Flemish cities) to the silting of the Zwin, and the want of adaptation in its waterways to the needs of great ships and modern navigation. The old sea entrance to Bruges was through the Zwin, by way of Sluys and Kadzand; up that channel came the Venetian merchant fleet and the Flemish galleys, to the port of Damme. By 1470, it ceased to be navigable for large vessels. The later canal is still open, but as it passes through what is now Dutch territory, it is little used; nor is it adapted to any save ships of comparatively small burden. Another canal, suitable for craft of 500 tons, leads through Belgian territory to Ostend; but few vessels now navigate it, and those for the most part only for local trade. The town has shrunk to half its former size, and has only a quarter of its mediæval population. The commercial decay of Bruges, however, has preserved its charm for the artist, the archeologist, and the tourist; its sleepy streets and unfrequented quays are among the most picturesque sights of bustling and industrial modern Belgium. The great private palaces, indeed, are almost all destroyed: but many public buildings remain, and the domestic architecture is quaint and pretty.

Jan Van Eyck - Ardolfini portrait

Bruges was the mother of the arts in Flanders. Jan van Eyck lived here from 1428 to 1440: Memling, probably, from 1477 till 1494. Caxton, the first English printer, lived as a merchant at Bruges (in the Domus Anglorum or English factory) from 1446 to

1476, and probably put in the press here the earliest English printed book (though strong grounds have been adduced in favour of Cologne). Colard Mansion, the great printer of Bruges at that date, was one of the leaders in the art of typography.

Those who desire further information on this most interesting town will find it in James Weale's Bruges et ses Environs, an admirable work, to which I desire to acknowledge my obligations.

Procession of the Holy Blood - Image: Alberto Fernandez Fernandez

At least two whole days should be devoted to Bruges: more if possible. But the hasty traveller, who has but time for a glimpse, should neglect the churches, and walk round the Grand' Place and the Place du Bourg to the Dyver: spending most of his time at the **Hôpital de St. Jean, which contains the glorious works of Memling. These are by far the most important objects to be seen in the city. The description in this Guide is written from the point of view of the more leisurely traveller.

Expect the frequent recurrence of the following symbols on houses or pictures: (1) the Lion of Flanders, heraldic or otherwise, crowned, and bearing a collar with a pendant cross; (2) the Bear of Bruges; (3) the Golden Fleece (Toison d'or), the device of the Order founded by Philippe le Bon in 1430, and appropriate to a country which owed its wealth to wool; it consists of a sheep's skin suspended from a collar. The Flemish emblem of the Swan is also common as a relief or decoration.

St. Donatian, Archbishop of Rheims, is the patron saint. His mark is a wheel with five lighted candles.

The Heart of Bruges

The original nucleus of Bruges is formed by the Place du Bourg, which stands near the centre of the modern city. In 865, Baldwin Bras-de-Fer, Count of Flanders, built a château or burg by the Reye, in a corner of land still marked by the modern canal of the Dyver, and near it a chapel, into which he transported the relics of St. Donatian.

Place du Bourg - Image: Donar Reiskoffer

This burg grew in time into the chief palace of the Counts of Flanders, now replaced by the Palais de Justice; while the chapel by its side developed into the first cathedral of Bruges, St. Donatian, now wholly demolished. A bridge hard by crossed the little river Reye; and from this bridge the town ultimately derives its name. The burg was built as a tête-du-pont to protect the passage. A town of traders gradually sprang up under the protection of the castle, and developed at last into the great trading port of Bruges. To this centre, then, we will first direct ourselves.

Go from your hotel, down the Rue St. Amand, or the Rue St. Jacques, to the Grand' Place or market-place of Bruges, noticing on your way the numerous handsome old houses, with high-pitched roofs and gable-ends arranged like steps, mostly of the 16th and 17th centuries. (Bruges is a Flemish-speaking town: note the true names of the streets in Flemish.)

The belfry in Bruges Markt - Image: L. Ellis

The very tall square tower which faces you as you enter the Grand' Place is the *Belfry, the centre and visible embodiment of the town of Bruges. The Grand' Place itself was the forum and meeting-place of the soldier-citizens, who were called to arms by the chimes in the Belfry. The centre of the Place is therefore appropriately occupied by a colossal statue group (modern) of Pieter de Coninck and Jan Breidel, the leaders of the citizens of Bruges at the Battle of the Spurs before the walls of Courtrai in 1302, a conflict which secured the freedom of Flanders from the interference of the Kings of France. The group is by Devigne. The reliefs on the pedestal represent scenes from the battle and its antecedents.

The majestic Belfry itself represents the first beginnings of freedom in Bruges. Leave to erect such a bell-tower, both as a mark of independence and to summon the citizens to arms, was one of the first privileges which every Teutonic trading town desired to wring from its feudal lord. This (brick) tower, the pledge of municipal rights, was begun in 1291 (to replace an earlier one of wood), and finished about a hundred years later, the octagon (in stone) at the summit (which holds the bells) having been erected in 1393-96. It consists of three stories, the two lower of which are square and flanked by balconies with turrets; the windows below are of the simple Early Gothic style, but show a later type of architecture in the octagon. The niche in the centre contains the Virgin and Child (restored, after being destroyed by the French revolutionists). Below it on either side are smaller figures holding escutcheons. From the balcony between these last, the laws and the rescripts of the Counts were read aloud to the people assembled in the square.

The Belfry can be ascended by steps. Apply to the concierge; 25 c. per person. Owing to the force of the wind, it leans slightly to the S.E. The *view from the top is very extensive and striking; it embraces the greater part of the Plain of Flanders, with its towns and villages: the country, though quite flat, looks beautiful when thus seen. In early times, however, the look-out from the summit was of practical use for purposes of observation, military or maritime. It commanded the river, the Zwin, and the sea approach by Sluys and Damme; the course of the various canals; and the roads to Ghent, Antwerp, Tournai, and Courtrai. The Belfry contains a famous set of chimes, the mechanism of which may be inspected by the visitor. He will have frequent opportunities of hearing the beautiful and mellow carillon, perhaps to excess. The existing bells date only from 1680: the mechanism from 1784.

The Halle en Belfort adjacent to the Belfry – Image: Smabs Sputzer

The square building on either side of the Belfry, known as Les Halles, was erected in or about 1248, and is a fine but sombre specimen of Early Gothic civic architecture. The wing to the left was originally the Cloth Hall, for the display and sale of the woollen manufactures of Ghent and Bruges. It is now used as municipal offices. A door to the left gives access to a small Museum of Antiquities on the ground floor, which may be safely neglected by all save specialist archæologists. The wing to the right is the meat market.

Now, stand with your back to the Belfry to survey the Square. The brick building on your right is the Post Office (modern); the stone one beyond it (also modern) is the Palace of the Provincial Government of Flanders. Both have been erected in a style suitable to the town. In the Middle Ages, ships could come up to this part of the Grand' Place to discharge their cargo. The quaint houses that face you, with high-pitched gable-ends, are partly modern, but mostly old, though restored. On the left (W.) side of the Place, at the corner of the Rue St. Amand, stands the square castle-like building known as Au Lion de Flandre and marked by its gold crest bearing lion.

Lion des Flanders statue - Image: Ludovic Péron

It is one of the best brick mediæval buildings in Bruges. According to a doubtful tradition, it was occupied by Charles II. of England during his exile, when he was created by the

Brugeois King of the Crossbowmen of St. Sebastian (see later). In the house beside it, known as the Craenenburg, the citizens of Bruges imprisoned Maximilian, King of the Romans, from the 5th to the 17th of February, 1488, because he would not grant the care of his son Philip, heir to the crown of the Netherlands, to the King of France. They only released him after he had sworn before an altar erected at the spot, on the Host, the true Cross, and the Relics of St. Donatian, to renounce his claim to the guardianship of his son, and to grant a general amnesty. However, he was treacherously released from his oath by a congress of Princes convened a little later by his father, the Emperor Frederic IV.

Bruges Provincial Government Palace and Post Office - Image: Brian Snelson

From the corner of the Post Office, take the short Rue Breydel to the Place du Bourg, the still more intimate centre and focus of the early life of Bruges. This Place contained the old Palace of the Counts of Flanders, and the original Cathedral, both now destroyed, as well as the Town Hall and other important buildings still preserved for us.

The tallest of the three handsome edifices on the S. side of the Square (profusely adorned with sculpture) is the **Hôtel de Ville, a beautiful gem of Middle Gothic architecture, begun about 1376, and finished about 1387. This is one of the finest pieces of civic architecture in Belgium. The façade, though over-restored, and the six beautiful turrets and chimneys, are in the main of the original design. The sculpture in the niches, destroyed during the French Revolution, has been only tolerably replaced by modern Belgian sculptors in our own day. The lower tier contains the Annunciation, on the right and left of the doorway, with figures of various saints and prophets. In the tiers above this are statues of the Counts of Flanders of various ages. The reliefs just below the windows of the first floor represent episodes from Biblical history:—David before Saul, David dancing before the Ark, the Judgment of Solomon, the Building of Solomon's Temple, and other scenes which the visitor can easily identify. The Great Hall in the interior is interesting only for its fine pendant Gothic wooden roof.

Bruges City Hall - Image: Wolfgang Staudt

The somewhat lower building, to the right of the Hôtel de Ville (Stadhuis, or City Hall), is the **Chapelle du Saint Sang. The decorated portal round the corner also forms part of the same building.

In the 12th and 13th centuries (age of the Crusades) the chivalrous and credulous knights of the North and West who repaired to the Holy Land, whether as pilgrims or as soldiers of the Faith, were anxious to bring back with them relics of the saints or of still more holy personages. The astute Greeks and Syrians with whom they had to deal rose to the occasion, and sold the simple Westerns various sacred objects of more or less doubtful authenticity at fabulous prices. Over these treasured deposits stately churches were often raised; for example, St. Louis of France constructed the Sainte Chapelle in Paris, to contain the Crown of Thorns and part of the True Cross, which he had purchased at an immense cost from Baldwin, Emperor of Constantinople.

Among the earlier visitors to the Holy Land who thus signalised their journey was Theodoric of Alsace, elected Count of Flanders in 1128; he brought back with him in 1149 some drops of the Holy Blood of the Saviour, said to have been preserved by Joseph of Arimathea, which he presented to his faithful city of Bruges. Fitly to enshrine them, Theodoric erected a chapel in the succeeding year, 1150; and this early church forms the lower floor of the existing building. Above it, in the 15th century, when Bruges grew richer, was raised a second and more gorgeous chapel (as at the Sainte Chapelle), in which the holy relic is now preserved. Almost all the works of art in the dainty little oratory accordingly bear special reference to the Holy Blood, its preservation, and its transport to Bruges. The dedication is to St. Basil, the founder of eastern monasticism—a Greek Father little known in the West, whose fame Theodoric must have learned in Syria. The nobles of Flanders, it must be remembered, were particularly active in organising the Crusades.

Basilica of the Holy Blood - Image: Jim Linwood

The exterior has a fine figure of St. Leonard (holding the fetters which are his symbol) under a Gothic niche. He was the patron of Christian slaves held in duress by the Saracens. The beautiful flamboyant portal and staircase, round the corner, erected in 1529-1533, in the ornate decorative style of the period, have (restored) figures of Crusaders and their Queens in niches, with incongruous Renaissance busts below.

The Museum of the Brotherhood of the Holy Blood, on the first floor, which we first visit, contains by the left wall the handsome silver-gilt Reliquary (of 1617), studded with jewels, which encloses the drops of the Holy Blood. The figures on it represent Christ (the source of the Blood), the Blessed Virgin, St. Basil (patron of the church), and St. Donatian (patron of the town). The Blood is exhibited in a simpler châsse in the chapel every Friday; that is to say, on the day of the Crucifixion. The great Reliquary itself is carried in procession only, on the Monday after the 3rd of May. Right and left of the châsse are portraits of the members of the Confraternity of the Holy Blood by P. Pourbus, 1556: unusually good works of this painter. A triptych to the right, by an unknown master of the early 16th century, figures the Crucifixion, with special reference to the Holy Blood, representing St. Longinus in the act of piercing the side of Christ (thus drawing the Blood), with the Holy Women and St. John in attendance; on the wings, the Way to Calvary, and the Resurrection.

The altar upon which the Holy Blood relic is presented - Image: Matt Hopkins

Between the windows is a curious chronological picture of the late 15th century, representing the History of Our Lady in the usual stages, with other episodes. To the right of it, a painting of the 15th century shows Count Theodoric receiving the Holy Blood from his brother-in-law, Baldwin, King of Jerusalem, and the bringing of the Holy Blood to Bruges.

On the right wall there is a famous *triptych by Gerard David (the finest work here), representing the Deposition in the Tomb, with the Maries, St. John, Nicodemus, and an attendant holding a dish to contain the Holy Blood, which is also seen conspicuously flowing from the wounds; the left wing shows the Magdalen with Cleophas; the right wing, the preservation of the Crown of Thorns by Joseph of Arimathea. The portrait character of the faces is admirable: stand long and study this fine work.

The original designs for the windows of the Chapel are preserved in a glass case by the window; behind which are fragments of early coloured glass; conspicuous among them, St. Barbara with her tower. On the exit wall is a fine piece of late Flemish tapestry, representing the bringing of the body of St. Augustine to Pavia, with side figures of San Frediano of Lucca and Sant' Ercolano of Perugia—executed, no doubt, for an Italian patron.

Basilica of the Holy Blood - main nave

The Chapel itself, which we next enter, is gorgeously decorated in polychrome, recently restored. The stained glass windows, containing portraits of the Burgundian Princes from the beginning of the dynasty down to Maria Theresa and Francis I., were executed in 1845 from earlier designs. The large window facing the High Altar is modern. It represents appropriately the history of the Passion, the origin of the Sacred Blood, its Transference to Bruges, and the figures of the Flemish Crusaders engaged in its transport. At the summit of the window, notice the frequent and fitting symbol of the pelican feeding its young with its own blood.

In the little side chapel to the right, separated from the main building by an arcade of three arches, is the tabernacle or canopy from which the Sacred Blood is exhibited weekly. To the right is hung a Crown of Thorns. Notice, also, the Crown of Thorns held by the angel at the top of the steps. The window to the left (modern) represents St. Longinus, the centurion who pierced the side of Christ, and St. Veronica, displaying her napkin which she gave to the Saviour to wipe his face on the way to Calvary, and which retained ever after the impress of the Divine Countenance. Almost all the other objects in the chapel bear reference, more or less direct, to the Holy Blood. Observe particularly in the main chapel the handsome modern High Altar with its coloured reliefs of scenes of the Passion. Such scenes as the Paschal Lamb on its base, with the Hebrew smearing the lintel of the door, are of course symbolical.

The Lower Chapel, to which we are next conducted, is a fine specimen of late Romanesque architecture. It was built by Theodoric in 1150. Its solid short pillars and round arches contrast with the lighter and later Gothic of the upper building. The space above the door of the eastern of the two chapels which face the entrance is occupied by an interesting mediæval relief representing a baptism with a dove descending. Notice as you pass out, from the Place outside, the two beautiful turrets at the west end of the main chapel.

Oude Civiele Griffie - Image: PMRMaeyaert

To the left of the Hôtel de Ville stands the ornate and much gilded Renaissance building known as the *Maison de l'Ancien Greffe – or Oude Civiele Griffie - originally the municipal record office. It bears the date 1537, and received due restoration complete with profuse gold decoration. Over the main doorway is the Lion of Flanders; on the architrave of the first floor are heads of Counts and Countesses; and the building is surmounted by a figure of Justice, with Moses and Aaron and emblematical statues. Note the Golden Fleece and other symbols. The interior is uninteresting.

Palais du justice - Image: sailko

The east side of the square is formed by the Palais de Justice, which stands on the site of an old palace of the Counts of Flanders, presented by Philippe le Beau to the Liberty of Bruges, and employed by them as their town hall of the Buitenpoorters, or inhabitants of the district outside the gate, known as the Franc de Bruges. The Renaissance building, erected between 1520 and 1608, was burnt down and replaced in the 18th century by the very uninteresting existing building. Parts of the old palace, however, were preserved, one room in which should be visited for the sake of its magnificent **chimney-piece. In order to see it, enter the quadrangle: the porter's room faces you as you enter.

The concierge conducts you to the Court-Room, belonging to the original building. Almost the entire side of the room is occupied by a splendid Renaissance chimney-piece, executed in 1529, after designs by Lancelot Blondeel of Bruges (a painter whose works are frequent in the town), and Guyot de Beaugrant of Malines, for the Council of the Liberty of Bruges, in honour of Charles V., as a memorial of the Treaty of Cambrai, in 1526. (This was the treaty concluded after the battle of Pavia, by which François Ier of France was compelled to acknowledge the independence of Flanders. Some of the figures in the background are allusive to the victory.) The lower part, or chimney-piece proper, is of black marble. The upper portion is of carved oak.

The marble part has four bas-reliefs in white alabaster by Guyot de Beaugrant, representing the History of Susannah, a mere excuse for the nude: (1) Susannah and the Elders at the Bath; (2) Susannah dragged by the Elders before the Judge; (3) Daniel before the Judge exculpating Susannah; (4) The Stoning of the Elders. The genii at the corners are also by Beaugrant. The whole is in the pagan taste of the Renaissance. The upper portion in oak contains in the centre a statue of Charles V., represented in his capacity as Count of Flanders (as shown by the arms on his cuirass): the other figures represent his descent and the accumulation of sovereignties in his person. On the throne behind Charles (ill seen) are busts of Philippe le Beau, his father, through whom he inherited the Burgundian dominions, and Johanna (the Mad) of Spain, his mother, through whom he inherited the united Peninsula.

The statues left and right are those of his actual royal predecessors. The figures to the left are his paternal grandfather, the Emperor Maximilian, from whom he derived his German territories, and his paternal grandmother, *Mary of Burgundy, who brought into the family Flanders, Burgundy, etc. Mary is represented with a hawk on her wrist, as she was killed at twenty-five by a fall from her horse while out hawking. (We shall see her tomb later at Notre-Dame.) The figures on the right are those of Ferdinand of Aragon and Isabella of Castile, the maternal grandfather and grandmother of Charles, from whom he inherited the two portions of his Spanish dominions. The medallions at the back represent the personages most concerned in the Treaty of Cambrai, and the Victory of Pavia which rendered it possible. (De Lannoy, the conqueror, to whom François gave up his sword, and Margaret of Austria.) The tapestry which surrounds the hall is modern; it was manufactured at Ingelmünster after the pattern of a few old fragments found in the cellars of the ancient building. The mediocre painting on the wall depicts a sitting of the court of the Liberty of Bruges in this room (1659).

The north side of the square is now occupied by a small Place planted with trees. Originally, however, the old cathedral of Bruges occupied this site. It was dedicated to St. Donatian, the patron of the city, whose relics were preserved in it; but it was barbarously destroyed by the French Revolutionary army in 1799, and the works of art which it contained were dispersed or ruined. Figures of St. Donatian occur accordingly in many paintings at Bruges. Jan van Eyck was buried in this cathedral, and a statue has been erected to him under the trees in the little Place. In order, therefore, mentally to complete the picture of the Place du Bourg in the 16th century, we must imagine not only the Hôtel de Ville, the Chapelle du Saint Sang, and the Ancien Greffe in something approaching their existing condition, but also the stately cathedral and the original

Renaissance building of the Franc de Bruges filling in the remainder.

The Bridge on Blind Donkey Street - Image: Jim Linwood

An archway spans the space between the Ancien Greffe and the Hôtel de Ville. Take the narrow street which dives beneath it, looking back as you pass at the archway with its inscription of S.P.Q.B. (for Senatus Populusque Brugensis). The street then leads across a bridge over the river Reye or principal canal, and affords a good view of the back of the earlier portion of the Palais de Justice, with its picturesque brick turrets, and a few early arches belonging to the primitive palace. I recommend the visitor to turn to the right after crossing the bridge, traverse the little square, and make his way home by the bank of the Dyver and the church of Notre-Dame. The view towards the Hôtel de Ville and the Belfry, from the part of the Dyver a little to the east behind the Belfry, is one of the most picturesque and striking in Bruges.

Ferraris' map of Bruges, circa 1775, depicts the city's nucleus

Old St. John's Hospital

The Hospital of St. John, one of the most ancient institutions in Bruges, or of its kind in Europe, was founded not later than 1188, and still retains, within and without, its mediæval arrangement. Its Augustinian brothers and nuns tend the sick in the primitive building, now largely added to.

The exterior of the old hospital of Saint John – Image: Jean-Pol Grandmont

Exterior aside, it derives its chief interest for the tourist from its small Picture Gallery, the one object in Bruges which must above everything else be visited. This is the only place for studying in full the exquisite art of Memling, whose charming and poetical work is here more fully represented than elsewhere. In this respect the Hospital of St. John may be fitly compared with the two other famous "one-man shows" of Europe—the Fra Angelicos at San Marco in Florence, and the Giottos in the Madonna dell' Arena at Padua. Many of the pictures were painted for the institution which they still adorn; so that we have here the opportunity of seeing works of mediæval art in the precise surroundings which first produced them.

The three Hans Memling panels upon the St. John altar

Hans Memling, whose name is also written Memlinc and Memlin, etc. (long erroneously cited as Hemling; through a mistaken reading of the initial in his signature) is a painter of whom little is known, save his work; but the work is the man, and therefore amply sufficient. He was born about 1430, perhaps in Germany, and is believed to have been a pupil of Roger van der Weyden, the Brussels painter, whose work we shall see later at Antwerp and elsewhere. Mr. Weale has shown that he was a person of some wealth, settled at Bruges in his own house (about 1478), and in a position to lend money to the town. He died in 1495. His period of activity as a painter is thus coincident with the earlier work of Carpaccio and Perugino in Italy; and he died while Raphael was still a boy.

In relation to the artists of his own country, whose works we have still to see, Memling was junior by more than a generation to Jan van Eyck, having been born about ten years before Van

Eyck died; he was also younger by thirty years than Roger van der Weyden; and by twenty or thirty years than Dierick Bouts; but older by at least twenty than Gerard David. Memling has been called the Fra Angelico of Flanders; but this is only true so far as regards Fra Angelico's panel works; the saintly Frate, when he worked in fresco, adopted a style wholly different from that which he displays in his miniature-like altar-pieces. It would be truer to say that Memling is the Benozzo Gozzoli of the North: he has the same love of decorative adjuncts, and the same naïve delight in the beauty of external nature.

Before visiting the Hospital, it is also well to be acquainted in outline with the history of St. Ursula, whose châsse or shrine forms one of its greatest treasures. The Hospital possessed an important relic of the saint—her holy arm—and about 1480-1489 commissioned Memling to paint scenes from her life on the shrine destined to contain this precious deposit. The chest or reliquary which he adorned for the purpose forms the very best work of Memling's lifetime.

St. Ursula was a British (or Bretonne) princess, brought up as a Christian by her pious parents. She was sought in marriage by a pagan prince, Conon, said to be the son of a king of England. The English king, called Agrippinus in the legend, sent ambassadors to the king of Britain (or Brittany) asking for the hand of Ursula for his heir. But Ursula made three conditions: first, that she should be given as companions ten noble virgins, and that she herself and each of the virgins should be accompanied by a thousand maiden attendants; second, that they should all together visit the shrines of the saints; and third, that the prince Conon and all his court should receive baptism. These conditions were complied with; the king of England collected 11,000 virgins; and Ursula, with her companions, sailed for Cologne, where she arrived miraculously without the assistance of sailors (but Memling adds them). Here, she had a vision of an angel bidding her to repair to Rome, the threshold of the apostles.

From Cologne, the pilgrims went up the Rhine by boat, till they arrived at Basle, where they disembarked and continued their journey on foot over the Alps to Italy. At length they reached the Tiber, which they descended till they approached the walls of Rome. There, the Pope, St. Cyriacus, went forth with all his clergy in procession to meet them. He gave them his blessing, and lest the maidens should come to harm in so wicked a city, he had tents pitched for them outside the walls on the side towards Tivoli. Meanwhile, prince Conon had come on pilgrimage by a different route, and arrived at Rome on the same day as his betrothed. He knelt with Ursula at the feet of the Pope, and, being baptized, received in exchange the name of Ethereus.

After a certain time spent in Rome, the holy maidens bethought them to return home again. Thereupon, Pope Cyriacus decided to accompany them, together with his cardinals, archbishops, bishops, patriarchs, and many others of his prelates. They crossed the Alps, embarked again at Basle, and made their way northward as far as Cologne. Now it happened that the army of the Huns was at that time besieging the Roman colony; and the pagans fell upon the 11,000 virgins, with the Pope and their other saintly companions. Prince Ethereus was one of the first to die; then Cyriacus, the bishops, and the cardinals perished. Last of all, the pagans turned upon the virgins, all of whom they slew, save only St. Ursula. Her they carried before their king, who, beholding her beauty, would fain have wedded her. But Ursula sternly refused the offer of this son of Satan; whereupon the king, seizing his bow, transfixed her breast with three arrows. Hence her symbol is an arrow; also, she is the patroness of young girls and of virgins, so that her shrine is particularly appropriate in a nunnery.

Both sides of the shrine of Saint Ursula

Most of the bones of St. Ursula and her 11,000 virgins are preserved at Cologne, the city of her martyrdom, where they are ranged in cases round the walls of a church dedicated in her honour; but her arm is here, and a few other relics are distributed elsewhere.

From the Grand' Place, turn down the Rue des Pierres, the principal shopping street of Bruges, with several fine old façades, many of them dated. At the Place Simon Stévin turn to the left, and go straight on as far as the church of Notre-Dame. The long brick building with Gothic arches, on your right, is the **Hospital of St. John the Evangelist.

First, examine the brick Gothic exterior. Over the outer doorway is the figure of a bishop with a flaming heart, the emblem of St.

Augustine, this being an Augustinian hospital. Continue on to the original main portal (now bricked up) with a broken pillar, and two 13th century reliefs in the tympanum. That to the right represents the Death of the Virgin, with the Apostles grouped around, and the figure of the Christ receiving her naked new-born soul as usual. Above is the Coronation of Our Lady. That to the left seems like a reversed and altered replica of the same subject, with perhaps the Last Judgment above it. It is, however, so much dilapidated that identification is difficult. (Perhaps the top is a Glory of St. Ursula.) Go on as far as the little bridge over the canal, to inspect the picturesque river front of the Hospital.

The pictures are collected in the former Chapter-house of the Hospital, above the door of which is another figure of St. Augustine.

St. Johns Hospital entrance - Image: Navy8300

The centre of the room is occupied by the famous châsse or **shrine containing the arm of St. Ursula, a dainty little Gothic chapel in miniature. It is painted with exquisite scenes from the legend, by Memling, with all the charm of a fairy tale. He treats it as a poetical romance. Begin the story on the side towards the window. (For a penetrating criticism of these works, see Conway.)

1st panel, on the left: St. Ursula and her maidens, in the rich dress of the Burgundian court of the 15th century, arrive at Cologne, the buildings of which are seen in the background, correctly represented, but not in their true relations. In a window in the background to the right, the angel appears to St. Ursula in a vision.

2nd panel: the Virgins arrive at Basle and disembark from the ships. In the background, they are seen preparing to make their way, one by one, across the Alps, which rise from low hills at the base to snowy mountains. From another ship Conon and his knights are disembarking.

**3rd panel: (the most beautiful:) the Maidens arrive at Rome. In the distance they are seen entering the city through a triumphal arch; in the foreground, St. Ursula kneels before St. Cyriacus and his bishops, with their attendant deacons, all the faces having the character of portraits. (Note especially the fat and jolly ecclesiastic just under the arch.) At the same time, her betrothed, Conon, with his knights, arrives at Rome by a different road, and is seen kneeling in a red robe trimmed with rich fur beside St. Ursula. (Fine portrait faces of Conon and an old courtier behind him.) The Pope and his priests are gathered under the portals of a beautiful round-arched building, whose exquisite architecture should be closely examined. To the extreme right, the new converts and Conon receive baptism naked in fonts after the early fashion. In the background of this scene, St. Ursula receives the Sacrament. (She may be recognised throughout by her peculiar blue-and-white dress, with its open sleeves.) To the left of her, Conon makes confession. In this, as in the other scenes, several successive moments of the same episode are contemporaneously represented. Look long at it.

Now, turn round the shrine, which swings freely on a pivot, to see the scenes of the return journey.

1st panel: (beginning again at the left:) the Pope and his bishops and cardinals embark with St. Ursula in the boat at Basle on their way to Cologne. Three episodes are here conjoined: the Pope cautiously stepping into a ship; the Pope seated; the ship sailing down the Rhine. All the faces here, and especially the timid old Pope stepping into the boat, deserve careful examination. In the background, the return over the Alps.

*2nd panel: the Maidens and the Pope arrive at Cologne, where they are instantly set upon by the armed Huns. Conon is slain by the thrust of a sword, and falls back dying in the arms of St. Ursula. Many of the maidens are also slaughtered.

*3rd panel: continuous with the last, but representing a subsequent moment: the Martyrdom of St. Ursula. The King of the Huns, in full armour, at the door of his tent, bends his bow to shoot the blessed martyr, who has refused his advances. Around are grouped his knights in admirably painted armour. (Note the reflections.) All the scenes have the character of a mediæval romance. For their open-air tone and make-believe martyrdom, see Conway.

At the ends of the shrine are two other pictures, (1) *St. Ursula with her arrow, as the protectress of young girls, sheltering a number of them under her cloak (not, as is commonly said, the 11,000 Virgins). Similar protecting figures of the saint are common elsewhere (Cluny, Bologna, etc.). At the opposite end, (2) the Madonna and Child with an apple, and at her feet two Augustinian nuns of this Hospital, kneeling, to represent the devotion of the order.

The roof of the shrine is also decorated with pictures. (1) St. Ursula receiving the crown of martyrdom from God the Father, with the Son and the Holy Ghost; at the sides, two angels playing the mandoline and the regal or portable organ; (2) St. Ursula in Paradise, bearing her arrow, and surrounded by her maidens, who shared her martyrdom, together with the Pope and other ecclesiastics in the background. (This picture is largely borrowed from the famous one by Stephan Lochner on the High Altar of Cologne Cathedral, known as the Dombild. If you are going on to Cologne, buy a photograph of this now, to compare with Meister Stephan later. His altar-piece is engraved in Conway. If you have it with you, compare them.) At the sides are two angels playing the zither and the violin. (The angels are possibly by a pupil.)

I have given a brief description only of these pictures, but every one of them ought to be carefully examined, and the character of the figures and of the landscape or architectural background noted. You will see nothing lovelier in all Flanders.

Near the window by the entrance is a **Triptych, also by Memling, commissioned by Brother Jan Floreins of this Hospital. The central panel represents the Adoration of the Magi, which takes place, as usual, under a ruined temple fitted up as a manger. The Eldest of the Three Kings (according to precedent) is kneeling and has presented his gift; Joseph, recognisable (in all three panels) by his red-and-black robe, stands erect behind him, with the presented gift in his hands. The Middle-aged King, arrayed in cloth of gold, with a white tippet, kneels with his gift to the left of the picture. The Young King, a black man, as always, is entering with his gift to the right.

The three thus typify the Three Ages of Man, and also the three known continents, Europe, Asia, Africa. On the left hand side of this central panel are figured the donor, Jan Floreins, and his brother Jacob. (Members of the same family are grouped in the well-known "Duchâtel Madonna," also by Memling, in the Louvre.) To the right is a figure looking in at a window and wearing the yellow cap still used by convalescents of the

Hospital, (arbitrarily said to be a portrait of Memling.) The left panel represents the Nativity, with our Lady, St. Joseph, and two adoring angels. The right panel shows the Presentation in the Temple, with Simeon and Anna, and St. Joseph (in red and black) in the background. (The whole thus typifies the Epiphany of Christ; left, to the Blessed Virgin; centre, to the Gentiles; right, to the Jews.) The outer panels, in pursuance of the same idea, have figures, right, of St. John Baptist with the lamb (he pointed out Christ to the Jews), with the Baptism of Christ in the background; and left, St. Veronica, who preserved for us the features of our Lord, displaying his divine face on her napkin. The architectural frame shows the First Sin and the Expulsion from Paradise. Note everywhere the strong character in the men's faces, and the exquisite landscape or architectural backgrounds. Dated 1479. This is Memling's finest altar-piece: its glow of colour is glorious.

By the centre window, a *triptych, doubtfully attributed to Memling, represents, in the centre, the Deposition from the Cross, with the Holy Blood conspicuous, as might be expected in a Bruges work. In the foreground are St. John, the Madonna, and St. Mary Magdalene; in the background, the preparations for the Deposition in the Tomb. On the wings: left, Brother Adrian Reins, the donor, with his patron saint, Adrian, bearing his symbol, the anvil, on which his limbs were struck off, and with his lion at his feet; right, St. Barbara with her tower, perhaps as patroness of armourers. On the exterior wings, left, St. Wilgefortis with her tau-shaped cross; right, St. Mary of Egypt, with the three loaves which sustained her in the desert.

On the same stand is the beautiful *diptych by Memling, representing Martin van Nieuwenhoven adoring the Madonna. The left panel represents Our Lady and the Child, with an apple, poised on a beautifully painted cushion. A convex mirror in the background reflects the backs of the figures (as in the Van Eyck of the National Gallery). Through the open window is seen a charming distant prospect. The right panel has the fine portrait of the donor, in a velvet dress painted with extreme realism. Note the admirable prayer-book and joined hands. At his back, a stained glass window shows his patron, St. Martin, dividing his cloak for the beggar. Below, a lovely glimpse of landscape. This is probably Memling's most successful portrait. Dated 1487: brought here from the Hospice of St. Julian, of which Martin was Master.

In all Flemish art, observe now the wooden face of the Madonna—ultimately derived, I believe, from imitation of painted wooden figures, and then hardened into a type. As a rule, the Madonna is the least interesting part of all Flemish painting; and after her, the women, especially the young ones. The men's faces are best, and better when old: character, not beauty, is what the painter cares for. This is most noticeable in Van Eyck, but is true in part even of Memling.

At the end of the room is the magnificent *triptych painted by Memling for the High Altar of the Church of this Hospital. This is the largest of his works, and it is dedicated to the honour of the two saints (John the Evangelist and John the Baptist) who are patrons of the Hospital. The central panel represents Our Lady, seated in an exquisite cloister, on a throne backed with cloth of gold. To the right and left are two exquisite angels, one of whom plays a regal, while the other, in a delicious pale blue robe, holds a book for Our Lady. Two smaller angels, poised in air, support her crown. To the left, St. Catherine of Alexandria kneels as princess, with the broken wheel and the sword of her martyrdom at her feet. The Child Christ places a ring on her finger; whence the whole composition is often absurdly called "The Marriage of St. Catherine." It should be styled "The Altarpiece of the St. Johns." To the right is St. Barbara, calmly reading, with her tower behind her. When these two saints are thus combined, they represent the meditative and the active life (as St. Barbara was the patroness of arms:) or, more definitely, the clergy and the knighthood.

Hence their appropriateness to an institution, half monastic, half secular. In the background stand the two patron saints; St. John Baptist with the lamb (Memling's personal patron), to the left, and St. John the Evangelist with the cup and serpent, to the right. (For these symbols, see Mrs. Jameson.) Behind the Baptist are scenes from his life and preaching. He is led to prison, and his body is burned by order of Julian the Apostate. Behind the Evangelist, he is seen in the cauldron of boiling oil. The small figure in black to the right is the chief donor, Brother Jan Floreins, who is seen further back in his secular capacity as public gauger of wine, near a great crane, which affords a fine picture of mercantile life in old Bruges. The left wing represents the life of St. John the Baptist.

In the distance is seen the Baptism of Christ. In a room to the left, the daughter of Herodias dances before Herod. The foreground is occupied by the episode of the Decollation, treated in a courtly manner, very redolent of the Burgundian splendour. Figures and attitudes are charming: only, the martyrdom sinks into insignificance beside the princess's collar.

Other minor episodes may be discovered by inspection. (The episodes on either wing overflow into the main pictures.) The right wing shows St. John the Evangelist in Patmos, writing the Apocalypse, various scenes from which are realistically and too solidly represented above him, without poetical insight. Memling here attempts to transcend his powers. He has no sublimity. On the exterior of the wings are seen the four other members of the society who were donors of the altar-piece; Anthony Zeghers, master of the Hospital, with his patron, St. Anthony, known by his pig and tau-shaped crutch and bell: Jacob de Cueninc, treasurer, accompanied by his patron, St. James the Greater, with his pilgrim's staff and scallop-shell: Agnes Casembrood, mistress of the Hospital, with her patron, St. Agnes, known by her lamb: and Claire van Hulsen, a sister, with her patron, St. Clara. Dated, 1479.

By the entrance door is a Portrait of Marie Moreel, represented as a Sibyl. She was a daughter of Willem Moreel or Morelli, a patron of Memling, whom we shall meet again at the Museum.

This is a fine portrait of a solid, plain body, a good deal spoiled by attempted cleaning. It comes from the Hospice of St. Julian.

As you go out, cast a glance at the fine old brick buildings, and note the cleanliness of all the arrangements.

It would be wise to return for another look prior to departure, and you should not be satisfied with a single visit.

The other pictures and objects formerly exhibited in this Hospital have been transferred to the Potterie and another building. They need only be visited by those whose time is ample.

Two nuns walk toward the Béguinage - Image: Josep Renalias

After leaving the Hospital, I do not advise an immediate visit to the Academy. Let the Memlings first sink into your mind. But the walk may be prolonged by crossing the canal, and taking the second turning to the right, which leads (over a pretty bridge of three arches) to the Béguinage, a lay-nunnery for ladies who take no vows, but who live in monastic fashion under the charge of a Superior. Above the gateway is a figure of St. Elizabeth of Hungary, (to whom the church within is dedicated) giving alms to a beggar. She wears her crown, and carries in her hand the crown and book which are her symbol. Remember these,—they will recur later.

Pass under the gateway and into the grass-grown precincts for an external glimpse of the quiet old-world close, with its calm white-washed houses. The church, dedicated to St. Elizabeth, is uninteresting. This walk may be further prolonged by the pretty bank of the Lac d'amour or Minnewater as far as the external canal, returning by the ramparts and the picturesque Porte de Gand.

Walks through Bruges

The town of Bruges itself is more interesting, after all, than almost any one thing in it. Vary your day by giving up the morning to definite sightseeing, and devoting the afternoon to strolls through the town and neighbourhoods, in search of picturesqueness and photo opportunities. I include here a few stray hints for such casual rambles.

First Walk

Set out from the Grand' Place, and turn down the Rue Breydel to the Place du Bourg. Cross the Place by the statue of Jan van Eyck; traverse the Rue Philippe Stock; turn up the Rue des Armuriers a little to the right, and continue on to the Place St. Jean, with a few interesting houses.

The famed statue of Jan Van Eyck in Bruges - Image: Steven Lek

Note here and elsewhere, at every turn, the little statues of the Virgin and Child in niches, and the old signs on the fronts or gables. The interesting Gothic turret which faces you as you go belongs to the old 14th Century building called De Poorters Loodge, or the Assembly Hall of the Noble Citizens within the Gate, as opposed to those of the Franc de Bruges.

Continue on in the same direction to the Place Jan van Eyck, where you open up one of the most charming views in Bruges over the canal and quays. The Place is "adorned" by a modern statue of Jan van Eyck. The dilapidated building to your left is that of the Académie des Beaux-Arts which occupies the site of the Citizens' Assembly Hall: the ancient edifice was wholly rebuilt and spoilt in 1755, with the exception of the picturesque tower, best viewed from the base of the statue. Opposite you, as you emerge into the Place, is the charming **Tonlieu** or Custom House, whose decorated façade and portal (restored) bear the date 1477, with the arms of Pieter van Luxemburg, and the collar of the Golden Fleece. The dainty little neighbouring house to the left, now practically united with it, has a coquettish façade: the saints in the niches are St. George, St. John Baptist, St. Thomas à Becket, (or Augustine?) and St. John the Evangelist.

The Tonlieu – or old Tollhouse – was formerly fitted up as the Municipal Library. It contains illuminated manuscripts and examples of editions printed by Colard Mansion. All round the Place are other picturesque mediæval or Renaissance houses.

The little street to the right (diagonally) of the Tonlieu leads on to the Marché du Mercedi, now called Place de Memling, embellished by a statue of the great painter. Cross the Place diagonally to the Quai des Espagnoles (Madonna and Child in front of you) and continue along the quay, to the left, to the first bridge; there cross and go along the picturesque Quai des Augustins to the Rue Flamande. (Quaint little window to the left, as you cross the bridge.) Follow the Rue Flamande as far as the Theatre, just before reaching which you pass, right, a handsome mediæval stone mansion, (formerly the Guild of the Genoese Merchants,) with a relief over the door, representing St. George killing the Dragon, and the Princess Cleodolind looking on. At the Theatre, turn to the right, following the tram-line, and making your way back to the Grand' Place by the Rue des Tonneliers.

The Tonlieu - Tollhouse - of Bruges - Image: Dennis Jarvis

As early as 1362, Bruges acquired its existing size, and was surrounded by ramparts, which still in part remain. A continuous canal runs round these ramparts, and beyond it again lies an outer moat. Most of the old gates have unhappily been destroyed, but four still exist. These may be made the objects of interesting rambles.

Second Walk

Go from your hotel, or from the Grand Place, by the Rue Flamande, as far as the Rue de l'Académie. Turn along this to the right, into the Place Jan van Eyck, noting as you pass the Bear of Bruges at the corner of the building of the old Academy. Follow the quay straight on till you reach a second canal, near the corner of which, by the Rue des Carmes, is an interesting shop selling decorative items.

Take the long squalid Rue des Carmes to the right, past the ugly convent of the English Ladies, with its domed church in the most painful taste of the later Renaissance (1736). The mediæval brick building on your right, at the end of the street, is the late Gothic Guild-house of the Archers of St. Sebastian.

The Little Bear of Bruges - Image: Derek Winterborn

Its slender octagonal tower has a certain picturesqueness. (St. Sebastian was of course the patron of archery.) Charles II. of England (see under the Grand' Place) was a member of this society during his exile: his bust is preserved here. So also was the Emperor Maximilian. Continue to the ramparts, and mount the first hill, crowned by a windmill,—a scene of a type familiar to us in many later Dutch and Flemish pictures. A picturesque view of Bruges is obtained from this point: the octagonal Belfry, the square tower of St. Sauveur, (the Cathedral), the tapering brick spire of Notre-Dame, with its projecting gallery and the steeple of the new church of the Madeleine are all conspicuous in views from this side. Follow the ramparts to the right, to the picturesque Porte de Ste. Croix, and on past the barracks and the little garden to the Quai des Dominicains, returning by the Park and the Place du Bourg or the Dyver.

Third Walk

Set out by the Grand Place and the Place du Bourg; then follow the Rue Haute, with its interesting old houses, as far as the canal. Do not cross it, but skirt the quay on the further side, with the towers of St. Walburge and St. Gilles in front of you. At the bridge, diverge to the right, round the church of St. Anne, and the quaint little Church of Jerusalem, which contains an unimportant imitation of the Holy Sepulchre at Jerusalem, founded by a burgomaster of Bruges in the 15th century.

It is just worth looking at. Return to the bridge, and follow the quay straight on to the modern Episcopal Seminary and the picturesque old Hospice de la Potterie, which now harbours the Museum of Antiquities belonging to the Hospital of St. John. I do not advise a visit. (It contains third-rate early Flemish pictures, inferior tapestry, and a few pieces of carved oak furniture. The entrance is by the door just beyond the church, Number F, 79. The church itself is worth a minute's visit.) This walk passes many interesting old houses, which it is not necessary now to specify. Return by the Porte de Damme, and the opposite side of the same canal, to the Pont des Carmes, whence follow the pretty canal on the right to the Rue Flamande.

Fourth Walk

Take the Rue St. Jacques, and go straight out to the Porte d' Ostende, which forms an interesting picture. Cross the canal and outer moat, and traverse the long avenue, past the gasometers, as far as the navigable canal from Bruges to Ostend. Then retrace your steps to the gateway, and return by the ramparts and the Railway Station to the Rue Nord du Sablon.

These four walks combined will show you almost all that is externally interesting in the streets and canals of the city.

The original Palace of the Counts of Flanders, we saw, occupied the site of the Palais de Justice. Their later residence, the Cour des Princes, in a street behind the Hôtel du Commerce, has now entirely disappeared. Its site is filled by a large ornate modern building, belonging to the Sisters of the Sacred Heart, who use it as a school for girls.

The water-system of Bruges is also interesting. The original river Reye enters the town at the Minnewater, flows past the Hospital and the Dyver, and turns northward at the Bourg, running under arches till it emerges on the Place Jan van Eyck.

This accounts for the apparently meaningless way this branch seems to stop short close to the statue of Van Eyck: also, for the medieval ships unloading at the Grand' Place. The water is now mostly diverted along the canals and the moat by the ramparts, with the craft upon these waterways mainly orientated to leisure and tourism.

The Churches

As previously mentioned, the original Cathedral of Bruges - St. Donatian - was destroyed by the French in 1799. Despite this, the town still possesses two fine medieval churches of considerable pretensions, as well as several others of lesser importance. Though of very ancient foundation, the two principal churches in their existing form date only from the most flourishing period of Bruges, the 13th, 14th, and 15th centuries.

St. Salvator

[This church is open 7 days a week. From Monday to Saturday it admits guests from 10am to 1pm, and is closed between 1pm and 2pm for lunch. It is reopened each day from 2pm to 5:30pm. The exception is Saturday, when the church closes at 3:30pm.

On Sunday opening times are narrower; 11:30am to 12pm (a mere half hour) during mornings, and from 2pm to 5pm in the afternoon.

Admission is free; however the church administration is appreciative of donations which aid in maintaining the order of the church and its artworks.]

A principle place of worship in Bruges, St. Salvator is most known for its well-maintained organ and striking, numerous stained glass Gothic archways.

St. Salvator Cathedral - Image: Christoph Radtke

St. Salvator or St. Sauveur, the larger, was erected into the Cathedral after the destruction of St. Donatian, whose relics were transferred to it. To this, therefore, we will first direct ourselves.

Go down the Rue des Pierres as far as the cathedral, which replaces a very ancient church built by St. Eligius (St. Éloy) in 646.

Externally, the edifice, which is built of brick, has rather a heavy and cumbrous effect, its chief good features being the handsome square tower and the large decorated windows of the N. and S. Transepts. The Choir and its chapels have the characteristic French form of a chevêt. The main portal of the N. Transept has been robbed of its sculpture. The Choir is of the late 13th century: the Nave and Transept are mainly in the decorated style of the 14th.

The best entrance is near the tower on the north side. Walk straight on into the body of the Nave, by the archway in the heavy tower, so as to view the internal architecture as a whole. The Nave and single Aisles are handsome and imposing, though the windows on the S. side have been despoiled of their tracery. Notice the curious high-pointed Triforium (1362), between the arches of the Nave and the windows of the Clerestory. The Choir is closed by a strikingly ugly debased Renaissance or rococo Rood-Screen, (1682), in black-and-white marble, supporting the organ. It has a statue of God the Father by the younger Quellin. The whole of the interior has been decorated afresh in somewhat gaudy polychrome by Jean Béthune. The effect is on the whole not unpleasing.

St Salvator - Stained glass archway and panes. Image: Javier Carro

The Cathedral contains few works of art of high merit, but a preliminary walk round the Aisles, Transept, and Ambulatory behind the Choir will give a good idea of its general arrangement. Then return to view the paintings. The sacristan takes you round and unlocks the pictures. Do not let him hurry you.

Begin with the Left Aisle.

The Baptistery, on your left, contains a handsome font. right and left of the entry to it are admirable brasses. In the Baptistery itself on the left wall are two wings of a rather quaint triptych, representing St. Martin dividing his cloak with the beggar; St. Nicholas raising to life the three boys who had been salted for meat; St. Mary Magdalen with the pot of ointment (in the distance, as Penitent in the Desert); and St. Barbara with her tower; dated 1613. Also a rude Flemish picture (16th century) of the lives of St. Joachim and St. Anna, and their daughter the Blessed Virgin:—the main episodes are the Marriage of the Virgin, Birth of the Virgin, and Rejection of St. Joachim from the Temple, with other scenes in the background.

The end wall of the Baptistery has Peter Pourbus's masterpiece, a *triptych painted for the Guild of the Holy Sacrament, attached to the church of St. Sauveur, and allusive to their functions. The outer wings, when closed, represent the Miracle of the Mass of St. Gregory, when the Host, as he consecrated it, was changed into the bodily Presence of the Saviour, to silence a doubter. It thus shows in a visible form the tremendous mystery of Transubstantiation, in honour of which the Guild was founded. Behind, the Brothers of the Confraternity are represented (on the right wing) in attendance on the Pope, as spectators of the miracle.

One of them holds his triple crown. These may rank among the finest portraits by the elder Pourbus. They show the last stage in the evolution of native Flemish art before it was revolutionized by Rubens. The inner picture represents, in the centre, the Last Supper, or rather, the Institution of the Eucharist, to commemorate which fact the Guild was founded. The arrangement of the figures is in the old conventional order, round three sides of a table, with Judas in the foreground to the left. The wings contain Old Testament subjects of typical import, as foreshadowing the Eucharist. Left, Melchisedec giving bread and wine to Abraham; right, Elijah fed by the angel in the Wilderness. All the faces have still much of the old Flemish portrait character.

On the right wall are the wings of a picture, by F. Pourbus (the son), painted for the Guild of Shoemakers, whose chapel is adjacent. The inside contains portraits of the members. On the outside are their patrons, St. Crispinus and St. Crispianus, with their shoemakers' knives.

Also, an early Crucifixion, of the school of Cologne (about 1400), with St. Catherine holding her wheel and trampling on the tyrant Maximin, by whose orders she was executed, and St. Barbara with her tower. (These two also occur together in Memling's great triptych.) The picture is interesting as the only specimen in Bruges of the precursors of Van Eyck on the lower Rhine. The Baptistery contains, besides, a fine old candlestick, and a quaint ciborium (for the Holy Oil) with coloured reliefs of the Seven Joys of Mary (1536).

The vistas from the North Transept are impressive. It terminates in the Chapel of the Shoemakers' Guild, with a fine carved wooden door of about 1470, and good brasses, as well as an early crucifix. It is dedicated to the patron saints of the craft, and bears their arms, a boot.

The first two chapels in the Ambulatory (behind the Choir) have good screens.

The third Chapel encloses the tomb of Archbishop Carondelet, in alabaster, (1544,) a fine work of the Italian Renaissance. The Descent from the Cross by Claeissens, with the Crown of Thorns and the Holy Blood in the foreground: on the wings, St. Philip, and the donor, under the protection of (the canonized) Charlemagne. Near this is a *triptych by Dierick Bouts, (falsely ascribed to Memling) representing, in the centre, St. Hippolytus torn to pieces by four horses. (He was the jailor of St. Lawrence, who converted him: see Mrs. Jameson).

The faces show well the remarkable power of this bourgeois painter of Louvain. On the left wing are the donors; on the right wing Hippolytus confesses himself a Christian, and is condemned to martyrdom. Over the altar, retable, a Tree of Jesse, in carved woodwork, with the family of Our Lady: on the wings, (painted,) the legend of St. Hubert and the stag, and the legend of St. Lucy.

In the Apse is the Chapel of the Host.

The next chapel, of the Seven Sorrows, has a Mater Dolorosa of 1460 (copy of one at Rome); a fine *brass; and the *portrait of Philippe le Beau, known as Philippus Stok (father of Charles V), and bearing the collar of the Golden Fleece.

The Choir, (admirable architecturally,) contains the *stalls and arms of the Knights of the Golden Fleece, with good carved Misereres.

The Cathedral contains many other pictures of interest, which, however, do not fall within the scope of these Guides.

The Chambre des Marguilliers, or Churchwardens' Vestry, contains manuscripts and church furniture, sufficiently described by the sacristan.

In the Sacristy are still preserved the relics of St. Donatian, with accompanying notes as to their origin and significance.

We now continue onward to the Church of Our Lady, with the guide overleaf assuming you have just departed St. Salvator.

Church of Our Lady

[This church is open from 9:30am to 5:00pm, Monday to Saturday. On Sundays tours are taken from 1:30pm to 5pm.

While entry to the nave is free, the museum section – and hence most of the major artworks I note herein, makes a charge of 6 euros. Children under 12 however go free, while seniors and young people under 26 receive discounts.]

On leaving the Cathedral, go round the south side, which affords an excellent view of the chapels built out from the apse. Then take the little Rue du St. Esprit as far as the Church of Our Lady, which replaced a chapel, built by St. Boniface, the Apostle of Germany, in 744, and enclosed in the town in 909.

The Gothic facade and archways of the Church of Our Lady - Image: Bernt Rostad

Stand opposite it, in the small Place on the north side, to observe the somewhat shapeless architecture, the handsome brick tower crowned by a tall brick steeple, and the beautiful little *porch or "Paradise," built out from the main structure in flamboyant Gothic of the 15th century. The portal of this porch has been walled up, and the area is now used as a chapel, approached from the interior. Notice the delicate tracery of the windows, the fine finials and niches, and the charming gable-end.

The picturesque building with turrets to the left of the church was originally the mansion of the family Van der Gruuthuus, one of the principal medieval stocks of Bruges. It had a passage communicating with the family gallery in the church of Notre-Dame. The building, recently restored, is now in course of being fitted up for the Town Museum of Antiquities. A Museum of Lace is already installed in it; the entrance is by a doorway over the bridge to the left.

Church of our Lady Nave and Organ - Image: Paul Hermans

Enter the church, and walk straight into the Nave, below the great West Window, a spot which affords a good view of the centre of the church, the vaulted double Aisles, and the angular Apse. The Choir is shut off from the body of the church by a very ugly marble Rood-Screen (1722), still bearing its crucifix, and with a figure of Our Lady, patroness of the church, enshrined above its central arch. Rococo statues of the Twelve Apostles, with their well-known symbols (1618), are attached to the pillars. (Note these symbols: they recur in similar situations everywhere.) In spite of hideous disfigurements, the main portion of the interior is still a fine specimen of good middle Gothic architecture, mainly of the 14th century.

Walk up the outer left Aisle. The last bay is formed by the Baptistery, originally the porch, whose beautiful exterior we have already viewed. Its interior architecture is also very charming. It contains the Font, and the usual figure of the patron, St. John the Baptist. This Aisle terminates in an apsidal chapel (of the Holy Cross) containing inferior pictures of the 17th century, representing the history of a relic of the True Cross preserved here.

The inner left Aisle leads to the Ambulatory or passage at the back of the Choir. The Confessionals to the right have fairly good rococo carved woodwork, 1689. On the left is the handsome mediæval woodwork gallery (1474), belonging to the Van der Gruuthuus family, originally approached by a passage from their mansion behind. Beneath it, is a screen of delicate early Gothic architecture, with family escutcheons above the door.

The windows of the Apse have good modern stained glass.

On the left, at the entrance to the Apse, Pourbus's Adoration of the Shepherds, a winged picture, closed. The sacristan will open it. On the wings are, left, the donor, Sire Josse de Damhoudere, with his patron, St. Josse, and his four sons; right, his wife, Louise, with her five daughters, and her patron St. Louis of France, wearing his crown and robe of fleurs-de-lis, and holding the main de justice. He is represented older than is usual, or indeed historical, and in features somewhat resembles Henri IV. This is a fine picture for its master. On the outer wings are the cognate subjects, the Circumcision and the Adoration of the Magi, in grisaille.

The chapel in the Apse, formerly the Lady Chapel, now contains the Host. It has a gaudy modern altar for the monstrance.

In the South Ambulatory, over a doorway, Foundation of the Church of Santa Maria Maggiore at Rome, by Claeissens.

The chapel to the left contains the celebrated **tombs of Mary of Burgundy and Charles the Bold, her father. Mary was the wife of Maximilian, and died by a fall from her horse in 1482, when only twenty-five. Her **monument was designed and executed by Peter Beckere of Brussels, by order of her son Philippe le Beau, in 1502.

The sarcophagus is of black marble: the statue of the Princess, in gilt bronze, lies recumbent upon it. The style is intermediate between that of the later Middle Ages and of the full Renaissance. Beside it is the *tomb of Charles the Bold, of far less artistic value. Charles was buried at Nancy, after the fatal battle, but his body was transported to St. Donatian in this town by his descendant Charles V, and finally laid here beside his daughter by Philip II, who had this tomb constructed for his ancestor in imitation of that of Mary.

(I advise the visitor after seeing these tombs and the great chimney-piece of the Franc de Bruges to read up the history of Charles the Bold and his descendants, down to Charles V.)

The east wall of this chapel, beyond the tomb of Charles the Bold, has a fine picture of Our Lady of Sorrows, enthroned, surrounded by smaller subjects of the Seven Sorrows. Beginning at the left, the Circumcision, the Flight into Egypt, Christ lost by his parents in the Temple, the Way to Calvary, (with St. Veronica holding out her napkin,) the Crucifixion, (with Our Lady, St. John, and Mary Magdalen,) the Descent from the Cross, and the Deposition in the Tomb. A fine work of its sort, attributed to Mostart (or to Maubeuge).

On the west wall are two wings from a triptych by Pourbus, with tolerable portraits, (centre-piece destroyed,) and an early Flemish painting of the Deposition from the Cross (interesting for comparison with Roger van der Weyden and Gerard David). In the foreground lies the vessel containing the Holy Blood. On the wings are the Crucifixion and the Resurrection. The whole is very rudely painted. Outside are portraits of the donor and his wife and children, with their patrons St. James (staff and scallop) and St. Margaret (whose dragon just appears in the background).

Michelangelo's Madonna - Image: Artmechanic

On an arcade, a little further on, is a very early fresco (1350?) of a saint (St. Louis of France?), and also a dainty small relief (about 1500) of a donor, introduced by his patron, St. Peter, adoring Our Lady.

The end chapel of the right aisle, that of the Holy Sacrament, contains a celebrated and noble white marble **Madonna and

Child, by Michael Angelo, enshrined in a black marble niche. The pensive, grave, and graceful face, the exquisite modelling of the dainty naked Child, and the beautiful infantile pose of its left hand, all betray a design of Michelangelo, though the execution may possibly have been left to pupils.

But the modelling is softer and more feminine than is usual with this great sculptor, except in his early period. In this respect, it resembles most the unfinished Madonna in the Bargello at Florence. Condivi mentions that Peter Mouscron of Bruges ordered of Michael Angelo a Madonna and Child in bronze: he was probably mistaken as to the material: and we have here doubtless the work in question. Apart from its great artistic value, this exquisite group is interesting as affording another link between Flanders and Italy.

The same chapel also contains some good 17th century pictures.

Near the confessional, as we return towards the West End of the church, we find a good diptych of Herri met de Bles, of 1520, containing, left panel, an Annunciation, with all the conventional elements; to the left, as usual, is the angel Gabriel; to the right, Our Lady. These relative positions are never altered. The lilies in the pot, the desk and book, the bed with its furniture, the arcade in the background, and the rich brocade, are all constant features in pictures of this subject. Look out for them elsewhere.

The right panel has the Adoration of the Magi, with the Old, Middle-aged, and Young Kings, the last-named a Moor. This quaint and interesting work of a Flemish painter, with its archaic background, and its early Italian reminiscences, also betrays the influence of Dürer. Among the other pictures may be mentioned a triptych in an adjacent small chapel: the central panel shows the Transfiguration, with the three apostles below, Moses, Elias, and the Eternal Father above (perhaps by Jan Mostart). On the wings (much later, by P. Pourbus), are the portraits of the donor, his wife, and their patron saints.

Prominently displayed is a famous but overrated Crucifixion by Van Dyck. Though possessing beauty of conception and composition, the work has been spoiled somewhat by restorations.

The West Wall of the church has several large pictures of the later Renaissance, which can be sufficiently inspected on their merits by those who care for them. The best of them are the Adoration of the Magi by Seghers, and De Crayer's Adoration of the Infant Jesus. I do not propose to deal at length with later Flemish art till we reach Brussels and Antwerp: at Bruges, it is best to confine oneself to the introductory period of Flemish painting—that of the Burgundian princes. I will therefore only call attention here to the meaningless way in which huge pictures like B. van Orley's Crucifixion, with subsidiary scenes from the Passion, reproduce the form of earlier winged pictures, which becomes absurd on this gigantic scale.

The Church of Saint Jacob / Sint-Jakobsberk

[Open during daytime hours from around 9am to 5pm, with shorter hours for visiting tourists on Sunday to allow for the morning services]

This church stands in the street of the same name, conveniently near the Hôtel du Commerce. It is also referred to as the Church of Saint James. It is quite notable for housing the tombstone of the great artist Peter Paul Rubens.

It is a good old mediæval building (12th century, rebuilt 1457-1518), but hopelessly ruined by alterations in the 17th century, and now, as a fabric, externally and internally uninteresting. Its architecture is in the churchwarden style: its decoration in the upholsterer's.

The carved wooden pulpit is a miracle of bad taste (17th century), surpassed only by the part-coloured marble rood-screen. A few good pictures and decorative objects, however, occur among the mass of paintings ranged round its walls as in a gallery. The best is a panel of the old Flemish School (by Dierick Bouts, or more probably a pupil), in the left aisle, just beyond the second doorway.

It tells very naïvely the History of St. Lucy (see Mrs. Jameson). Left, she informs her mother that she is about to distribute her goods to the poor, who are visibly represented in a compact body asking alms behind her. Centre, she is hailed before the consul Paschasius by her betrothed, whom she refuses to marry.

 She confesses herself a Christian, and is condemned to a life of shame. Right, she is dragged away to a house of ill-fame, the consul Paschasius accompanying; but two very stumpy oxen fail to move her. The Holy Ghost flits above her head. The details are good, but the figures very wooden and dated, 1480.

Beside it is an extravagant Lancelot Blondeel of St. Cosmo and St. Damian, the doctor saints, with surgical instruments and pots of ointment. The central picture shows their martyrdom.

Further on hangs a good Flemish triptych (according to Waagen, by Jan Mostart), representing, the prophecies of Christ's coming: centre, the Madonna and Child; with King Solomon below, from whom a genealogical tree rises to bear St. Joachim and St. Anna, parents of Our Lady. right and left of him, Balaam and Isaiah, who prophesied of the Virgin and Christ: with two Sibyls, universally believed in the Middle Ages to have also foretold the advent of the Saviour. The stem ends in the Virgin and Child. Left, the Tiburtine Sibyl showing the Emperor Augustus the vision of the glorious Virgin in the sky: right, St. John the Evangelist in Patmos beholding the Apocalyptic vision of the Woman clothed with the Sun. This is a fine work of its kind, and full of the prophetic ideas of the Middle Ages.

Pass round the Ambulatory and Choir to the first chapel at the east end of the right Aisle. It contains an altar with the Madonna and Child in Della Robbia ware, probably by Luca. Also, a fine tomb of Ferry de Gros and his two wives, the first of whom reposes by his side and the second beneath him. This is a good piece of early Renaissance workmanship (about 1530). The church also contains a few excellent later works by Pourbus and others, which need not be specified. This was the church of the Florentine merchants at Bruges (whence perhaps the Della Robbia) and particularly of the Portinari, who commissioned the great altar-piece by Van der Goes now in the Hospital of Santa Maria Nuova at Florence.

The other churches of Bruges need not detain the tourist, though all contain a few objects of interest for the visitor who has a week or two at his disposition.

Groeningemuseum

[The museum is closed on Mondays – between Tuesday and Sunday the opening hours are from 9:30am to 5pm.

Adults pay an admission fee of 8 euros, with children under 12 years admitted free. Those of senior age or under 26 receive a discounted rate of 6 euros.]

The Groeningemuseum is situated at Djiver, and was conceived as a means of uniting the hitherto scattered artworks of Bruges into a single, encompassing destination. Among the institutions it replaced almost a century ago was the renowned Academy of the Rue St. Catherine.

While the museum encompasses many neoclassical works, as well as modern art from the recent post-World War 2 era, the artistic centerpieces without doubt belong to Jan van Eyck, Hans Memling and the other Flemish Primitive era painters. I have chosen to describe in detail the most notable works showcased in the rooms of this altogether reasonable gallery.

Jan van Eyck. **Altar-piece, ordered by George van der Palen, for the High Altar of the original Cathedral of St. Donatian, of which he was a canon. The centre of the picture is occupied by the Madonna and Child, the face of Our Lady somewhat recalling German models. She sits in the apse of a church, probably St. Donatian. The Child, whom it is the fashion to describe as "aged-looking," fondles a parrot and grasps a bunch of flowers. To the left stands St. Donatian the Archbishop, patron saint of the church for which this altar-piece was painted. He bears his usual symbol, the wheel with five lighted candles (as in the beautiful panel by Gerard David in the National Gallery at London). This is a fine and finely-painted figure. To the right, St. George, in full armour, admirably represented, but in an affected attitude, lifts his casque somewhat jauntily as he presents his namesake the Canon George to Our Lady. In all this we get a touch of Burgundian courtliness: the event is represented as a state ceremonial. With his left hand the Saint supports his Red Cross banner. The portrait of the kneeling Canon himself,—asthmatic, pudding-faced—is very admirable and life-like, but by no means flattered. He grips his prayer-book with an old man's tremulous hand. (For a profound criticism of this fine picture, see Conway.) The insipid Madonna, the rather foolish St. George, the fine portrait of the Canon, are all typical of Van Eyck's manner. The accessories of architecture, decoration, and background, should also be carefully noted. The capitals of the columns and the knobs of glass in the window, as well as St. George's costume, are elaborated in Van Eyck's finest fashion.

(2.) Jan van Eyck. *Portrait of his wife, painted for presentation to the Bruges Guild of Painters, together with one of the artist himself, now undiscoverable. This is a fine though evidently unflattered portrait of a capable housewife, very stiffly arrayed in her best church-going costume. It deserves close inspection.

Above it, (3.) Head of Christ, ascribed to Jan van Eyck, but in reality a poor and reduced copy of the picture at Berlin.

(4.) Memling. **Triptych painted for Willem Moreel or Morelli, a member of a wealthy Savoyard family settled at Bruges. Like Jan van Eyck's portrait of the two Arnolfini in London, and Hugo van der Goes's triptych of the Portinari at Florence, this picture marks well the cosmopolitan character of old Bruges. In the central panel, St. Christopher (whose altar in the church of St. Jacques it adorned) wades with his staff through the water, feeling as he goes the increasing burden of the Christ-Child on his shoulder. (For the legend, see Mrs. Jameson.) To the left, above, is the diminutive figure of the hermit with his lantern, which always accompanies St. Christopher. The left foreground of the picture is occupied by St. Maurus, in his Benedictine costume; to the right is St. Giles (St. Egidius) the hermit, with the wounded doe, the arrow piercing the arm of the saint.

The left wing represents the donor, Willem Moreel, under the care of his patron, St. William, who wears a hermit's dress above his coat of armour. (When a saint places his hand on a votary's shoulder it usually implies that the votary is a namesake.) Behind are Moreel's five sons. All these portraits, but particularly that of the donor and his eldest son, who closely resembles him, are admirable. The right wing represents the donor's wife, Barbara, under the protection of her patron, St. Barbara, with her tower, showing as usual three windows (emblematic of the Holy Trinity). Behind the lady are her two daughters, one of whom is habited as a Benedictine nun, whence, doubtless, the introduction of St. Maurus into the main altar-piece. This fine triptych originally decorated an altar of St. Christopher in Moreel's private chapel in the church of St. Jacques.

One of his daughters is the "Sibylla Sambetha" represented at the Hospital. The wings at the back represent in grisaille St. John the Baptist with the lamb, and St. George with the dragon. It was usual to paint the outer wings in grisaille or in low tones of colour, so that the splendour of the interior hues might burst upon the spectator as the triptych was opened.

Gerard David has a *triptych, painted for Jean des Trompes, for the High Altar of the lower chapel of the Holy Blood. The central panel represents the Baptism of Christ. In the middle, the Saviour wades in the water of a diminutive Jordan, where the concentric circles show the increased careful study of nature.

On the right-hand side of the picture, St. John-Baptist, patron saint of the donor, pours water on his head. The relative positions of these two figures, and of the angel to the left holding a robe, are conventional: they have descended from a very early period of art. (In the Ravenna mosaics, the place of the angel is filled by the river-god of the Jordan with his urn, afterwards transformed and Christianized into an angel with a towel. Look out in future for similar arrangements.) The central figures are weak; but the robe of the angel is painted with Flemish minuteness. So are the flowers and leaves of the foreground. Above, the dove descends upon the head of the Saviour, while the Eternal Father pronounces from the skies the words, "Behold my Beloved Son in whom I am well pleased."

In the background are two other episodes: on the left is the preaching of St. John-Baptist (where Oriental costumes indicate the heathen); right, St. John-Baptist pointing out Christ to his disciples with the words, "Behold the Lamb of God." The distance shows two towns and a fine landscape. Observe the admirable painting of the trees, with their good shadows; also the ivy climbing up the trunk of one to the right. This picture is among the earliest in which the gloom of a wood is accurately represented: in many other respects it well illustrates the rise of landscape-painting. (For an exhaustive criticism, see Conway.) The left wing has a portrait of the donor, with his other patron, St. John the Evangelist, holding the cup. Beside the donor kneels his little son Philip. This portrait, the face and foot of the Evangelist, the fur of the donor's robe, the crane in the background, and many other accessories deserve close attention.

Two figures in the background dimly foreshadow Teniers. The right wing has a portrait of the donor's wife, Elizabeth, with her four daughters. Behind her stands her patroness, St. Elizabeth of Hungary, in Franciscan robes, with the crown on her head and the double crown and book in her hands, as on the statuette at the door of the Béguinage. The painting of a rosary here is excellent. The outer wings (turn them back) show, on the left, the Madonna and Child with a bunch of grapes; on the right, the donor's second wife Madeleine, introduced by her patroness, St. Mary Madeleine, who holds the alabaster pot of ointment. By the lady's side kneels her daughter. The background consists of a view, probably in the Bruges of that period. Painted about 1507.

Arguably the most striking work by Gerard David, The Punishment of the Unjust Judge, is present. These two panels are of a type commonly set up in courts of justice as a warning to evil-doers. They were ordered by the Bruges magistracy. You will see a similar pair by Dierick Bouts in Brussels. The story, a horrid one, is taken from Herodotus. Sisamnes was a judge in Persia whom King Cambyses detected receiving a bribe and ordered to be flayed alive. The king then stretched his skin on the seat of judgment, and appointed the son of Sisamnes to sit in his father's place, that he might remember to avoid a like fate. The first picture represents, in the background, the bribery. In the foreground, King Cambyses, in a rich embroidered robe, demonstrates on his fingers the guilt of the unjust judge. Sisamnes is seized on his tribunal by a man of the people; courtiers, lawyers, and burgesses looking on. The expression on his face and the painting of all the accessories is admirable.

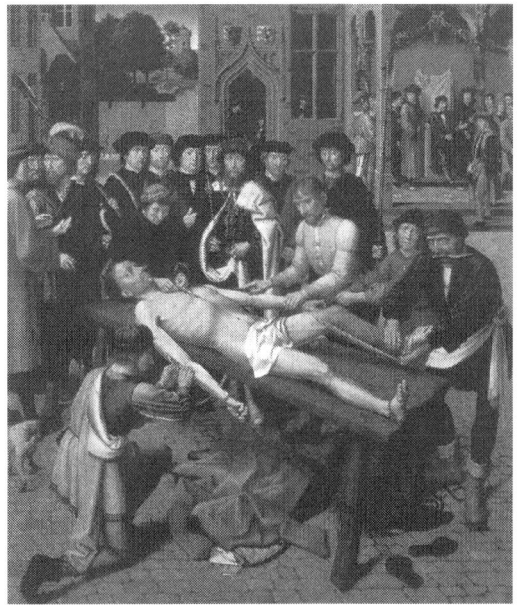

In the second picture we have the flaying of the unjust judge, a horrible scene, powerfully rendered. Cambyses stands by, holding his sceptre, surrounded by courtiers who recall the last age of the Burgundian dominion. In the background (as a subsequent episode) the son of Sisamnes is seen sitting in his father's place: behind him hangs the skin of the father. Architecture, landscape, ropes, and all other accessories of this painful picture should be carefully noted.

15. J. Prévost. Last Judgment. Below, the dead are rising, half naked, from the tomb, girt only with their shrouds; the good receiving garments from angels, and the bad hurried away to a very Flemish and unimpressive Hell. Above, Christ as Judge holds the sword. Two angels blow out the words of blessing or malediction. On the spectator's left, Our Lady shows the breast that suckled the Redeemer. Behind her are St. Peter with the key, St. Paul with the sword, St. Bartholomew with the knife, and other saints. On the right are St. John-Baptist with the lamb, King David with the harp, Moses, horned (as always), with the tables of the law, and a confused group of saints. This picture is rather curious than beautiful. Above it is a later treatment of the same subject by Van Coornhuuse, interesting for

comparison as showing the usual persistence of types and the conventional grouping of the individual figures. Compare especially the corresponding personages in the lower left-hand corners.

A few other pictures deserve passing notice. There is Death and the Miser, of the School of Quentin Matsys. Lancelot Blondeel, the architect of the great chimney-piece of the Franc de Bruges, represents St. Luke painting Our Lady, in one of the fantastic frames in which this painter delighted. Blondeel also has a St. George and the Dragon, with the Princess Cleodolind looking on. Around it are four smaller scenes of his martyrdom: (he was boiled, burnt with torches, dragged by a horse, and finally decapitated).

Other works include a good diptych of the Flemish school, by an unknown contemporary of Gerard David. It represents, left, a donor, with his patron St. John the Almoner, holding his symbol, a sheaf of corn. On the right, his wife with her patroness, St. Godeliva. 28, is an Adoration of the Magi, where the Three Kings again illustrate the three ages of man and the three continents. Beside it is a Nativity which exhibits all the traditional features already noted.

You may also behold a tolerably good Adoration of the Magi, of the German School, 15th century. Note once more the Three Kings, of whom the youngest is a Moor. Further drawings by Jan van Eyck of St. Barbara should be closely inspected. She holds a palm of martyrdom. In the background, workmen build her tower. It is interesting as a scene of real life at this period. This is a replica of the well-known picture at Antwerp. To the right, two coloured drawings by Gerard David from the life of St. John-Baptist. Above these hangs a tolerable P. Pourbus of the Last

Judgment, valuable for comparison with the two previous treatments of the same subject on the principal wall. Go from one to the other once or twice. Later painters of the Renaissance use this solemn theme as a mere excuse for obtruding the nude—and often the vulgar nude—into churches. On the same wall are a good triptych in grisaille by P. Pourbus (Way to Calvary, Descent from the Cross, Resurrection: from Notre-Dame at Damme), and other pictures.

The remaining walls have portraits and other works, from the 17th century downwards, most of which need no explanation. A few of them, indeed, are not without merit. But, as I have before observed, it is best in medieval Bruges to confine oneself to the 13th, 14th, 15th, and early 16th centuries, leaving the rise of the Renaissance, and the later Flemish School of painting, to occupy us at Antwerp, where they can be studied to far greater advantage.

As mentioned earlier, both within and outside the Groeningemuseum there are many artworks of later periods. Cubist and expressionist influences abound, with notable Magritte and Delvaux pieces providing interesting if comparatively trivial differentiation to the Medieval and Renaissance era works which outstrip them in significance.

Ghent

A Panoramic view of Ghent - Image: Michael Schmalenstroer

The modern Ghent is an attractive and commonly overlooked city and capital of East Flanders. Somewhat overshadowed by its close neighbor Bruges, Ghent as city nevertheless boasts a greater size and scope with its civic contours bending around the one uniting feature of Flanders – its waterways.

Picturesque scenes and architecture may be beheld alongside the River Leie, with the old city centre and Graslei locality of great interest to visitors. As well as the majestic scenes unfolding in the centre, the enchanting gothic spires of the city's cathedral and old town.

Recent modernization of the tramways and bus system have made navigation easier. Owing to this and steady promotional efforts, tourist numbers continue to trend upward. Many visitors, privy to the fact the town's social, economic and religious heritage are so intertwined with its architectural achievements and beauty, are keen to absorb the many artistic works and designs which populate the major attractions.

Origins of Ghent

Flanders owes everything to its water communications. At the junction of the Schelde with the Lys or Lei, there grew up in the very early Middle Ages a trading town, named Gent in Flemish, and Gand in French, but commonly Anglicised as Ghent. It lay on a close network of rivers and canals, formed partly by these two main streams, and partly by the minor channels of the Lieve and the Moere, which together intersect it into several islands. Such a tangle of inland waterways, giving access to the sea and to Bruges, Courtrai, and Tournai, as well as less directly to Antwerp and Brussels, ensured the rising town considerable importance in early eras.

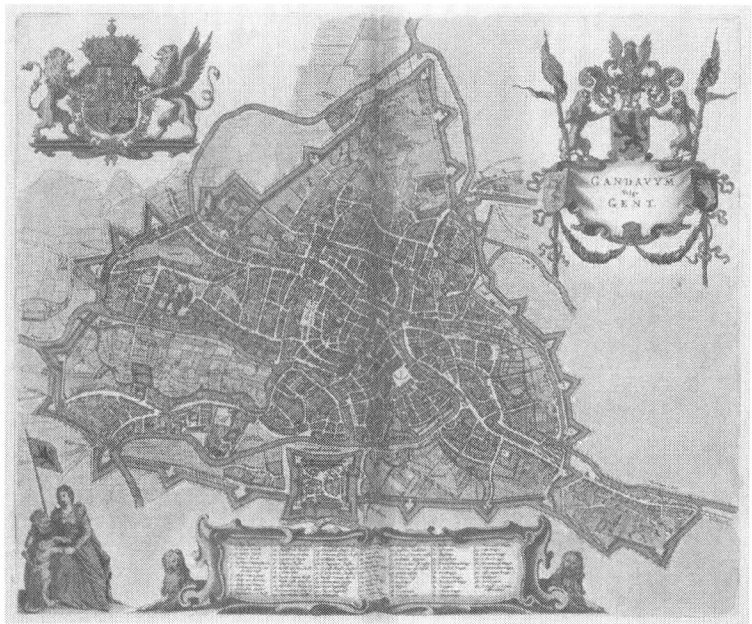

It formed the centre of a radiating commerce. Westward, its main relations were with London and the English wool ports;

eastward with Cologne, Maastricht, the Rhine towns, and Italy. Ghent was always the capital of East Flanders, as Bruges or Ypres were of the Western province; and after the Counts lost possession of Arras and Artois, it became in the 13th century their principal residence and the metropolis of the country. The trade in weaving grew rapidly in importance, and the Ghenters received from their Count a charter of liberties of the usual mediæval burgher type.

Battle of the Spurs sketch from the Royal Society of Antiquaries depicting an engagement of militia and cavalry

As time went on, and the city advanced in wealth, its subjection to its sovereigns became purely nominal. Ghent equipped large bodies of citizen soldiers, and repulsed a considerable English army under Edward I. The Ghenters were also determined opponents of the claims of the French kings to interfere in the internal affairs of Flanders; thus they were mainly instrumental in winning the famous Battle of the Spurs in 1302, when the citizens of Bruges and Ghent put to flight the army of France under the Count of Artois before the walls of Tournai, and dedicated as trophies 700 golden spurs, worn by the French knights whom they had routed. This battle, memorable as one of the chief triumphs of nascent industrial freedom over the chivalry and royalty of medievalism, secured the liberties of the Flemish towns against French aggression.

Early in the 14th century, the burghers of Ghent, under their democratic chief, Jacob or Jacques Van Artevelde, attained practical independence. Till 1322, the Counts and people of Flanders had been united in their resistance to the claims of France; but with the accession of Count Louis of Nevers, the aspect of affairs changed. Louis was French by education, sympathies, and interests, and aristocratic by nature; he sought to curtail the liberties of the Flemish towns, and to make himself despotic. The wealthy and populous burgher republics resisted, and in 1337 Van Artevelde was appointed Captain of Ghent. Louis fled to France, and asked the aid of Philip of Valois.

Thereupon, Van Artevelde made himself the ally of Edward III. of England, then beginning his war with France; but as the Flemings did not like entirely to cast off their allegiance—a thing repugnant to medieval sentiment—Van Artevelde persuaded Edward to put forward his trumped-up claim to the crown of France, and thus induced the towns to transfer their fealty from Philip to his English rival. It was therefore in his character as King of France that Edward came to Flanders. The alliance thus formed between the great producer of raw wool, England, and the great manufacturer of woollen goods, Ghent, proved of immense commercial importance to both parties. But as Count Louis sided with Philip of Valois, the breach between the democracy of Ghent and its nominal sovereign now became impassable. Van Artevelde held supreme power in Ghent and Flanders for nine years—the golden age of Flemish commerce—and was treated on equal terms by Edward, who stopped at Ghent as his guest for considerable periods. But he was opposed by a portion of the citizens, and his suggestion that the Black Prince, son of Edward III., should be elected Count of Flanders, proved so unpopular with his enemies that he was assassinated by one of them, Gerard Denys. The town and states immediately repudiated the murder; and the alliance which Van Artevelde had brought about still continued. It had far-reaching results; the woollen industry was introduced by Edward into the Eastern Counties of England, and Ghent had risen meanwhile to be the chief manufacturing city of Europe.

The sun sets over the river Lys in Ghent - Image: Graham Richter

The quarrel between the democratic weavers and their exiled Counts was still carried on by Philip van Artevelde, the son of Jacques, and godson of Queen Philippa of England, herself a Hainaulter. Under his rule, the town continued to increase in wealth and population. But the general tendency of later medieval Europe towards centralised despotisms as against urban republics was too strong in the end for free Ghent. In 1381, Philip was appointed dictator by the Democratic Party, in the war against the Count, son of his father's old opponent, whom he repelled with great slaughter in a battle near Bruges. He then made himself Regent of Flanders. But Count Louis obtained the aid of Charles VI. of France, and defeated and killed Philip Van Artevelde at the disastrous battle of Roosebeke in 1382. That was practically the end of local freedom in Flanders. Though the cities continued to revolt against their sovereigns from time to time, they were obliged to submit for the most part to their Count and to the Burgundian princes who inherited from him by marriage.

The subsequent history of Ghent is that of the capital of the Burgundian Dukes, and of the House of Austria. Here the German king, Maximilian, afterwards Emperor, married Mary of Burgundy, the heiress of the Netherlands; and here Charles V. was born in the palace of the Counts. It was his principal residence, and he was essentially a Fleming. Other historical reminiscences will be pointed out in the course of our peregrinations.

The old waterways, partially artificial, between Ghent and the sea, other than the circuitous route by the shallow Schelde, had silted up by 1827, when a ship canal was constructed to Terneuzen. This canal has since been widened and deepened so as to admit vessels of 1,700 tons; for a time this helped to some small degree to save the town from the commercial decline suffered by Bruges. In the 21st century however, it took several enhancements of the port and sea facilities in order for the city to retain its commercial reputation. But as its mouth lies in what is now Dutch territory, and as heavy tolls are levied, it is comparatively little used. Another and somewhat frequented canal leads to Bruges; but Ghent owes most of its existing prosperity to its manufactures (cotton, linen, engines, leather) and to its central position on the railway system.

The important points for the tourist to bear in mind are these, however. Ghent during the Middle Ages was a merchant republic, practically independent, with its guilds and its belfry, the last of which was used to summon the citizens to arms in case of danger. It was also the chief manufacturing town in Europe, as Bruges was the chief commercial centre. By treaty with Edward III., Bruges was made the "staple" or sole port of entry for English wool: and this wool was woven into cloth for the most part at Ghent.

Further details of the vicissitudes of Ghent can be found in Van Duyse, Gand, Monumental et Pittoresque.

The chief objects of interest at Ghent are the Cathedral, with its great Van Eyck; and the Town Hall and Belfry. These can be tolerably seen in one day: but a stay of three or four days will not be too much to explore the curious nooks of the early city.

The Core of Ghent

The old town of Ghent lies on the island formed by the junction of the Lys and the Schelde, with their various backwaters (all now largely artificial). Near this point, but beyond the Lys, the Counts of Flanders early erected a strong castle, the Gravensteen or Oudeburg, beneath whose protection, aided by the two navigable rivers, merchants and weavers gradually settled. As at Bruges, the heart of the town, however, is purely municipal and mercantile in its architecture. The Town Hall, which was the meeting-place of the citizens, and the Belfry, which summoned them to arms or council, are the chief points of interest in the city. The Schelde is still tidal to its very centre.

A vibrant market takes place in The Kouter - Image: Demeester

As many visitors will probably stop in one of the hotels on the the Kouter, near the southern end of older Ghent, I shall frankly take that square as our starting-point. Formerly termed the Place D'Armes, The Kouter is an ideal base from which to explore the greater city. To the right of The Kouter is swiftly sighted the large square tower; that of the Cathedral, while the tapering spire, crowned by a gilt dragon, belongs to the Belfry.

Go first on a tour of orientation through early Ghent. If you follow these directions implicitly, you can see everything important in one short walk. Cross the Kouter diagonally to the northeast corner, and follow the small and narrow streets which run due north to the front of the Cathedral. Walk round the south side of this, to form a first general impression, but do not enter it at present.

Exterior of St. Bavos Cathedral - Image: Mylius

Then, from the West Front of the Cathedral, take the Rue St. Jean straight before you. The tower with the gilded dragon which faces you as you walk is that of the Belfry. It was designed in 1183, about a century earlier than that of Bruges, but only erected between 1321 and 1339; it is a fine work in the Early Gothic style. Its windows have been walled up. The tapering turret which crowns the tower is unfortunately modern, and of iron. On the very summit stands a huge gilded dragon, which universal tradition represents as having been brought from St. Sophia at Constantinople to Bruges by the Crusader Baldwin of Flanders, (1204), and removed as a trophy by the people of Ghent (under Philip van Artevelde) in 1382. It certainly appears to be of Oriental origin, but is stated on documentary evidence (discovered by M. Vuylsteke) to have been made in Ghent itself in 1380. If so, it would seem at least to be based on an Oriental model.

Ghent Belfry and cloth hall - Image: Donarreiskoffer

The relatively small building at the foot of the Belfry, is the Cloth Hall, erected in 1424, a graceful but not very important Gothic edifice (of the Decorated period), with niches vacant of their statues. The concierge of the Belfry now has a room in it, with entry possible upon request.

The view is extensive and beautiful, but not quite so striking as that at Bruges. The principal buildings of the city lie just below you: beyond, all Flanders. The chimes are celebrated. The chief bell is known as Roelandt.

The Botermarkt in Ghent - Image: Demeester

Now turn round into the Botermarkt or Marché au Beurre to the right, and inspect the Belfry again from the little bay in the corner opposite. This is the best near view of the tower. The portal to the right was formerly the entry to the town prison, beneath the Belfry, now in course of complete restoration. In its gable is a too-famous 18th century relief (the Mammelokker) representing the Roman daughter feeding her father from her breast at the window of a prison, and doubtless intended to excite the charity of passers-by. It certainly serves no other function, for it is neither beautiful nor decorative.

The Mammelokker depicts a Roman named Pero, a prisoner, breast-fed by his daughter to ward off starvation.

Cross over to the right side of the market. The building on the left, in two totally distinct portions, is the Hôtel-de-Ville. The part at which you first arrive, (latest in point of time,) was rebuilt in the early Renaissance style in 1595-1628. It is one of the earliest and in many ways the best example of Renaissance architecture in Belgium, in part because it retains certain good features of local domestic building, such as the pointed gable-ends (round the corner to the left) and the projecting windows with dormers on the main façade. (Look out for their origin elsewhere.) It has three storeys, with projecting half colonnades, the columns being Doric on the ground floor, Ionic on the first floor, and Corinthian on the second. Recollect the gable-ends and dormers for comparison with others in old houses in Ghent hereafter.

Now, continue on to the corner, where we arrive at the earlier Gothic portion of the Hôtel-de-Ville, erected in 1518-1535 by Dominic de Waghemakere, who also built in part the cathedral at Antwerp. The projecting polygonal corner, with its handsome balcony, is very noticeable. The work is of the latest and most florid Gothic, somewhat lacking in grace and dignity, but ornate in its splendour. Observe the depressed arches, the noble cornice, the rich decoration of garlands. A few of the niches have now been filled with modern statues of saints. From the corner opposite, a good view is obtained of both parts of the Hôtel-de-Ville and also of the Belfry.

Turn to the left into the Rue Haut-Port, to observe the main front of this earlier Gothic building, with its fine projecting windows above, its empty niches, its handsome entrance staircase and main portal, its beautiful little balcony for addressing the people below, and the large projecting window of its ancient chapel near the centre. Note how well the façade is thus broken up and diversified. This is the finest specimen of florid Gothic in Belgium. Beyond it comes another Renaissance portion, and then a handsome Renaissance dwelling-house. The street also contains several fine early houses, the best of which (a Gothic guildhall, known as the Cour St. Georges) stands at the corner to the left, facing the Hôtel-de-Ville.

The interior of the Hôtel-de-Ville need not be visited, though it has a handsome Gothic staircase (demolished, sold, built into a private house, re-erected) and some fine halls and internal courts, interesting to those who have plenty of time at their disposal.

Now, return to the Belfry and continue straight down the left-hand side of the Rue de la Catalogne. The church on the right, round the base of which houses have been allowed to cluster, is St. Nicolas—the oldest in the town. This is one of the most solid pieces of architecture at Ghent. It has a fine decorated tower, which has happily escaped restoration, besides small turrets to the Transepts, and two, rather larger, to the gable of the Nave.

The ever-lively Korenmarkt - Image: PMRMaeyaert

Go on into the Koornmarkt or Marché aux Blés, to the right; stand there for a moment, at the end of the Rue de la Catalogne, to observe the fine coup d'œil, which takes in St. Nicolas, the Belfry, and the tower of the Cathedral. The main façade of St. Nicolas faces the Koornmarkt. Over the door is a modern figure of the Saint himself, raising the three boys who were salted down for meat. Nicolas was the popular saint, the patron of the merchants and burgesses; and the prominent position of his church on the Corn Market is very characteristic of the burgher spirit of Ghent.

A hasty glance will suffice for the interior, which is a characteristic specimen of the Belgian church, with figures of the Twelve Apostles, as always, against the pillars of the Nave; an ugly carved pulpit; short Transepts; an Apse with bad glass; and the vaulting of Nave, Aisles, and Choir concealed by plaster. The tawdry decorations render what might be a fine interior wholly unimpressive. The High Altar has an altar-piece by Liemakere, representing, in the confused style of the School of Rubens, the election of St. Nicholas as Bishop of Myra. Above is an 18th century figure of the Saint, raising the three boys from the tub. The early pillars of the Choir are really handsome.

On emerging from the front of the church, continue straight on to the bridge which crosses the Lys, affording a good view to the left of the Apse of St. Michel. Then, go along the side of this handsome church, with late Gothic windows resembling English Perpendicular. It has a solid but unfinished tower, and a good West Portal, robbed of its sculpture and cruelly mutilated. A glimpse at the interior, which has been scraped and renovated, will show at once the fine architecture. The Nave has impressive round pillars, windows in the clerestory, and excellent brick vaulting. The vaulted Aisles are surrounded by chapels.

The Choir is very handsome. Walk round the Transepts and Ambulatory. There are some good works of the School of Rubens.

Now, continue along the quay, on the same side as St. Michel, (observing as you go that the early town extended to both banks of the river), in order to view the façade of the handsome Maison des Bateliers, or Guild House of the Skippers, erected in 1531 for the masters of the shipping of Ghent, in somewhat the same florid late-Gothic style as the Hôtel-de-Ville. This is the finest existing specimen of old Flemish houses. Over the doorway is an appropriate relief of a ship, somewhat antiquated and heraldic in character. By the side of this Guild-house are two others, less interesting: the first, the Guild House of the Grain Measurers; the next, very old and dilapidated, the Staple House of Corn, Romanesque, said to be the earliest civil building in Belgium. Several fine gable-ends are seen to the left, including one with Renaissance architecture, on this side of the Lys. At the moment of writing, the houses next to the Skippers' Guild are in course of demolition, exposing a bare side of the old Hall most unpicturesquely.

Now, retrace your steps over the Bridge, and through the Corn Market, almost wholly modernized, with the exception of a few gabled houses.

Cafe terraces at the Grande Boucherie - Image: Stephane Mignon

The next little square at which we arrive is the Marché aux Herbes. Its W. side is occupied by the ancient but uninteresting Grande Boucherie. Turn to the left by the corner of the

Boucherie, with Our Lady and Child in a niche, and cross the bridge to the other side of the Lys. On the left are two handsome old houses. In front rise the gateway and bastions of the Oudeburg, or Castle of the Princes. This was the primitive palace of the Counts of Flanders in Ghent.

The castle has recently been cleared from the numerous modern houses which encumbered and hid it. The first stronghold on this site was erected in 868. The existing ruins of the gateway, with round Romanesque arches, date back to 1180; the square keep behind is of the 10th century. In this palace Jacob van Artevelde entertained Edward III. When Edward returned to England, he left Queen Philippa here, and during his absence she bore (in the Monastery of St. Bavon) her third son, John of Gaunt, who took his well-known surname from the place of his birth. It was on Edward's return to Flanders, accompanied by the ladies of Philippa's suite, that he found the French fleet drawn up near Sluys to prevent his entry into the port of Bruges, on which occasion he gained the first great English naval victory. The Castle, which is now in course of partial restoration, is closely bound up with the greatness of Van Artevelde and the heroic period in the history of Ghent.

Walk round it to note its extent and its commanding position at the point where the bridge crosses the Lys to the main part of the town.

The opposite corner of the c has a Renaissance gateway, re-erected in imitation of the original by Arthus Quellin, and adorned with sculptures of Neptune, the Schelde, and the Lys, the sources of Ghent's greatness. It leads to the Fish-market. Around are several good old houses.

Continue along the quay on the same side of the river as the Oudeburg, as far as the Pont du Laitage, just before reaching which you pass on your left two 17th century houses with reliefs, (the Works of Charity, a Flying Hart, etc.). Cross the bridge and turn to the right as far as the big cannon, known as Dulle Griete or Mad Margaret, dating back to the 14th century. By the touch-hole are the Cross of St. Andrew and the Arms of Phillipe le Bon of Burgundy.

Turn into the large square in front of you. The building which faces you at the end of the street as you advance (with a tower at the corner and high gables) is one of the best old medieval houses in Ghent, the Collacie-Zolder, or Municipal Council-Room, of the 13th or 14th century. It has an interesting little pulpit or balcony at its corner, with a bell, from which addresses could be made to the people. The towers that face you a little to the left are those of St. Jacques, to be visited presently.

Statue of Jacob van Artevelde in Vrijdagmarkt - Image: David Huang

Continue into the square, at the corner of which is the Municipal Council-Room. This is the Vrijdagmarkt or Marché du Vendredi, in which a strikingly picturesque market is still held every Friday morning. If possible, visit it. The square was the forum of old Ghent and the meeting-place of the citizens. A few fine old buildings in the native local style still surround it. The centre is appropriately occupied by a modern colossal statue of Jacob van Artevelde, addressing the citizens in his famous speech when he excited them to opposition to the Count of Flanders with his Gallicising policy. At the base are allegorical figures of Flanders, and of the Belgian towns, wearing mural crowns.

The reliefs represent Van Artevelde's three chief diplomatic triumphs,—the League of Ghent with Bruges and Ypres; the League of Flanders and England; the League of Flanders, Brabant, and Hainault. In this square the most important events in the history of early Flanders took place. Here the citizens of Ghent took the oath of allegiance to each new Count on his accession, after they had compelled him to swear in good old Teutonic style "to uphold and see upheld all the standing wits (laws), fore-rights (regulations), freehoods, and wonts of the Countship and town of Ghent."

The guilds which had their halls around met here to oppose arbitrary action on the part of their sovereign. Here, too, the parties within the town itself frequently joined issue in civil contest. In later times, the Duke of Alva perpetrated most of his shameful executions on this spot. The site of the statue of Van Artevelde was originally occupied by one of Charles V., who was born in Ghent, in a palace now destroyed, and whose history (see later) is intimately connected with this town, always one of his principal residences. The statue was destroyed in 1794 by the French invaders: (picture in the Museum).

St. James Church exterior - Image: Paul Hermans

Turn up at the corner by the Municipal Council-Room and take the first street to the left, which leads you into the Place St. Jacques, occupied by the Church of St. Jacques. The façade, with the two towers, was Romanesque, but has been restored in such a wholesale way as to destroy its interest. The remainder of the church is Gothic. Walk round it so as to observe its features, noticing in particular the quaint stone spire of the right-hand tower.

The interior might be good, were it not spoiled by tawdry decorations. The pulpit has a marble figure of the patron, St.

James, with the pilgrim's staff and gourd, emblematic of his connection with the great place of pilgrimage of Santiago de Compostella. The vaulting has been freed from excrescences, and is excellent of its kind. The High Altar has a figure of St. James above, and a painting of his martyrdom beneath.

This walk will have led you through the principal part of early Ghent. Hence you may return either by the Cathedral, or by the chief line of business streets which runs direct from the Pont du Laitage to the modern Palais de Justice and the Place d'Armes.

Saint Bavo's Cathedral

[Official website: http://www.sintbaafskathedraal.be/

Opening hours are between 9:30am and 5pm during the summer season, while during the winter season from the hours of 10:30pm to 4pm. Year round on Sundays the chapel is open from 1pm until the evening.

An ordinary visit and tour costs 4 Euros, with discounted rates available for groups and students.

There is an audio guide available which explains some of the artworks within the premises.]

The local patron saint of Ghent is St. Bavo, a somewhat dubious personage, belonging to the first age of Christianity in Flanders, of whom little is known.

Legend describes him as a "Duke of Brabant" in the 7th century, which is of course an anachronism. He seems to have been a nobleman of Hesbaie who spent his life as a soldier "and in worldly pleasures"; but when he was 50, his wife died. Overwhelmed with grief, he gave up all his possessions to be distributed among the poor, and entered a cell or monastery in Ghent, of which St. Amand (see later) was the founder. Of this he became abbot.

Saint Bavo's Cathedral exterior - Image: Michal Osmenda

At last, finding the monastic life not sufficiently austere, the new saint took refuge in a hollow tree in a forest, and there spent the remainder of his days. His emblem is a falcon. The monastery of St. Bavon long existed at Ghent; some of its ruins still remain, and will be described hereafter. To this local saint, accordingly, it might seem fitting that the Cathedral of Ghent should be dedicated. But in reality the building first functioned as a parish church under the invocation of St. John the Baptist, and only received the relics and name of St. Bavon after 1540, when Charles V. destroyed the monastery, as will be described hereafter.

The real interest of the Cathedral centres, however, not in the ruins of St. Bavon, nor in his picture by Rubens, but in the great polyptych of the Adoration of the Lamb, the masterpiece of Jan van Eyck and his brother Hubert, which forms in a certain sense the point of departure for the native art of the Netherlands. This is therefore a convenient place in which to consider the position of these two great painters. They were born at Maaseyck or Eyck-sur-Meuse near Maastricht; Hubert, the elder, about 1360 or 1370; Jan, the younger, about 1390.

Ruins of the Virgin's crypt - St. Bavon's Abbey

The only undoubted work of Hubert is the altar-piece in St. Bavon, and even this is only his in part, having been completed after his death by his brother Jan. Hubert probably derived his teaching from the School of the Lower Rhine, which first in the North attained any importance, and which had its chief exponents at Maastricht and Cologne. Of this School, he was the final flower. Though not, as commonly said, the inventor of oil-painting, he was the first artist who employed the process in its developed form, and he also made immense advances in naturalness of drawing and truth of spirit.

Jan was probably a pupil of Hubert; he lived at Ghent while the great picture of the Adoration of the Lamb was still being completed; later, he was painter by appointment to the court of the Dukes of Burgundy, and had a house at Bruges, where he died in 1440. He was also employed on various missions abroad, accompanying embassies as far as to Portugal. His painting, though less ideal and beautiful than that of his great successor Memling, is marvellous in its truth: it has an extraordinary charm of purity of colour, vividness of delineation, and fine portrayal of character. Indeed, all the early Flemish artists were essentially portrait painters; they copied with fidelity whatever was set before them, whether it were fabrics, furniture, jewellery, flowers, or the literal faces and figures of men and women.

Hubert and Jan van Eyck, however, were not so much in strictness the founders of a school as the culminating point of early German art, to which they gave a new Flemish direction. Their work was almost perfect in its own kind. Their successors did not surpass them: in some respects they even fell short of them.

The Adoration of the Lamb is by far the most important thing to be seen at Ghent. But it is viewed at some disadvantage in the church, and is so full of figures and meaning that it cannot be taken in without long study. I strongly advise you, therefore, to buy a photograph of the entire composition beforehand, and try to understand as much as possible of the picture by comparing it with the account here given, the evening before you visit the picture. You will then be able more readily to grasp the actual work, in form and colour, when you see it.

Go straight from your hotel to the Cathedral,—built as the parish church of St. John about 1250-1300; re-dedicated to St. Bavon, 1540; erected into a Bishop's see, 1599. Stand before the West Front at a little distance, to examine the simple but massive architecture of the tower and façade.

The great portal has been robbed of the statues which once adorned its niches. Three have been "restored": they represent, centre, the Saviour; on the left is the patron, St. Bavon, recognisable by his falcon, his sword as duke, and his book as monk; he wears armour, with a ducal robe and cap above it; right, St. John the Baptist, the earlier patron.

Then, walk, to the right, round the south side, to observe the external architecture of the Nave, Aisles, and Choir. The latter has the characteristic rounded or apsidal termination of Continental Gothic, whereas English Gothic has usually a square end. Enter by the S. portal.

The interior, with single Aisles and short Transepts, (Early Gothic) is striking for its simple dignity, its massive pillars, and its high arches, though the undeniably noble effect of the whole is somewhat marred to English eyes by the unusual appearance of the unadorned brick walls and vaulting. The pulpit, by

Delvaux (1745), partly in oak, partly in marble, represents Truth revealing the Christian Faith to astonished Paganism (figured as an old and outworn man:) it is a model of all that should be avoided in plastic or religious art. The screen which separates the Choir from the Transepts is equally unfortunate. The apsidal end of the Choir, however, with its fine modern stained glass, forms a very pleasing feature in the general coup d'œil.

Begin the examination in detail with the left or north Aisle. The 1st chapel, that of the Holy Cross, contains a Pietà by Janssens and a Descent from the Cross by Rombouts, good works of the school of Rubens. The 3rd chapel, that of St. Macarius or St. Macaire (an object of local worship whom we shall meet again elsewhere at Ghent), has a modern statue of the saint, and a pleasing decoration in polychrome. The right or S. Aisle has nothing of importance.

A short flight of steps leads to the Ambulatory, whose black-and-white marble screen, on the side toward the Choir, is not without dignity.

The sacristan opens the locked Chapels in the Ambulatory (flamboyant), beginning at the steps on the right or south side of the Choir. You will find him in the Sacristy, in the N. Transept. Do not let him hurry you.

The 1st chapel contains a tolerable triptych by F. Pourbus (son of Peter), with the Finding of Christ in the Temple for its central subject, and the Circumcision and Baptism on the inner wings. Notice in the last the conventional attitudes of the Baptist, the Saviour, and the angel with the towel, as in the Gerard David and all old examples of this subject: but the semi-nude figure undressing in the foreground is an unhappy innovation of the Renaissance. Many of the heads in the central picture are portraits: Alva, Charles V., Philip II., and Pourbus himself. On the outer wings is a good *portrait of the donor (Viglius) adoring the Saviour (1571).

3rd chapel. Crucifixion, by Gerard van der Meire, of Ghent. On the left wing, Moses striking the Rock, symbolical of the fountain of living water, Christ. On the right wing, the Elevation of the Brazen Serpent, symbolical of the Crucifixion. This is a mystic "typical" picture, interesting only for its symbolism. Note the Flemish love of such subjects.

The 4th chapel contains a good tomb of Cornelius Jansen and Willem Lindau, the two first bishops of Ghent (bishopric founded only in 1599) with fair recumbent figures of the early 17th century.

5th chapel. Coxcie. Lazarus and Dives: a mediocre picture.

Mount the steps to the Upper Ambulatory.

The 6th chapel (of the Vydts family) contains the famous altarpiece of the **Adoration of the Lamb, by Hubert and Jan van Eyck, to study which is the chief object of a visit to Ghent. See it more than once, and examine it carefully. Ask the Sacristan to let you sit before it for some time in quiet, or he will hurry you on. You must observe it in close detail.

St Bavo's Cathedral interior and ceilings - Image: Michal Osmenda

As a whole, the work before you is not entirely by the two Van Eycks. The Adam and Eve on the outer upper shutters of the interior (originally by Hubert) have been altogether removed, and are now in the Museum at Brussels, where we shall see them in due course. Their place has been filled, not by copies (for the originals were nude), but by skin-clad representations of the same figures, whose nudity seemed to the Emperor Joseph II. unsuitable for a church. The lower wings, which were principally (it is believed) by Jan van Eyck, have also been removed, and sold to Berlin. They are replaced by very tolerable copies, made in the early 16th century by Michael Coxcie. Thus, to form an idea of the detail of the original in its full totality it is necessary to visit, not only Ghent, but also Brussels and Berlin. Nevertheless, I describe the whole picture here as it stands, as this is the best place to observe its general composition. I shall say a few words later as to variations of this work from the original. There is a good copy of the whole picture in the Museum at Antwerp, where you will be able to inspect it at greater length and under easier conditions. The remaining portions of the original still left here are believed to be for the most part the work of Hubert van Eyck. Jan must rather be studied in many scattered places,—Bruges, Brussels, Berlin, Paris, Madrid, and London.

The altar-piece was commissioned from Hubert van Eyck by Josse Vydts (Latinised as Jodocus), a gentleman of Ghent, and his wife, Isabella, about the year 1420. Hubert died while the polyptych was still unfinished, and Jan completed it in 1432. Too much importance has been attached by critics, I fancy, to the rhyming hexameter inscribed upon it, (with the words "De Eyck" unmetrically introduced:) "Pictor Hubertus major quo nemo repertus," etc. They have been twisted into a deliberate expression of belief on the part of Jan that Hubert was a greater painter than himself. If so, it seems to me, Jan was a worse critic than painter. They are probably due, however, to a somewhat affected modesty, or more probably still, to a priestly poet who was in straits to find a rhyme for Hubertus.

I proceed to a detailed explanation of the picture.

The subject, in its entirety, is the Adoration of the Lamb that was Slain, and it is mainly based on the passage in the Apocalypse: "I looked, and lo, a Lamb stood on the Mount Zion, and with Him an hundred and forty and four thousand, having His Father's name written in their foreheads. . . . And I heard the voice of harpers harping with their harps." Elsewhere we read: "I beheld, and, lo, a great multitude, which no man could number, clothed with white robes, and palms in their hands. . . . These are they which came out of great tribulation, and have washed their robes, and made them white in the blood of the Lamb. Therefore are they before the throne of God; and He shall feed them, and shall lead them to living fountains of waters, and shall wipe away all tears from their eyes." Much of the imagery, however, I believe, is also taken from the Te Deum.

Lower Tier

The central panel (original: attributed to Hubert) represents in its middle the altar, hung with red damask, and covered with a white cloth, on which the Lamb of God is standing. His blood flows into a crystal chalice. (This part is clearly symbolical of the Eucharist.) Upon Him, from above, descends the Holy Ghost, in the form of a dove, sent out by the Eternal Father, who occupies the central panel on top. Around the altar are grouped adoring angels, with many-coloured wings, holding the instruments of the Passion—the Cross, the Spear, the Sponge, and the Column to which Christ was fastened for flagellation. In front of it, two angels swing censers.

The flowery foreground is occupied by the Fountain of Life, from which pure water flows limpid, to irrigate the smiling fields of Paradise. Four bands of worshippers converge towards this centre. On the left-hand side, stand, kneel, or ride, a group of worshippers representing, as a whole, the secular aspect of the Christian Church—the laity. The foreground of this group is occupied by the precursors of Christ. Conspicuous among them are the Jewish prophets in front, and then the Greek poets and philosophers,—Homer, Plato, Aristotle—whom mediæval charity regarded as inspired in a secondary degree by the Spirit of Wisdom. Homer, in white, is crowned with laurel. The group also includes kings and other important secular personages. The right-hand side, opposite, is occupied by representatives of the Church, showing the religious as opposed to the secular half of the Christian world. In the front rank kneel 14 persons, the Twelve Apostles (with Paul and Matthias) in simple robes, barefooted; behind them are ranged all the orders of the hierarchy—canonized popes, with their attendant deacons; archbishops, bishops, and other dignitaries.

The background shows two other groups, one of which (to the left) consists of the Martyrs, bearing their palms of martyrdom, and including in their number popes, cardinals, bishops, and other ecclesiastics. The inner meaning of this group is further emphasized by the symbolical presence of a palm tree behind them. To balance them on the right advance the Virgins conspicuous among whom are St. Agnes with her lamb, St. Barbara with her tower, St. Catherine, and St. Dorothy with her roses: many of them carry palms of martyrdom. These various groups thus illustrate the words of the Te Deum, representing "the glorious company of the apostles," "the goodly fellowship of the prophets," "the noble army of martyrs," "the Holy Church throughout all the world," etc., in adoration of the Lamb that was Slain. (A chorus of Apostles, of Prophets, of Martyrs, of Virgins is common in art.)

The more distant background is occupied by towered cities, typifying perhaps the New Jerusalem, but adorned with Flemish or Rhenish turrets and domes, and painted with Flemish minuteness and exactitude.

On the front of the altar are written in Latin the words, "Behold the Lamb of God that taketh away the sins of the world."

The Left Wings (inferior copy by Coxcie: originals, probably by Jan, now at Berlin) form a continuation of the scene of the Prophets and the secular side of Christendom in the central panel, and represent, in the First or Inner Half, the Orders of Chivalry and the mediæval knighthood riding, as on a crusade or pilgrimage, towards the Lamb that was Slain. At their head go the soldier saints, St. George, St. Adrian, St. Maurice, and St.

Charlemagne (for the great emperor Karl is also a canonized person). The action of the horses throughout is admirable. The Second or Outer Half (ill described as "the Just Judges") represents the Merchants and Burgesses, among whom two portraits in the foreground are pointed out by tradition as those of Hubert and Jan van Eyck: (Hubert in front, on a white horse: Jan behind, in a dark brown dress, trimmed with fur). But this detail is unimportant: what matters is the colour and composition on one hand, the idea on the other. These two panels, therefore, with the group in front of them, are to be taken as representing the Secular World—learned, noble, knightly, or mercantile—in adoration of the central truth of Christianity as manifested in the Holy Eucharist.

The corresponding Right Wings (copy by Coxcie: originals, probably by Jan, at Berlin) show respectively the Hermits and Pilgrims—the contemplative and ascetic complement of the ecclesiastical group in front of them: the monastic as opposed to the beneficed clerics. The First or Inner Half shows the Eremites, amongst whom are notable St. Anthony with his crutch, and, in the background, St. Mary Magdalen with her box of ointment, emerging from her cave, (the Sainte Baume) in Provence, in her character as the Penitent in the Desert. On the Second or Outer Half, the body of Pilgrims is led by the gigantic form of St. Christopher, with his staff and bare legs for wading; behind whom is a pilgrim with a scallop-shell, and many other figures, not all of them (to me) identifiable. Here again the presence of palms in the background marks the esoteric idea of martyrdom.

I need not call attention throughout to the limpid sky, the fleecy clouds, the lovely trees, the exquisite detail of architecture and landscape.

Upper Tier

The three Central Panels (original) are attributed to Hubert. That in the middle represents, not (I feel sure) as is commonly said, Christ, but God the Father ("Therefore they are before the throne of God") wearing the triple crown (like the Pope), holding the sceptre, and with his right hand raised in the attitude of benediction. His face is majestic, grave, passionless: his dress kingly: a gorgeous morse fastens his jewelled robe of regal red. At his feet lies the crown of earthly sovereignty. He seems to discharge the Holy Ghost on the Lamb beneath him. The word Sabaoth, embroidered on his garments, marks him, I think, as the Father: indeed, the Son could hardly preside at the sacrifice of the Lamb, even in the Eucharist.

On the right of the Father, in the panel to the (spectator's) left (Hubert: original), Our Lady, crowned, as Queen of Heaven, sits reading in her blue robe. Her face is far more graceful than is usual in Flemish art: indeed, she is the most charming of Flemish Madonnas. Behind her is stretched a hanging of fine brocade.

The panel to the right (Hubert: original) shows St. John the Baptist, with his camel-hair garment, covered by a flowing green mantle. The folds of all these draperies in Hubert's three figures, though simple, have great grandeur.

The Outer Wing to the left (substituted clothed figure, not a copy: original, by Hubert, at Brussels) has Adam, as typical (with Eve) of unregenerate humanity: a sense further marked by the Offerings of Cain and Abel above it.

The Outer Wing to the right has an Eve with the apple, (similarly clad, not copied from the original, by Hubert, now at Brussels:) above it, the First Murder.

The Inner Left Wing (copy: the original, attributed to Jan, is at Berlin) has a beautiful group of singing angels.

The Inner Right Wing (copy: the original, likewise attributed to Jan, is also at Berlin) has an angel (not St. Cecilia) playing an organ, with other angels accompanying on various musical instruments.

Taking it in its entirety, then, the altar-piece, when opened, is a great mystical poem of the Eucharist and the Sacrifice of the Lamb, with the Christian folk, both Church and World, adoring. It was in order to prepare your mind for recognition of this marked strain of mysticism in the otherwise prosaic and practical Flemish temperament, that I called your attention at Bruges to several mystic or type-emphasising pictures, in themselves of comparatively small æsthetic value.

The composition contains over 200 figures. Many of them, which I have not here identified, can be detected by a closer inspection, which, however, I will leave to the reader.

Now, ask the sacristan to shut the wings. They are painted on the outer side (all a copy) mainly in grisaille, or in very low tones of colour, as is usual in such cases, so as to allow the jewel-like brilliancy of the internal picture to burst upon the observer the moment the altar-piece is opened.

The lower wings have (in this copy) representations of the Four Evangelists, in niches, in imitation of statuary. Observe the half-classical pose and costume of Luke, the Beloved Physician. These figures, however, were not so arranged in the original, as I shall afterwards explain.

The upper wings represent on their first or lowest tier, the Annunciation, a frequent subject for such divided shutters. In the centre is the usual arcade, giving a glimpse of the town of Ghent where Hubert painted it. (The scene is said to be Hubert's own studio, which stood on the site of the Café des Arcades in the Place d'Armes: the view is that which he saw from his own windows.) To the left as always is the angel Gabriel, with the Annunciation lily; to the right is Our Lady, reading. The Dove descends upon her head. The ordinary accessories of furniture are present—prie-dieu, curtain, bed-chamber, etc. Note this arrangement of the personages of the Annunciation, with the empty space between Our Lady and the angel: it will recur in many other pictures. Observe also the Flemish realism of the painter, who places the scene in his own town at his own period: and contrast it with the mysticism of the entire conception. The uppermost tier of all is occupied by figures of two Sibyls (universally believed in the Middle Ages to have prophesied of Christ) as well as two half-length figures of the prophets Zachariah and Micah, (also as foretellers of the Virgin birth).

In several details the outer shutters in this copy differ markedly from the originals at Berlin. Jan's picture had, below, outer panels (when shut), portraits of Josse Vydts and his wife: inner panels, imitated statues (in grisaille) of St. John the Baptist and St. John the Evangelist, patrons at that time of this church. If you are going on to Berlin, you will see them: if back to London, then go to the Basement Floor of the National Gallery, where you will find the water-colour copy done for the Arundel Society, which will give you an excellent idea of the work in its original condition.

A few words must be given to the external history of this great altar-piece. It was begun by Hubert about 1420. His death in 1426 interrupted the work. Jan probably continued to paint at it till 1428, when he went to Portugal. On his return, he must have carried it to Bruges, where he next lived, and there completed it in 1432. It was then placed in this the family chapel of Josse Vydts. During the troubles of the Reformation it was carried to the Hôtel-de-Ville, but after the capitulation to the Duke of Parma it was restored to the chapel of the Vydts family.

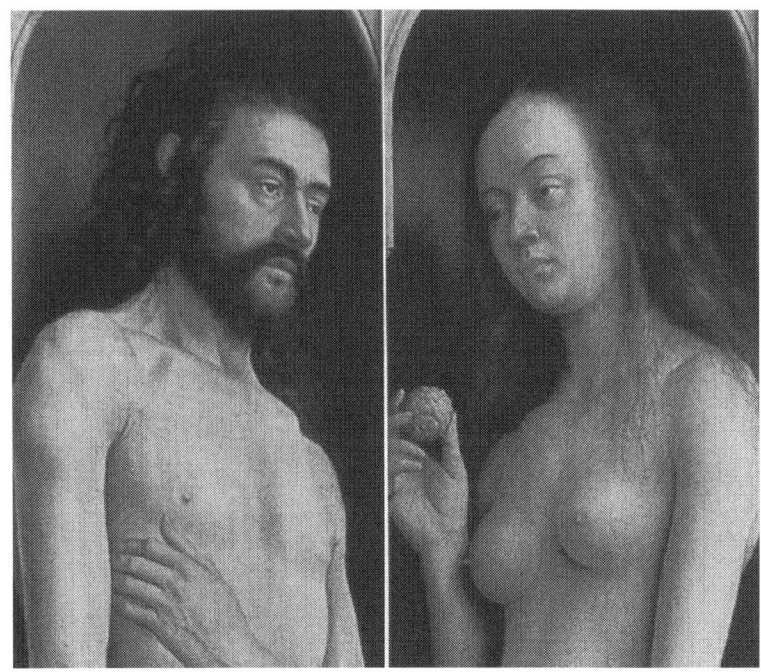

Adam and Eve

Philip II. wished to carry it off, but had to content himself with a copy by Coxcie, the wings of which are now in this chapel. The panels with Adam and Eve were removed in 1784, after Joseph II. had disapproved of them, and hidden in the sacristy. In 1794, the remaining panels were carried to Paris: after the peace, they were returned, but only the central portions were replaced in the chapel. The wings, save Adam and Eve, were sold to a Brussels dealer, and finally bought by the King of Prussia, which accounts for their presence at Berlin. As for Adam and Eve, the church exchanged them with the Brussels Museum for the wings of Coxcie's copy. These various vicissitudes will explain the existing condition of the compound picture. Do not be content with seeing it once. Go back to your hotel, rest and re-read this description, and come again to study this immortal art afresh tomorrow. The chapel of the Holy Sacrament, in the Apse, has very ugly rococo monuments to bishops of the 18th century, in the worst style of the debased Renaissance, and other monstrosities.

The 10th chapel has a famous *altar-piece by Rubens, St. Bavon renouncing his worldly goods to embrace the monastic life. The Saint is seen, attired as a Duke of Brabant of the 17th century, in his armour and ducal robes, attended by his pages, making his profession at the door of a stately Renaissance church, such as certainly did not exist in the North in his time, and received with acclamation by a dignified body of nobly-robed ecclesiastics, including St. Amand (see later, under the Monastery of St. Bavon). The features of the patron saint are said to be those of Rubens; they certainly resemble his portrait of himself at Florence. The foreground is occupied by a group of poor, to whom St. Bavon's worldly goods are being profusely scattered.

On the left are two ladies, in somewhat extravagant courtly costumes, who are apparently moved to follow the Saint's example. They are said to be the painter's two wives, but the resemblance to their known portraits is feeble. This is a fine specimen of Rubens's grandiose and princely manner, of his feeling for space, and of his large sense of colour; but it is certainly not a sacred picture. It was appropriately painted for the High Altar in the Choir (1624), after the church was dedicated to St. Bavon and erected into a cathedral, but was removed from that place of honour in the 18th century to make room for a vulgar abomination by Verbruggen. (I defer consideration of Rubens and his school till we reach Brussels and Antwerp.) Fair monument of a 17th century bishop.

Choir and altar of Saint Bavo Cathedral - Image: Edward Webster

Descend the steps again. Enter the Choir, a very fine piece of architecture: it has beautiful grey stone arches (dating to about 1300), a handsome Triforium, and excellent brick vaulting. The lower portion, however, is still disfigured by black-and-white marble screens and several incongruous rococo tombs, some of which have individual merit. (That to the left, Bishop Triest by Duquesnoy, is excellent in its own genre.) Over the High Altar flutters a peculiarly annoying and flyaway 17th century figure of the Apotheosis of St. Bavon, the patron saint of the Cathedral, who of course thus occupies the place of honour. It is by Verbruggen. The huge copper candlesticks, bearing the royal arms of England as used by Charles I, belonged to his private oratory in Old St. Paul's in London, and were sold by order of Cromwell. At this point, you can enjoy an impressive view down the Nave.

The City and Outskirts of Ghent

Old Ghent occupies for the most part the island which extends from the Palais de Justice on one side to the Botanical Gardens on the other. This island, bounded by the Lys, the Schelde, and an ancient canal, includes almost all the principal buildings of the town, such as the Cathedral, St. Nicolas, the Hôtel-de-Ville, the Belfry, and St. Jacques, as well as the chief Places, such as the Marché aux Grains, the Marché aux Herbes, and the Marché du Vendredi. It also extended beyond the Lys to the little island on which is situated the church of St. Michel, and again to the islet formed between the Lieve and the Lys, which contains the château of the Counts and the Place Ste. Pharailde.

Ghent botanical gardens

In the later middle ages, however, the town had spread to nearly its existing extreme dimensions, and was probably near as populous as it is in the 21st century. But its ancient fortifications have been destroyed, and their place has been taken by boulevards and canals. The line may still be traced on the map, or walked round through a series of shipping suburbs; but it is uninteresting to follow, a great part of its course lying through the more squalid portions of the town. The only remaining gate is that known as the Rabot (1489), a very interesting and picturesque object, situated in a particularly apartment ridden suburb. It can best be reached by crossing the bridge near the church of St. Michel, and continuing along the Rue Haute to the Boulevard du Béguinage, (where stood originally the Grand Béguinage, whose place is now occupied by modern streets.) Turn there along the boulevard to the right, till you reach the gate, which consists of two curious round towers, enclosing a high and picturesque gable-end. Owing to the unpleasant nature of the walk, I do not recommend this excursion.

The Rabot gate - Image: Traveler100

The S. quarter of the town, beyond the Cathedral and St. Nicolas has been much modernized during the last two centuries. Its only interesting points are the recent Palais de Justice and the Kouter or Place d'Armes, (once the archery ground) in which a pretty flower-market is held on Friday and Sunday mornings. The Café des Arcades, at its E. end, occupies the site of Hubert van Eyck's studio.

The rest of the inner town contains little that throws light on its origin or history.

There is, however, one small excursion which it would be well for those to take who have a morning to spare, and who desire to understand the development of Ghent—I mean to the Monastery of St. Bavon, which alone recalls the first age of the city. Every early mediæval town had outside its walls a ring of abbeys and monasteries, and Ghent was particularly rich in this respect.

St Bavos Abbey - Image: Paul Hermans

St. Amand was the apostle of Flanders and the surrounding countries. He was sent by the pious king Dagobert to convert the Flemings en bloc, and is said to have built, about 630, a little cell by the bank of the Lys, N.E. of the modern city. In 651, St. Bavon entered this infant monastery, which henceforth took his name. The abbey grew to be one of the most important in Flanders, and occupied a large area on the N.E. of the town, near the Antwerp Gate. Eginhard, the biographer and son-in-law of Charlemagne, was abbot in the 9th century. The Counts of Flanders had rights of hospitality at St. Bavon's; hence it was here, and not in the Oudeburg as usually stated, that Queen Philippa gave birth to John of Gaunt.

In 1539 however, Charles V, a headstrong despot, angry at the continual resistance of his native town to his arbitrary wishes, dissolved the monastery in the high-handed fashion of the 16th century, in order to build a citadel on the spot. As compensation for disturbance to the injured saint, he transported the relics of

St. Bavon to what was then the parish church of St. John, which has ever since borne the name of the local patron. Around the dismantled ruins, the Emperor erected a great fort, afterwards known as the Spaniards' Castle, (Château des Espagnols, or Het Spanjaards Kasteel.) This gigantic citadel occupied a vast square space, still traceable in the shape of the modern streets; but no other relic of it now remains. The ruins of the Abbey are in themselves inconsiderable, but they are certainly picturesque and well worth a visit from those who are spending some days in Ghent. The hurried tourist may safely neglect them.

The direct route from the Kouter to the Abbey is by the Quai du Bas Escaut, and the Rue Van Eyck. A pleasanter route, however, is by the Rue de Brabant and the Rue Digue de Brabant to the Place d'Artevelde, passing through the handsomest part of the modern town. (In the Place itself stands the fine modern Romanesque Church of St. Anne, the interior of which is sumptuously decorated in imitation of mosaic.) Thence, follow the Quai Porte aux Vaches to the Place Van Eyck. Cross the bridges over the Upper and Lower Schelde, and the Abbey lies straight in front of you.

St. Anne's Church - Image: Limowreck

Walk past the ivy-clad outer wall of the ruins to the white house at the corner of the street beyond it, where you will find the concierge (notice above the door). The concierge conducts you over the building, which has a picturesque cloister, partly Romanesque, but mainly 15th century. The centre of the quadrangle is occupied by a pretty and neatly-kept garden of the old sweet-scented peasant flowers of Flanders. The most interesting part of the ruins, however, is the octagonal Romanesque Baptistery or, a fine piece of early vaulting, with round arches, very Byzantine in aspect. The chapel rests on massive piers, and its Romanesque arches contrast prettily with the transitional Gothic work of the cloister in the neighbourhood. Within are several fragments of Romanesque sculpture, particularly some *capitals of columns, with grotesque and naïve representations of Adam and Eve with the Lord in the Garden, and other similar biblical subjects. (Examine closely.) There is likewise an interesting relief of St. Amand preaching the Gospel in Flanders, and a man-at-arms in stone, of Artevelde's period, removed from the old coping of the Belfry.

We next go on to the Crypt, the tombs of the monks, the monastery cellars, etc., where are collected many pieces of ancient sculpture, some found in the ruins and others brought from elsewhere. The Refectory at the end, which for some time served as the Church of St. Macaire, is now in course of transformation into a local Museum of Monumental Art. It contains some good old tombs, and an early fresco (of St. Louis?) almost obliterated. But the garden and cloister are the best of the place, and make together a very pretty picture. You can return by the Quai and the Rue St. Georges, or by the Place St. Bavon and the Archiepiscopal Palace. (The castellated building to the left, much restored, near the Cathedral, known as the Steen of Gérard le Diable, is the sole remaining example of the mediæval fortified houses in Ghent.)

Another monastery, a visit to which will lead you through the extensive southern portion of the city, is the (wholly modernized) Benedictine Abbey of St. Peter's. This is open from 10am to 6pm, with a tour featuring a film available at 4 euro. To reach it, you take the Rue Courte du Jour and the Rue Neuve St. Pierre, to the large square known as the Plaine St. Pierre, partly obtained by demolition of the monastery buildings. It is situated on rising ground, which may pass for a hill in Flanders. This is, in its origin, the oldest monastery in Ghent, having been founded, according to tradition, by St. Amand himself, in 630, on the site of an ancient temple of Mercury.

The existing buildings, however, hardly date in any part beyond the 17th century. The Church of Notre-Dame de St. Pierre was erected between 1629 and 1720, in the grandiose style of the period. It is vast, and not unimposing. The interior has a certain cold dignity. The pictures are mostly of the school of Rubens, many of them dealing with St. Peter and St. Benedict; among them are good specimens. The best, by De Crayer, shows the favourite Benedictine subject of St. Benedict recognising the envoy of King Totila, who personated the king.

The Plaine de St. Pierre is used for the events on the yearly calendar, from Mi-Carême to Easter.

On the way back from the Picture Gallery, you pass on your left the Rue Longue des Pierres, down which, a little way on the right, is a small Museum of Antiquities. I do not advise a visit to this. It contains one good brass, and some silver badges worn by ambassadors of Ghent, but otherwise consists, for the most part, of third-rate bric-à-brac.

Most visitors to Ghent go to see the Grand Béguinage. This was originally situated in a little district by itself, close to the gate of the Rabot, where its church, uninteresting, (dedicated, like that of Bruges, to St. Elizabeth of Hungary), still stands; but the site has been occupied by the town for new streets. The present Grand Béguinage lies on the road to Antwerp. It is a little town in miniature, enclosed by wall and moat, with streets and houses all very neat and clean, but of no archæological interest. Yet it forms a pleasant enough end for a short drive. And you can buy lace there. The description in Baedeker is amply sufficient.

Bruges is full of memories of the Burgundian Princes. At Ghent it is the personality of Charles V., the great emperor who cumulated in his own person the sovereignties of Germany, the Low Countries, Spain and Burgundy, that meets us afresh at every turn. He was born here in 1500, and baptized in a font (otherwise uninteresting) which still stands in the north Transept of the Cathedral. Ghent was really, for the greater part of his life, his practical capital, and he never ceased to be at heart a Ghenter. That did not prevent the citizens from justly rebelling against him in 1540, after the suppression of which revolt Charles is said to have ascended the Cathedral tower, while the executioner was putting to death the ringleaders in the rebellion, in order to choose with his brother Ferdinand the site for the citadel he intended to erect, to overawe the freedom-loving city. He chose the Monastery of St. Bavon as its site, and, as we have seen, built there his colossal fortress, now wholly demolished. The Palace in which he was born and which he inhabited frequently during life, was known as the Cour du Prince. It stood near the Ancien Grand Béguinage, but only its name now survives in that of a street. The Spaniard's Castle was long the standing menace to freedom in the Low Countries. Within its precincts Egmont and Hoorn were imprisoned in 1568 for several months before their execution.

During the early Middle Ages, the Oudeburg was the residence of the Counts of Flanders in Ghent. Later on, that castellated building grew out of keeping with the splendour of the Burgundian Princes, and its place as a royal residence was taken by the Cour du Prince, already mentioned, which was inhabited by Maximilian and his wife, Mary of Burgundy, as well as by Philippe le Beau and Johanna of Spain, the parents of Charles V. No direct memorials of the great Emperor now exist in Ghent, his statue in the Marché du Vendredi having been destroyed; but a modern street commemorates his name, and mementoes of him crop up at every point in the city.

Though the Ghenters were rebellious subjects, Charles V. was proud of his capital, and several of his very bad bon mots, punning on the words Gand and gant, have been preserved for us. As Baedeker repeats these imperial jests, however, I need not detail them.

Ghent Museum of Fine Arts

[Official webpage: http://www.mskgent.be/en/

Closed on Mondays, open between 10am and 6pm Tuesday to Sundays. Enquiries are taken via email: museum.msk@gent.be

This museum is located on the eastern side of the Citadelpark, a short 15 minute walk from Saint Peter's station.]

Given that its library of works dates from the 15th century onward, there is comparatively little by way of interest in the Ghent Museum of Fine Arts in the context of this handbook which is primarily occupied with Flemish Renaissance era works. There are however a few works displayed which are of interest, which I note herein. Should you be enthused about art of later periods, this gallery (formed to follow the unifying pattern of the Groeningemuseum in Bruges) has plenty to behold.

Ghent Museum of Fine Art - Image: Paul Hermans

The structure of the museum itself is in the main neoclassical in design, following the trends of the 19th century period to which it dates. It was designed by Charles van Rysselberghe, with construction finished shortly after 1900. Successive renovations, the latest of which concluded in 2007, have rendered the gallery's interior modern and quite bare aside from the portraiture within each room.

The works of Hieronymus Bosch receive a limited representation, with his Christ Carrying the Cross by far the most significant work on permanent display. Painted around 1510, the painting is a great jumble of faces wearing different expressions. Aside from these and the cross, there is no background as such – a conspicuous black envelops the scene in the painting's upper portions.

Some of the figures present are paying attention to the spectacle of Christ, others are seemingly distracted or engaged in their own business. Christ together with Veronica on the bottom left have closed their eyes, and wear plain and calm expressions in contrast to most of the faces around which are variously contorted. The image attempts and succeeds to contrast the serenity of faith with the chaos and hellishness of those without or apathetic toward belief.

In the Baroque sphere, a few notables likewise present themselves. Of good significance is Peter Paul Rubens *The Flagellation of Christ* – this is a sketch made in preparation for the full and complete work which today sits within St. Paul's Church in Antwerp. The later concluded work is part of the revered Antwerp canvas, in itself visual panoply of artistic achievement.

Additionally we have Anthony Van Dyck's Jupiter and Antiope. An early work by the artist, completed when he was merely twenty, the depiction is of the supreme God Jupiter making his intention of impregnating Antiope clear. The usual eagle watches intently, craning its neck if itself observing art, placing the viewer in the discomforting position of voyeur. For admirers of Anthony Van Dyck, this work has something of a milestone significance – betraying the young painter's evident imitation of his master Rubens, yet evidencing the wonderful talent yet to emerge in true splendour.

There are several less significant works of the Baroque era from lesser artists which can be readily beheld and interpreted. There is however one work of local significance to Ghent, being as it was commissioned by the Bishop Triest.

Theodore Rombouts *The Allegory of the Five Senses* is representative of the 17th century enthrallment with the allegorical. An era which advanced and chronicled so many of the folk tales we today enjoy, this fascination with the symbolic persists in our popular consciousness to this day.

The casual observer would see a group of friends, convivially enjoying a leisurely day of merriment. However, closer inspection reveals each gentleman to correspond to the five human senses of Sight, Sound, Taste, Touch and Smell. Thus the deceptively relaxed serenity actually carries greater meaning.

Brussels

Panorama of Brussels' *Grote Markt* - Image: Steve Collis

The mighty and historic capital of Belgium has a magisterial finesse unique and in some respects unequalled by other cities comparable in influence. As the seat of the European Union, the city's political significance cannot be understated. Aside from the artistic and aesthetic, visitors appreciate the highly developed transportation and the impressive selection of foods at the city's many restaurants and eateries.

For art, Brussels enjoys true distinction – its historic ties to the Dutch culture have ensured its galleries are populated healthily with works by French, Flemish and Dutch masters. Those eager to take in the ecclesiastical history will be pleased by its churches and cathedrals, while purveyors of architecture can spend potentially weeks in study of the many styles its edifices display, from Medieval to Neoclassical to Rococo to Modernist.

Many visit the Belgian capital with only a vague desire to fulfill a yearning for culture, falling short at the time to appreciate in true depth the creations amassed within its majestic streets and structures. Fortunately our pages catalogue and discuss the finest and most ancient of artworks; be they paintings, sculpture or relics, to be found in Brussels' older quarters.

Origins of Brussels

Brussels was in a certain sense the ancient capital of Brabant, as Bruges and Ghent were the ancient capitals of West and East Flanders. It grew up (as early as the 8th century) on the banks of the little river Senne, whose course through its midst is now masked by the modern Inner Boulevards, built on arches above the unseen stream. The Senne is one of the numerous rivers which flow into the Schelde, and the original town clustered close round its banks, its centre being marked by the Grand' Place and the church of St. Nicolas.

The Senne running through Rebecq - Image: Jean-Pol Grandmont

Unlike Bruges and Ghent, however, Brussels has always been rather an administrative than a commercial centre. It is true, it had considerable trade in the Middle Ages, as its fine Hôtel-de-Ville and Guild Houses still attest; but it seems to have sprung up round a villa of the Frankish kings, and it owed at least as much to its later feudal lords, the Counts of Louvain, afterwards Dukes of Brabant, and to their Burgundian successors, as to its mercantile position.

The diminutive Senne was never a very important river for navigation, though, like most of the Belgian waterways, it was ascended by light craft, while a canal connected the town with the Schelde and Antwerp: but the situation of Brussels on the great inland trade route between Bruges or Ghent and Cologne gave it a certain mercantile value. Bruges, Ghent, Brussels, Louvain, Maastricht, and Aix-la-Chapelle all formed stations on this important route, and all owed to it a portion of their commercial prestige.

The burgher town which was thus engaged in trade and manufactures was Flemish in speech and feeling, and lay in the hollow by the river and the Grand' Place. But a lordly suburb began to arise at an early date on the hill to eastward, where the Counts of Louvain built themselves a mansion, surrounded by those of the lesser nobility. After 1380, the Counts migrated here from too democratic Louvain. Later on, in the fifteenth century, the Dukes of Burgundy (who united the sovereignty of Brabant with that of Flanders) often held their court here, as the population was less turbulent and less set upon freedom than that of purely commercial and industrial Bruges and Ghent. Thus the distinctive position of Brussels as the aristocratic centre and the seat of the court grew fixed.

Again, the Dukes of Burgundy were French in speech, and surrounded themselves with French knights and courtiers; to suit the sovereigns, the local nobility also acquired the habit of speaking French, which has gradually become the language of one-half of Belgium. But the people of the Old Town in the valley were, and are still, largely Flemish in tongue, in customs, in sympathies, and in aspect; while the inhabitants of the Montagne de la Cour and the court quarter generally are French in speech, in taste, and in manners. We will trace in the sequel the gradual growth of Brussels from its nucleus by the river (the Lower Town), up the side of the eastern hill to the Palace district (the Upper Town), and thence through the new Quartier Léopold and the surrounding region to its modern extension far beyond the limits of the medieval ramparts.

Choose a hotel in the airy and wholesome Upper Town, as near as possible to the Park or the Place Royale.

St. Michael statue in the Cathedral nave - Image: Viktorhauk

St. Michael the Archangel is the patron saint of Brussels: he will meet you everywhere, even on the lampposts. For the patroness, St. Gudula, see under the Cathedral.

The Heart of Brussels

The nucleus of Brussels, as of Paris, was formed by an island, now no longer existing. Round this islet ran two branches of the little river Senne, at present obliterated by the Inner Boulevards. Brussels, in short, has denied its parentage; the Senne, which is visible north and south of the Outer Boulevards, being covered over by arches within the whole of the Inner City.

The Goriksmarkt in the Place St. Gery - Image: Johan Bakker

The centre of the island is marked by the little Place St. Géry, which the reader need not trouble to visit. Here, at the end of the 6th century, St. Géry, Bishop of Cambrai and apostle of Brabant, built a small chapel, succeeded by a church, now demolished. The true centre of Brussels, however, may be conveniently taken as the existing Bourse. Close by, as the town grew, the Grand' Place or market-place was surrounded by noble medieval and Renaissance buildings. To this centre then, the real heart of Brussels in the Middle Ages, we first direct ourselves.

Go from your hotel to the Grand Place, it may be reached by either of two convenient roads; from the Place Royale by the Montagne de la Cour and the Rue de la Madeleine, or from the Park by the Montagne du Parc (which takes various names as it descends), and the Galérie St. Hubert. Either route brings you out at the end of the Galérie, whence a short street to the left will land you at once in the Grand' Place, undoubtedly the finest square in Europe, and the only one which now enables us to reconstruct in imagination the other Grand's Places of Belgium and the Rhine country.

The Grand Place in Brussels - Image: Mats Halldin

The most conspicuous building in the Place, with the tall tower and open spire, is the Hôtel-de-Ville, with one possible exception (Louvain) the handsomest in Belgium. It consists of a tapering central tower, flanked by two wings, their high-pitched roof covered with projecting windows. The ground floor is arcaded. The first and second floors have Gothic windows, altered into square frames in a portion of the building. The edifice is of different dates. The original Hôtel-de-Ville consisted only of the wing to your left, as you face it, erected in 1402.

Hôtel de Ville - Town Hall - of Brussels - Image: Ben2

The right wing, shorter in façade, and architecturally somewhat different, was added in 1443. The style of the whole, save where altered, is Middle Gothic "Decorated"). The beautiful open spire should be specially noticed. On its summit stands a colossal gilt metal figure (1454) of the Archangel Michael, patron of the city. The statues in the niches are modern, and not quite in keeping with the character of the building. Observe, over the main portal, St. Michael, patron saint of the town, with St. Sebastian, St. Christopher, St. George, and St. Géry. Below are the Cardinal Virtues. The figures above are Dukes of

Brabant. Inspect the whole façade carefully. You will hardly find a nobler piece of civic architecture in Europe. The carved wooden door has also a figure of St. Michael. The gargoyles and the bosses near the staircase entrance to the left are likewise interesting.

Now, go round the corners to the left and right, to inspect the equally fine façades, facing the Rues de l'Hôtel-de-Ville and de la Tête-d'Or. The back of the building is 18th century and uninteresting. You may also pass rapidly through the courtyard, which however has very little character. But you need not trouble to inspect the interior, unless you are an abandoned sight-seer.

Maison du Roi - Image: Harald Hoyer

The other important and beautiful building which faces the Hôtel-de-Ville is the Maison du Roi, formerly used as the Halle au Pain or Broodhuis. It is of late florid Gothic, verging towards Renaissance (1514, restored:) and is in three storeys, two of them arcaded. The first floor has an open gallery, like the loggia of a Venetian palace, whence ladies could view processions and ceremonies in the square below. The building terminates in a high roof, with projecting windows, and a handsome open tower and lantern. The whole has been recently rebuilt and profusely gilded. Within, is a small Communal Museum (open free daily, 10 to 4). Come again often to view these two noble halls.

The third principal building on the eastern side of the Square is known as the Maison des Ducs. It was once the Public Weighing House, constructed in a debased Renaissance style, and also profusely gilded. It bears the date 1698, but is now unworthily occupied by shops.

The whole of the remaining space in this glorious square is surrounded by magnificent storefronts and offices of various corporations.

Maison des brasseurs - Image: Romainberth

Beginning on the south side (that occupied by the Hôtel-de-Ville), we have first on the left, two high-gabled houses of good 17th century domestic architecture. Next to them on the right, comes the Hôtel des Brasseurs, dated 1752. This was originally the Guild Hall of the Brewers, and as such there is a small 'museum' which I do not recommend given the lack of substance – the petty sum of its unexplained exhibits is scarcely made up for by the short presentational video and beer samples.

After that, again, rises the house known as "The Swan," which once belonged to the corporation of butchers. The small building at the corner, next the Hôtel-de-Ville, with an open loggia, now in course of restoration, is known as the Maison de l'Étoile: a gilt star surmounts its gable.

The finest group of houses, however, is that to the W. side of the Square (right of the Hôtel-de-Ville), unoccupied by any one prominent building. Beginning on the left, we have, first, the house known as "The Fox" (Le Renard), dated 1699: it is surmounted by a figure of St. Nicholas resuscitating the three boys, and is adorned with statues of Justice and the Four Continents on its first floor.

A closer view of the Swan house

Then comes the Guild Hall of the Skippers, or Maison des Bateliers, its gable constructed somewhat like the poop of a ship. The symbolism here is all marine—sailors above; then

Neptune and his horses, etc. right of this, we see the house known as "La Louve," bearing as a sign Romulus and Remus with the wolf. This was originally the Guild Hall of the Archers. It shows an inscription stating that it was restored, after being burnt down, by the Confraternity of St. Sebastian (patron of archers). Its relief of the Saint with a bow is appropriate. The two remaining houses are "La Brouette," dated 1697, and "Le Sac," bearing on its gable a medallion with three faces.

The Pigeon - formerly the Hall of the Painters - Image: Claire Stodola

The houses on the north side, (that occupied by the Maison du Roi,) are less interesting, except those on the extreme right Next to the Maison du Roi itself come two pretty little decorated houses. One of whom is known as The Pigeon and was formerly the Guild of the Painters. It acquired fame as the residence of Victor Hugo during his exile.

The other structure is called "La Taupe," – this was once the Hall of the Tailors. The two last at the corner of the street have undergone several restorations over the years. Several other fine houses of the same period close the vista of the streets round the corner.

This imposing group of former Guild Halls dates, however, only from the end of the 17th century, mostly about 1697. The reason is that in 1695 the greater part of the Grand' Place was destroyed by Marshal de Villeroi during the siege. Two years later, the Guild Houses were rebuilt in the ornate and somewhat debased style of the Louis XIV. period. Fortunately, the two great mediæval buildings, which stood almost isolated, did not share the general destruction.

Continue your stroll through the Lower Town.

The modernised Church of St. Nicholas - Image: EmDee

From the Grand' Place, take the Rue au Beurre, which leads west towards the Bourse. On your right you will pass the now uninteresting and entirely modernized Church of St. Nicolas. In its origin, however, this is one of the oldest churches in Brussels, and though it has long lost almost every mark of antiquity, it is instructive to recognise here again (as at Ghent) the democratic patron saint of the merchants and burgesses in close proximity to their Town Hall and their former Guild Houses. The Bourse itself, which faces you, is a handsome and imposing modern building. Go past its side till you reach the line of the Inner Boulevards, which lead north and south between the Gare du Nord and the Gare du Midi.

The Bourse - Brussels Stock Exchange - Image: Ben2

This superb line of streets, one of the finest set of modern boulevards in Europe, has been driven straight through the heart of the Old Town, and the authorities offered large money prizes for the best façades erected along the route. Content yourself for the moment with a glance up and down, to observe the general effect, and then continue on to your left along the Boulevard, where the first street on the right will lead you to the little Place St. Géry, now occupied by a market, but originally the centre of Old Brussels. A stroll through the neighbouring streets is interesting, past the Halles Centrales, and the modern Church of St. Catherine, close by which stands the old Tower of St. Catherine, built into a modern block of houses. A little further on is the picturesque Tour Noire, the only remaining relic of the first fortifications of the city. You may prolong this walk to the Place du Béguinage, with a tolerable church. The quarter has no special interest, but it will serve to give you a passing idea of the primitive nucleus of medieval Brussels.

Church of St. Catherine - Image: Romaine

I will interpolate here a few remarks about the more modern portion of the Old Town. The best way to see it is to take the tram along the Inner Boulevards from the Gare du Midi to the Gare du Nord. You will then pass, first, the Outer Boulevards (see later): next, right, the Palais du Midi; on the left is the Place d'Anneessens, with a statue of Anneessens, the intrepid and public-spirited magistrate of Brussels who was put to death in 1719 for venturing to defend the privileges of the city against the Austrian authorities. Just opposite this, you get a glimpse, right, of the Place Rouppe, to be noticed later. Passing the Place Fontainas, where many streets radiate, you arrive at the Bourse, already noticed.

The handsome corner building (with dome) in front of you, which forms so conspicuous an element in the prospect as you approach, is the Hôtel Continental. Just in front of it expands a small new square, the Place de Brouckere, on which a monument is now erected to a late burgomaster (De Brouckere.)

At this point, the Boulevard divides, the western branch following the course of the Senne (which emerges to light just beyond the Outer Boulevards,) while the eastern branch goes straight on to the Gare du Nord, passing at the first corner a handsome narrow house with gilt summit, which won the first prize in the competition instituted by the Municipality for the best façades on the new line of streets.

The Art Deco tower of Brussels Gare du Nord - Image: Dr Leslie Sachs

After reaching the Gare du Nord, you can return to the Gare du Midi by an alternative line of main streets, which also cuts through the heart of the Old Town, a little to the E. of the Inner Boulevards. It begins with the Rue Neuve, where a short street to the left conducts you straight to the Place des Martyrs, a white and somewhat desolate square of the 18th century, (1775) adorned later with a Monument to the Belgians who were killed during the War of Independence in 1830.

Shortly after this (continuing the main line) you pass two covered galleries, right and left, and then arrive at the Place de la Monnaie. On your right is the handsome building of the Post Office; on your left, the white Ionic-pillared Grand Théâtre or Théâtre de la Monnaie, (opera, etc.). You then pass between St. Nicolas on the left, and the Bourse on the right, and continue on to the Place Rouppe, (ornamented with a fountain and a statue of Brussels personified): whence the Avenue du Midi leads you straight to the Place de la Constitution, in front of the South Station.

The remainder of the Western Half of the town is, for the most part, poor and devoid of interest, though it contains the principal markets, hospitals, and barracks, as well as the basins for the canals which have superseded the Senne.

Royal Museums of Fine Arts of Belgium

[Refer to the Museum's website for the latest outlay of works: http://www.fine-arts-museum.be/en/

The gallery is closed on Mondays, and opens on Tuesdays to Fridays from 10am to 5pm. It is open on weekends from 11am to 6pm.

Adults over 26 are admitted to the gallery and associated museums for 8 euros. Children and young adults under 26 are admitted for 2 euros, senior citizens are discounted at 6 euros, while children under 5 are admitted for free.]

I include here an account of the Royal Museums of Fine Arts of Belgium, because it is the most important object to be seen in the town, after the Grand' Place and its neighbourhood.

Royal Museum of the Fine Arts – Image: Michel Wal

You must pay it several visits—three at the very least—and you may as well begin early. Follow the roughly chronological order here indicated, and you will understand it very much better. Begin again next time where you left off last: but also, revisit the rooms you have already seen, to let the pictures sink into your memory. Intersperse these visits with general sight-seeing in the town and neighbourhood. Note that not all of the works I describe may be present – many are shuffled about the major galleries of Belgium and the Netherlands, to afford their visitors enjoyment through part of the year.

The Royal Museums form an excellent continuation to the works of art at Bruges and Ghent. In the first place, it gives us some further examples of the Old Flemish masters, of the Van Eycks and of Memling, as well as several altar-pieces belonging to the mystical religious School of the Brussels town-painter, Roger Van der Weyden, who was Memling's master. These have been removed from churches at various times, and gradually collected by the present Government. It also affords us an admirable opportunity of becoming well acquainted with the masterpieces of Dierick Bouts, or Dierick of Haarlem, an early painter, Dutch by birth but Flemish by training, who was town painter in democratic Louvain, (which town may afterwards be made the object of an excursion from Brussels).

But, in the second place, besides these painters of the early school, the Brussels Gallery is rich in works of the transitional period, and possesses in particular a magnificent altar-piece by Quentin Massys, the last of the old Flemish School, and the first great precursor of the Renaissance in the Low Countries. He was practically an Antwerp man (though born at Louvain), and his place in art may more fitly be considered in the Antwerp Museum.

From his time on we are enabled to trace, in this Gallery, the evolution of Flemish art to its third period, the time of Rubens (also better seen at Antwerp) and his successors, the great Dutch painters, here fairly represented by Rembrandt, Frans Hals, Van der Helst, Gerard Dou, and Teniers.

In the following list of the most noteworthy works of each School, I have adhered, roughly speaking, to a chronological order, but without compelling the reader unnecessarily to dance up and down the various rooms of the collection from one work to another. The Gallery itself is one of the most splendid in Europe. Please note that its contents are subject to rearrangement and reorganization, in accordance with exhibitions.

Paul de Vigne sculptures to the right of the Museum of Fine Arts entrance - Image: DimiTalen

The national collection of pictures by Old Masters occupies the very handsome building known as the Palais des Beaux-Arts in the Rue de la Régence, immediately after passing through the Place Royale. Four large granite columns in front: bronze sculpture groups to right and left.

Enter by the big door with the four large granite columns. In the vestibule, turn to the right, and mount the staircase. Then pass through Room III. and Corridor A, to Room V. on the right, and on into Room I.

Room I - Hall of the Old Flemish Masters

This room contains the most interesting works in the Gallery.

(You may also, if you like, pass through the collection of Sculpture in the Hall below, entering by Corridor D; in which case, turn to the left into Rooms VIII. and II., and then to the right into Room I., as above. This is the handsomer entrance. Much of the sculpture has great merit: but being purely modern, it does not fall within the scope of these Historical Guides.)

Begin in the middle of the wall, with No. 170, **Hubert van Eyck: the two outer upper shutters from the Adoration of the Lamb at Ghent, representing Adam and Eve, whose nudity so shocked Joseph II. that he objected to their presence in a church. These fine examples of the unidealized northern nude are highly characteristic of the Van Eycks' craftsmanship. The Adam is an extremely conscientious and able rendering of an ordinary and ill-chosen model, surprisingly and almost painfully true in its fidelity to nature. The foreshortening of the foot, the minute rendering of the separate small hairs on the legs, the large-veined, every-day hands, the frank exhibition of the bones and sinews of the neck, all show the extreme northern love of realism, and the singular northern inattention to beauty.

Compare this figure with the large German panels on a gold ground in the corners diagonally opposite (No. 624), if you wish to see how great an advance in truth of portraiture was made by the Van Eycks. The Eve is an equally faithful rendering of an uninteresting model, with protruding body and spindle legs. Above, in the lunettes, are the Offerings of Cain and Abel, and the Death of Abel, in grisaille. The backs of the shutters will be opened for you by the attendant. They exhibit, above, two Sibyls, with scrolls from their prophecies; below, the central portion of the Annunciation in the total picture, with a view through the window over the town of Ghent, and the last words of the angelic message, truncated from their context. This portion of the picture is, of course, only comprehensible by a study of the original altar-piece at Ghent.

Continue now along this wall to the right of the Adam and Eve.

24. J. Gossart, called Mabuse (1470-1541), triptych with a Glorification of the Magdalen, given by a special votary. The central panel contains the chief event in her history—the Supper at the House of Simon the Pharisee. The host and one guest are admirably represented by Flemish portraits, exquisitely robed, and reproduced in marvellous detail. The figure of the Christ is, as usual, insipid. Beneath the table, the Magdalen, as central figure, with her alabaster box of ointment, kisses the feet of Christ. To the right, Judas, with his traditional red hair, and bearing the purse, asks, with a contemptuous gesture, Why this was not sold and given to the poor? In the background are the Apostles. Conspicuous amongst them is the conventional round face of St. Peter. The whole scene takes place in a richly decorated interior, with charming colouring and a finely rendered clock, curtain, and other accessories. Gossart visited Italy, and was one of the earliest Flemings to be influenced by the Italian Renaissance. You will not overlook the half-Gothic, half-Renaissance architecture, nor the chained squirrel, nor the semi-grotesque episodes in the background, very domestic and Flemish. (Moses above the Pharisee's head marks his devotion.

The left panel has another principal event in the Magdalen's life, the Resurrection of Lazarus. Here also the Christ is insipid, but the Peter behind him, in a green robe, is finely characterized; and the John, affected. Beside are the Magdalen (same dress as before) and Martha, with a group of women and bystanders in singular head-dresses. In the background rises a very ideal Bethany. The right panel represents the kneeling donor (an unknown Premonstratensian abbot); on his book is written, "Mary Magdalen, pray for us." Above him is seen the floating figure of the Magdalen, clad only in her own luxuriant hair, and raised aloft by angels from her cave, the Sainte Baume, in

Provence, to behold the Beatific Vision. The background has Stations of the Cross, actually copied (with the rest of the landscape) from those at the Sainte Baume, which Gossart must have visited at his patron's instance. On the backs of the wings, yet another scene in the life of the Saint, Christ and the Magdalen in the Garden. All this triptych is finely modelled and well-coloured.

552. Three panels attributed to Roger van der Weyden, of Tournai, town painter of Brussels, and teacher of Memling—a highly symbolical and religious master. Scenes from the Life of the Virgin. In the centre, the Presentation of the Virgin in the Temple. The foreground is occupied by St. Joachim and St. Anna, parents of the little Virgin, who is seen mounting the regulation fifteen steps of the Temple, assisted by a somewhat unusual angel. At the head of the steps stands the High Priest. Within, the Virgins of the Lord are seen reading. To the right, still in the same panel, is the Annunciation, with the usual features, angel to the left, Madonna to the right, prie-dieu, bed, Annunciation lily, and arcade in the foreground. The left panel has the Circumcision; and the right, Christ among the Doctors in the Temple, with some excellent portraits in the background. (For Van der Weyden's place in art, see Conway; for the Madonna ascending the steps, Legends of the Madonna.)

554. Also attributed to Roger van der Weyden: parts of the same series, Way to Calvary and the Crucifixion. The first has the usual brutal soldiers and a suffering but not very dignified Christ. (Study for comparison with others.) Beside the Virgin kneels the donor. The second has the conventional figures of the fainting Madonna, St. John, the Magdalen, and the other Maries: sun and moon darkened. In the distance of both, Flemish towns. (Good trees and landscape.)

105a. Fine Madonna with Child, and an apple by Van Clive.

159. A crowded Calvary of the German School (late 15th century) with an emaciated Saviour, writhing and distorted thieves, and rather wooden spectators. Observe the St. Longinus in armour on the bay horse, piercing the side of Christ, for comparison hereafter with such later conceptions as Rubens's at Antwerp. To the left is the group of the Madonna, St. John, and the two Maries. The red eyes of St. John are characteristic of this scene, and descend to Van Dyck. The Maries are unmitigated German housewives. The Magdalen embraces the foot of the Cross. On the right are spectators and

a brawl between soldiers. The background is full of characteristic German devils and horrors: also St. Veronica, Peter and Malchus, Judas hanging himself, etc.

Above it, 523, German School, attributed to Wolgemut, Christ and the Apostles: gold background. Very flavourless: shows the tendencies from which the Van Eycks revolted.

517. Roger van der Weyden: head of a Woman Weeping. Perhaps a portion of a large composition, or a study for one. More likely, a copy by a pupil. Much damaged.

Now, return along the same wall, beyond the great Van Eyck in the centre.

335. Bernard van Orley (transitional). Triptych (sawn in two), with the Patience of Job inside, and Lazarus and Dives outside. In the centre panel, the house falling upon the sons of Job. In the background, Job and his comforters: his house in flames, etc. Left panel, the flocks and herds of Job driven off by the Sabeans, with Satan before the Almighty at the summit. Right panel, Job in his last state more blessed than formerly: his comforters ask him to intercede for them. Beyond this again,

the outer shutters (the panels having been sawn through): extreme left, Lazarus at the Rich Man's gate; above, his newborn soul borne aloft to Heaven. Below, cooks, servants, etc. Extreme right, the Rich Man dying, attended by his physician (compare the Dropsical Woman by Gerard Dou in the Louvre). Below, Dives in Torments (in a very Flemish Hell) calling to Lazarus. Above, Lazarus in Abraham's bosom. This is a good characteristic example of the transitional period between the early and later Flemish art, greatly influenced by the Italian Renaissance. Van Orley travelled in Italy, and imitated Raphael in composition and drawing.

Beyond it, attributed to Roger van der Weyden, 553 (3 panels arbitrarily placed together). In the centre panel, two subjects. Left, the Nativity, elements all conventional: ruined temple, shed, ox and ass (extremely wooden), and St. Joseph in background. (He frequently bears a candle in this scene in order to indicate that the time is night.) Right, the Adoration of the Three Kings, old, middle-aged, young, the last a Moor. St. Joseph examines, as often, the Old King's gift. Note his costume; it recurs in Flemish art. Left panel, Joseph of Arimathea with the Crown of Thorns, Nicodemus with the three nails, St. John, and the three Maries at the sepulchre. Right panel, Entombment, with the same figures: the Crown of Thorns and nails in the foreground. Great importance is always attached to these relics, preserved in the Sainte Chapelle, and at Monza, near Milan.

350. Patinier. Repose on the Flight into Egypt, with fine landscape background.

122. Cranach the Elder. Hard portrait of a very Scotch looking and Calvinistic Elder.

10. Amberger; German School, 16th century; excellent portrait of a gentleman; good beard.

569. Fine portrait of a man, by unknown artist. Flemish School, 16th century.

Above these, 618, Flagellation and Ascension, German School, with gilt backgrounds.

The skied pictures on this wall are only interesting as specimens of the later transitional period; when Flemish Art was aiming ill at effects unnatural to it.

Continue along the wall in the same direction.

By the door, 557, *portrait of Johanna of Spain (the Mad), mother of Charles V.: fine 15th century work.

531 and 532. Excellent old Flemish portraits.

Above these, 541, Scenes from the Life of the Virgin, with a donor. On the left is the Nativity. Note the conventional elements. On the right is the Circumcision. Above, Angel and patron saints.

557. *Portrait of Philippe le Beau, father of Charles V., companion to his wife opposite. Observe the collar of the Golden Fleece, and the united arms of Spain, Burgundy, etc., on his doublet. These portraits were originally the wings of a triptych.

544. A Holy Family and St. Anne, with the donor, a Franciscan monk, by a feeble imitator of Memling.

334. Tolerable portrait of a doctor, by Bernard Van Orley.

Next it, unnumbered, *Virgin and child. Gérard David. Our Lady feeds Christ with a characteristic Flemish wooden spoon.

348. Patinier, a painter chiefly memorable for his landscapes (of which this is a poor example). St. Jerome in the Desert, beating his breast with a stone before a crucifix. Beside him, his cardinal's hat and lion. Not a good example of the master.

641. Holbein the Younger. Portrait of *Sir Thomas More.

Above, 575. Triptych, Flemish School, early 16th century. Centre panel, Miracle of St. Anthony of Padua and the Mule. (The Saint, carrying the Host, met a scoffer's mule, which knelt till it passed.) Above, St. Bonaventura, attired as bishop, praying. These must be the chief objects of the donor's devotion: they are also represented on the outer wings. Right and left, the donor (whose name was Tobias), with his personal patron, St. Raphael the Archangel (accompanying the young Tobias), and his wife, with St. Margaret and the Dragon. (For Tobias and the Fish, see Book of Tobit.)

174, skied, is a Last Judgment by Floris, also transitional and useful for comparison with others elsewhere. To right and left, the Fall of the Damned and the Just Ascending recall early examples at Bruges.

534. Triptych of the Flemish School (Hugo van der Goes?); Centre panel, Assumption of Our Lady. Round the empty tomb are gathered the apostles; conspicuous among them, St. Peter with a censer, and St. James. Above, Our Lady taken up in a glory by Christ and the Holy Ghost, represented as like Him. In the background, her Funeral, St. Peter, as Pope, accompanying. Note the papal dress of St. Peter; St. James holds the cross as Bishop of Jerusalem. Left wing, the chief donor, accompanied by his guardian angel and two of the apostles, one of whom holds St. Peter's tiara, as if part of the main picture. In the background, St. Thomas receiving the Holy Girdle from an Angel, a common treatment in Flemish art, though Italians make him receive it from Our Lady in person. (See my Guide to

Florence.) Right wing, donor's son and wife, with guardian angel. This triptych closely resembles No. 535 (which see later), except that that picture is in one panel, instead of three. I think 535 must have been painted first, and this taken from it, but made into a triptych; which would account for the unusual flowing over of the main subject into the wings.

419. Martin Schongauer (of Colmar, a German largely influenced by Roger van der Weyden), *Ecce Homo, painted like a miniature.

349. Patinier: another Repose on the Flight into Egypt. Observe persistence of the main elements. Notice in particular, as compared with the similar picture (350) close by, the staff, basket, etc., in the right foreground.

546. School of Memling, perhaps by the master: a Bishop preaching: M. Fétis thinks, exhorting the Crusade in which Pope Nicholas V. wished to interest the princes of Europe after the fall of Constantinople.

621. School of Dürer: Fine and thoughtful portrait of a man, perhaps Erasmus.

Above it, 577, Flemish triptych (school of Van der Weyden) of the Adoration of the Magi, the elements in which will by this time be familiar to you. Right and left, Adoration of the Shepherds and Circumcision. The exceptional frequency of the subject of the Adoration of the Magi in the Low Countries and the Rhine district is to be accounted for by the fact that the relics of the Three Kings are preserved in Cologne Cathedral, and are there the chief object of local cult.

At the corner, 84 and 255, two good portraits by the German de Bruyn (early 16th cent.). Transitional: show Italian influence.

Between them, 619, unknown German, Wedding Feast at Cana. That you may have no doubt as to the reality of the miracle, a servant is pouring water into the jars in the foreground. He is much the best portion of the picture. Behind are Christ, St. John, and Our Lady. Next to them, the bride and bridegroom. (Compare the Gerard David in the Louvre.)

Above it, 624, a very quaint St. George and St. Catherine, early German School, with gold background. St. George is stiffly clad in armour, and painfully conscious of his spindle legs, with a transfixed dragon and broken lance at his feet. St. Catherine looks extremely peevish, with a Byzantine down-drawn mouth: she holds the sword of her martyrdom, and has a fragment of her wheel showing behind her. Her face is highly characteristic of the severity and austerity of early German art. Companion piece (624) at opposite corner.

Now proceed to the next wall.

539. Fine portraits of a donor and his wife, with their patron saints, Peter and Paul. The tops of both have been sawn off.

549 and 643. Two Madonnas. Not very important.

545. Between them, **unknown German Master (Lafenestre says, Flemish). Panel with Our Lady and Virgin Saints, what is called a "Paradise Picture," apparently painted for a church or nunnery in Cologne, and with the chief patronesses of the city churches or chapels grouped around in adoration. Our Lady, with her typical German features, sits in front, in a robe of blue, before a crimson damask curtain upheld by angels. Her face is

sweetly and insipidly charming. She holds a regal court among her ladies. In front of her kneels the Magdalen, with her long hair and pot of ointment. To the left is St. Catherine of Alexandria, crowned as princess, and with her wheel embroidered in pearls on her red robe as a symbol. The Infant Christ places the ring on her finger.

Further left is St. Cecilia with a bell, substituted in northern art (where the chimes in the belfry were so important) for the organ which she holds in Italy. Then, St. Lucy, with her eyes in a dish, and St. Apollonia, holding her tooth in a pair of pincers. In front of these two, in a richly brocaded dress, and beautiful crown, St. Ursula, the great martyr of Cologne, with the arrows of her martyrdom lying at her feet. To Our Lady's right, St. Barbara, in a purple robe trimmed with ermine and embroidered with her tower (of three windows), offers a rose to the Infant. Her necklet is of towers. As usual in northern art, she balances St. Catherine. Beside her kneels St. Agnes, in red, with her lamb, and her ruby ring: beyond whom are St. Helena with the cross (wearing a simple Roman circlet), St. Agatha, holding her own severed breast in the pincers, and St. Cunera with the cradle and arrow, one of the martyred companions of St. Ursula. In the background, the True Vine on a trellis, the garden of roses ("is my sister, my spouse"), and a landscape of the Rhine, in which St. George kills the dragon. This is a particularly fine composition of the old German School.

65 and 66. **Dieric Bouts: Two companion panels, life-size figures, known as the Justice of the Emperor Otho, and painted for the Council-Room of the Hôtel-de-Ville at Louvain, as a warning to evil-doers, perjurers, or unjust magistrates. (Compare the Gerard David of the Flaying of Sisamnes in the Academy at Bruges.) It is first necessary to understand the story. During the absence of the Emperor Otho in Italy (according to tradition), his empress made advances to a gentleman of the court, who rejected her offers. Piqued by this rebuff, the empress denounced him to Otho on his return as having attempted to betray her honour. Otho, without further testimony, had the nobleman beheaded. His widow appeared before the Emperor's judgment-seat, bearing her husband's head in her hands, and offered to prove his innocence by the ordeal of fire. She therefore held a red-hot iron in her hand unhurt.

Otho, convinced of his wife's treachery by this miraculous evidence, had the perjured empress burned alive. The first panel, to the right, represents the scene in two separate moments. Behind, the nobleman, in his shirt and with his hands tied, walks towards the place of execution, accompanied by his wife in a red dress and black hood, as well as by a Franciscan friar. In the foreground, the executioner (looking grimly stern) has just decapitated the victim, and is giving the head to the wife in a towel. The headless corpse lies on the ground before him. The neck originally spurted blood; flowers have been painted in to conceal this painful element. All round stand spectators, probably portraits of the Louvain magistrates, admirably rendered in Bouts's dry and stiff but life-like manner.

Behind them, within a walled garden belonging to a castle in the background, stand the Emperor with his sceptre and crown, and the faithless Empress. Good town and landscape to the left is The second panel, and to the left, separated from this by a large triptych, represents the nobleman's wife appearing before the enthroned Otho. In her right hand she holds her husband's head; with her left she grasps the red-hot iron, unmoved. The brazier of charcoal in which it has been heated stands on the parti-coloured marble floor in the foreground. Around are several portraits of courtiers. Behind is represented the scene of the empress burning, which closes the episode. I need not call attention to the admirable painting of the fur, the green coat, Otho's flowered red robe, the dog, the throne, and all the other accessories. This is considered Dierick Bouts's masterpiece. (Go later to Louvain to complete your idea of him.)

Between these two pictures are arranged five of the finest works in the collection.

292 and 293. Memling: **Portraits of William Moreel (or Morelli), Burgomaster of Bruges, and his wife Barbara, the same persons (Savoyards) who are represented in the St. Christopher triptych in the Academy at Bruges. Their daughter is the Sibyl

Sambetha of the St. John's Hospital. Both portraits, but especially the Burgomaster's, are good, hard, dry pictures.

515. Memling: **Triptych: perhaps painted in Italy (if I permitted myself an opinion, I would say, doubtfully by Memling). At any rate, it is for the Sforza family of Milan. Central panel, the Crucifixion, with Our Lady and St. John. Beautiful background of a fanciful Jerusalem. Sun and moon darkened. In the foreground kneel Francesco Sforza in armour, his wife Bianca Visconti, and his son Galeazzo-Maria. Behind the duke, his coat of arms. Left panel: the Nativity.

In the foreground St. Francis with the Stigmata, as patron saint of Francesco, and St. Bavon with his falcon. Right panel: St. John the Baptist, as patron saint of Giovanni Galeazzo. Below, St. Catherine with her sword and wheel, and St. Barbara with her tower, two charming figures. I do not know the reason of their introduction, but they are common pendants of one another in northern art. You can get an attendant to unfasten the outer wings of the triptych for you, but they are not important. They contain, in grisaille, to the left is St. Jerome and the lion; and to the right St. George and the dragon. (The presence of St. Bavon in this enigmatic picture leads me to suppose it was painted for a church at Ghent. But what were the Sforza family doing there? Perhaps it has reference to some local business of the Sforzas in Flanders.)

190. **Roger van der Weyden: Portrait of Charles the Bold of Burgundy, wearing the Golden Fleece. An excellent and characteristic piece of workmanship. The arrow has a meaning: it is the symbol of St. Sebastian, to whom (as plague-saint) Charles made a vow in illness, and whomever after he specially reverenced.

294. Memling: **Portrait of an unknown man, which may be contrasted for its comparative softness of execution with the harder work of his master beside it. Above these:—

211. Triptych, by Heemskerck (early Dutch School), representing, Centre, the Entombment, Christ borne, as usual, by Nicodemus and Joseph of Arimathea. In front, the crown of thorns. Behind, the Magdalen; then the Madonna and St. John, the two Maries, and an unknown man holding a vase of ointment. Left and right the donor and his wife, with their patron saints Peter and Mary Magdalen (keys, box of ointment).

542. *Dierick Bouts of Louvain: The Last Supper. A fine and characteristic example of the town painter of Louvain. The faces are those of peasants or small bourgeois. To the right are the

donors, entering as spectators: their faces are excellent. Judas sits in front of the table. The Christ is insipid. Note the admirable work of the pavement and background. The servant is a good feature. If you have Conway with you, compare this picture with the engraving of the very similar one by Bouts at Louvain, (p. 277:) only, the architecture there is Gothic, here Renaissance.

139. *Descent from the Cross (Van der Weyden or his school). Notice the white sheet on which the body is laid, as later in the great Rubens. Nicodemus and Joseph of Arimathea support the body, St. John and one of the Maries holds the fainting Madonna. Left, the Magdalen, with her long hair. By her feet, her box of ointment. Close beside it, the nails, hammer and pincers. (M. Lafenestre, following Bode, attributes this picture to Petrus Christus, but with a query.)

29. Pleasing transitional Madonna, School of Van Orley, somewhat Italian in feeling, in a pretty arcade, with nice landscape background.

Above these, 109, a triptych, by Coninxloo. Centre, Family of St. Anne. Interesting for comparison with the great Quentin Matsys in the centre of the room. On the left is Joachim's offering rejected in the Temple (small episodes behind). On the right, the death of St. Anne. Come back to the central panel after you have viewed the Quentin Matsys. (The component personages are explained there.)

543. Tolerable triptych, Flemish school, representing the events of the Infancy. Centre, Adoration of the Shepherds, with the usual conventional features (ruined temple, shed, ox and ass, etc.), and St. Joseph holding his candle, as often, to indicate night time. Left, Annunciation, with the usual position of the

angel reversed. Otherwise, the portico and other features persist. Compare the great Van Eyck at Ghent, from which some elements here are borrowed. Right, the Circumcision. Symbolical figure of Moses on altar, full of the symbolism of Van der Weyden's school. (Outer shutters, uninteresting, SS. Catharine and Barbara.)

585. Above it, good family group of a donor and his sons, with St. George; and his wife and daughters, with St. Barbara. (The crucifixes mark monks and nuns.)

At the corner, 624, German school. St. Mary Magdalen and St. Thomas, on gold background. Companion piece to 624. At opposite end.

626. School of Martin Schongauer: Christ and the Magdalen in the house of the Pharisee. Very contorted. Compare with the Gossart.

Above it, 106, Flemish school. Mass of St. Gregory, with the Crucified Christ appearing on the altar. (Recall the Pourbus at Bruges.) A most unpleasant picture. Behind, are the elements of the Passion. To the left is the donors; on the right, Souls in Purgatory, relieved by masses. Many minor episodes occupy the area.

On either side of it, *27, 28, beautiful soft-toned German portraits (? by Beham) of two children, Maximilian II. and his sister Anne of Austria.

563. Lombard: Unimportant picture, meaninglessly described as Human Misfortunes. It seems to commemorate an escape from shipwreck and from plagues by the same person. On the left panel: A ship sinking; a man saved on the shore. In the

background, under divine direction of an angel, he finds his lost gold in a fish's body. In the right hand panel he lies ill of plague, while above is seen the miracle of St. Gregory and the Angel of the Plague (Michael) sheathing his sword on the Castle of St. Angelo.

540. Virgin and Child. Attributed without much certainty to Petrus Christus.

535. Good unknown Flemish picture of the *Assumption of Our Lady (closely resembling No. 534, which see again). The empty tomb stands in the midst, with lilies; around, St. Peter and St. James, and the other apostles; above, Our Lady ascending, borne by a duplicated figure of Christ (one standing for the Holy Ghost), in an almond-shaped glory. On the right is her Funeral, with St. Peter wearing the triple crown; On the left is St. Thomas receiving the girdle from an angel. Compare with 534, which Lafenestre judges to be the work of a different artist.

567. Good portrait attributed to Bernard Van Orley.

596. Six panels: Flemish School. Ornate, but not interesting. (1) The Lord creating Eve; in the background the Temptation. (2) Abraham, Sarah, and Isaac; in the background in three successive scenes, Abraham's Sacrifice. (3) Noah and his Family with the Ark. (4) Esau asks the Blessing of Isaac. (5) Meeting of Jacob and Esau. Note the grotesquely urban conception of the Semitic nomads. (6) The Nativity.

559. Attributed to Van Orley. Pietà, with the usual group, and family of donors. Interesting as a work of transition.

Above it, 580. Triptych, with Descent from the Cross, Flemish school. Usual figures; identify them. On the left hand wings are,

Agony in the Garden, Kiss of Judas, Peter and Malchus: To the right is The Resurrection. Noli Me Tangere, Disciples at Emmaus, etc.

107. P. Coecke, 16th century: A Last Supper. Only interesting as showing transition. Compare with Dierick Bouts.

Above it, 300. Patinier: Dead Christ on the knees of the Virgin (Our Lady of the Seven Sorrows), painfully emaciated. A sword pierces Our Lady's breast (and will recur often). Around it, the rest of the Seven Sorrows. Note the landscape, characteristic of the painter.

12. (Old number; no new number.) Coninxloo: Joachim and Anna, with the rejected offering. From them, a genealogical tree bears the Madonna and Child. To the left and right is the Angel appearing to Joachim, and Joachim and Anna at the Golden Gate. (Read up the legend.) Curious architectural setting.

301. Good portrait by an unknown (transitional) Fleming (Van Orley?), probably of a lawyer; the charters seem to indicate a secretary of Maximilian and Charles V.

The place of honour in the centre of the room is occupied by 299, a magnificent **triptych by Quentin Matsys, one of the noblest works of the transitional school, strangely luminous, with very characteristic and curious colouring. It represents the favourite Flemish subject of the Family of St. Anne. (It was painted for the Confraternity of St. Anne at Louvain, and stood as an altar-piece in the church of St. Pierre.) Central panel: An arcade, in the middle arch of which appears St. Anne, in red and purple (throughout), offering grapes to the Divine Child, who holds a bullfinch, and is seated on the lap of Our Lady. On the right is Mary Salome, with her two sons James and John. While on the left, Mary Cleophas, with her sons James the Less, Simon, Thaddæus, and Joseph the Just. Behind the parapet, beside St. Anne, her husband Joachim; and beside Mary Salome, her husband Zebedee. Beside Our Lady, her husband Joseph; beside Mary Cleophas, her husband Alphæus. Beautiful blue mountain landscape. Left panel: The angel appearing to Joachim, in a magnificent blue landscape. Joachim's dress is constant. The angel's robe is most delicious in colour. The right hand panel is The Death of St. Anne, with Our Lady and the other Maries in attendance. Behind, their husbands. The young Christ gives the benediction.

Now, go round to the back of the picture, to observe the outer wings. On the left is St. Joachim driven from the Temple by the High Priest On the right (chronologically the first), Joachim and Anna (much younger), making their offerings (on marriage) to the High Priest in the Temple. (Same High Priest, younger; same dresses.) The portrait behind recalls the earlier Flemish manner; otherwise, the work is full of incipient transition to the Renaissance. Little episode of Joachim and Anna distributing alms in the background. (When the triptych is closed, this wing comes in its proper place as first of the series.)

191. Jan van Eyck: (attribution doubtful; probably a later artist, perhaps Gerard David): The Adoration of the Magi. Another good example of this favourite Flemish subject. In the foreground, the Madonna and Child: one of Van Eyck's most pleasing faces (if his). Then, the Old King, kneeling; the Middle-aged King, half-kneeling; and the Young King, a Moor, with his gift, behind. (The Old King in such pictures has almost always deposited his gift.) In the background, Joseph, and the retinue of the Magi. Ruined temple, shed, ox, ass, etc., as usual.

291. Dierick Bouts: *Martyrdom of St. Sebastian. Characteristic peasant face; admirable cloak and background.

Now go into the next hall, which is marked as Room II on the gallery plan.

Room II

This room mainly contains German and Flemish pictures of the transition.

Right of the door, 338. Very Raphaelesque Holy Family by Bernard Van Orley, showing in the highest degree the Italian influence on this originally quite Flemish painter.

Above it, 92 and 92A. Portraits of the Micaul family.

105. J. Joest: St. Anne enthroned, Joseph, Our Lady, the Infant. Early transitional.

193. Jean Gossaert, Adam and Eve. Good later Flemish nude.

50. J. Bosch: Appalling Flemish Temptation of St. Anthony, with perhaps the silliest and most grotesquely repulsive devils ever painted.

2. Aertsen: *The Dutch Cook. A famous picture, showing well the earlier stages of Dutch genre development.

217. Van Hemessen: Genre piece, absurdly given the name of The Prodigal Son, by a sort of prescription, but really a Flemish tavern scene of the sort which afterwards appealed to Dutch artists. A characteristic work: transitional, but with good humorous faces, especially to the right. Painters still thought all pictures must pretend to be sacred.

591. German Adoration of the Magi. A fragment only.

603. Herri met de Bles: The Temptation of St. Anthony. Figures and landscape show Italian influence.

336. Transitional Adoration of the Shepherds. Observe the growing Renaissance feeling and Italian influence.

247, 248. Excellent portraits by Adrien Key.

41. Lancelot Blondeel: St. Peter enthroned as Pope: in one of his usual extravagant architectural frameworks. In circles above, his Imprisonment and Crucifixion.

Close by, unnumbered, two excellent portraits.

81. P. Brueghel the Younger: absurdly called The Census at Bethlehem. In reality a Flemish winter scene.

318. Sir Anthony More: *Portrait of the Duke of Alva, with the firm lips and cruel eyes of the ruthless Spaniard. One understands him.

359. Good portrait by Pourbus of a plump and well-fed Flemish gentleman.

80. P. Brueghel the Younger: Described as the Massacre of the Innocents. Flemish winter. The beginning of genre painting.

Most of the pictures skied above these are of some interest for comparison with earlier examples of the same subjects.

565. Unknown French portrait of Edward VI. of England. Hard and dry and of little artistic value.

566. Tolerable Flemish portrait of Guillaume de Croy (Golden Fleece).

573. Good Flemish portrait of a woman, dated 1504.

555. Flemish school: Annunciation. Chiefly interesting for its conventional features, and its very quaint figure of St. Mary of Egypt, with her three loaves, in the right hand panel.

124b. (Old number; no new number given.) Unusual combined picture of St. Jerome, uniting the subjects usually known as St. Jerome in the Desert and St. Jerome in his Study.

622. Fine German portrait of the early 17th century.

316. Good strong portrait, by Sir Anthony More, of Hubert Goltzius.

123. Cranach the Elder (German 16th cent.): *Adam and Eve. Fine specimens of the later northern nude of the early Renaissance, interesting for comparison with the cruder realism of Van Eyck. As yet, however, even the figure of Eve has relatively little idealism or beauty. Excellent stag in the background.

361. A good Pourbus. Beyond the door, 536, Flemish school: (Hugo Van der Goes?). Donor, a lady in a nun's dress (?), with her name-saint, St. Barbara, bearing her palm as a martyr: in the background, her tower with the three windows. To balance it, 536, Her brother (?) or husband, with his patron, St. James. (Staff and scallop-shell.)

Above, 84, Triptych by Jan Coninxloo of the History of St. Nicholas. (The wings are misplaced.) On the right wing (it should be the left), St. Nicholas, three days old, stands up in his bath to thank God for having brought him into the world. Central panel, the young St. Nicholas enthroned as Bishop of Myra. Upon the left wing (should be the right), The Death of St. Nicholas, with angels standing by to convey his soul to Heaven. A good transitional Flemish picture. Beneath, tolerable portraits.

361a. A late Flemish Virgin, with portrait of the donor and St. Francis receiving the stigmata.

572. Sir Anthony More. Portrait. Above it, 595, an Entombment, where note again the conventional grouping.

337. Wings of a triptych by Bernard van Orley. The centre is missing. On the left is the Martyrdom of St. Matthias. On the right is The Doubting Thomas. In the background, Lazarus and Dives, and other episodes. Renaissance architecture.

4. Van Alsloot: The Procession of the Body of St. Gudula at Brussels: of the Spanish period, with the guilds named. Interest purely archæological. Each guild carries its mace and symbol. (The second part comes later.)

586. Above this, skied, are four good female saints, transitional, named on labels.

574. Portrait, of the school of Van Orley: lady with a pink, pleasing. Italian influence is obvious.

505. Portrait of a lady, by M. De Vos. Early 17th century, marking the latest transitional period. It belongs to a destroyed triptych.

79. Breughel the Elder: St. Michael the Archangel conquering the devils. A hideous nightmare of a morbid and disordered imagination.

627. Crucifixion, by an unknown German, with small figures of donors, and Rhine background.

597. German school. Tree of Jesse, of purely symbolical interest.

504. *Portrait by M. De Vos. Probably husband of (and pendant to) the previous one. It was the other wing of the same triptych.

5. Van Alsloot: Remainder of the Procession of St. Gudula, with a quaint dragon, and the Maison du Roi in the background. Observe, near the centre, the personification of the patron, St. Michael: elsewhere are St. Christopher, Ste. Gudule, etc.

561. Two panels from a triptych attributed to Van Orley. Centre, missing. To the left witness The Birth of the Virgin. Note this for the conventional features: St. Anne in bed; attendant feeding

her: bath for infant. In the background presentation of the Virgin in the Temple: Joachim and Anna below: the Virgin ascending: the High Priest welcoming her: the Virgins of the Lord by the side. On the right, Joachim's offering is rejected. In the background, the meeting of Joachim and Anna at the Golden Gate, and the angel foretelling the Birth of the Virgin. Compare this with the great Quentin Matsys, observing especially the money falling from the table.

76. Another example of a later Last Judgment.

584. Mostart: Two stories from the life of St. Benedict. (1) The miracle of his dinner. (2) As a youth, he mends by prayer the dish broken by his nurse. (See Mrs. Jameson's Monastic Orders.)

Now pass through Room [VIII.], containing chiefly late Italian and French pictures (which we'll neglect for the present) and go on into Corridor A, to the left, overlooking the Sculpture Gallery. This takes us at once into the Later Flemish school of Rubens and his followers, whose works fill all these large corridors, which are admirably adapted for them. Begin to the right of the door. (Remember that I do not attempt criticism, but confine myself to historical indications.)

230. Jordaens: Fine landscape, with city to the right. As yet, however, landscape dare not stand entirely on its own merits. Therefore, we have here in the foreground figures of Eleazar and Rebecca at the well, which retain the tradition that pictures must have some sort of sacred purpose.

194a. Unknown. Interior of a picture-gallery, with well-known pictures.

Left of the door. 465. Van Thulden: Flemish Wedding Feast. Landscape is beginning to triumph now; it gets rid of all pretence of sacredness, but still retains small figures in the foreground. Landscape for landscape's sake is hardly yet dreamed of.

135. De Crayer, one of the best imitators of Rubens: *Adoration of the Shepherds, in the master's manner.

379. Rubens: **Coronation of the Virgin by God the Father and the Son, the Holy Ghost hovering above in a glory. This altar-piece, for an altar of Our Lady, is a magnificent specimen of the

master's rich and luminous colouring. The crimson robe of the Christ, the blue and lilac harmony on the Madonna, and the faint yellow of the Father's robe, are admirably contrasted. So are the darkness of the lower clouds and the luminosity of the upper region, recalling Titian's famous Assumption at Venice. The little boy angels are sweet and characteristic. Here you may begin to appreciate the force, the dash, the lavish wealth of Rubens. (According to Rooses, however, the work of a pupil, touched up by the master.)

Then, unnumbered, Jordaens: *Susannah and the Elders: a very Flemish and matronly Susannah. The nude of Rubens, without the glorious touch of the master: but a good picture.

392. Study by the same for the ceiling in Whitehall.

386. Fine *portrait by Rubens of a fair man (J. C. de Cordes). "Inferior work." (Fromentin.)

390. Rubens: **Charming little Madonna and Child (called "Our Lady of the Forget-me-not"), in a garden of roses (the landscape by J. Brueghel). One of his best small pictures, in a careful style.

387. Rubens: *Portrait: Wife of the last: in his finest and richest portrait manner, which contrasts in many ways with his larger and freer allegorical style. (Fromentin thinks poorly of it.)

389. In the corner, four Fine *Heads of Negroes, a study for the Magi, by Rubens. Not caricatured, but full of genuine negro character.

Above it, 219. An Adoration of the Magi by Herreyns: Interesting only as showing the persistence of the school into the 18th century.

235. Jordaens: *An Allegory of Abundance. Studies from the nude in the style of the school: meritorious.

Pass the door of the Dutch school. Beyond it, more Still Life, excellently painted.

240. Next door, Jordaens: *Nymph and Satyr. (This corridor is largely given up to works by Jordaens, who was a Protestant, and preferred heathen mythological subjects to Catholic Christian ones.

434. Snyders: 17th century: *Still Life, which now begins to be painted on its own merits. This last is by the great animal painter of the Flemish school.

238. Jordaens: Very Flemish *family group, with a somewhat superfluous satyr. (Subject nominally taken from the fable of the Satyr and the Wayfarer.)

302. Vandermeulen: View of Tournai and landscape, with the siege by Louis XIV. introduced for the sake of figures in the foreground.

Above it, 240 (? old number). De Crayer: St. Anthony and St. Paul the Hermit. Interesting for persistence of the typical figures.

The other pictures in this corridor are, I think, self-explanatory.

Room III

Right hand, further corner from door, Still Life by Snyders.

100. Good portrait by Philippe de Champaigne.

387a. Splendid *portrait by Rubens (according to Rooses, by Van Dyck).

This room also contains several fine pictures by Teniers (father or son) and other late Flemish painters, deserving of attention, but needing no explanation. (Portraits, etc.) Do not imagine because I pass them by that you need not look at them.

Now enter Corridor B

Left of the door, good works by De Crayer and others.

166. Van Dyck (the greatest pupil of Rubens, leading us on to the later Dutch school). *St. Francis in ecstasy before the Crucifix. From the Franciscan Capuchin Church in Brussels.

288. P. Meert, good portraits.

165. Companion to 166. Another Franciscan picture by Van Dyck. *St. Anthony of Padua holding the Infant Jesus. (In neither is he seen to great advantage.)

In the centre, 378, Rubens: **Assumption, high altar-piece from the Carmelite Church in Brussels. A fine picture, of Ruben's early period, smooth of surface and relatively careful, with the apostles looking into the empty tomb, whence women are picking roses (See Legends of the Madonna). To the right, the youthful figure of St. Thomas, stretching his hands. Observe the fine contrast of colour between the lower and upper portions. This is a noble specimen of the master's bold and dramatic treatment, but without his later ease of execution.

503. *Good portraits, by C. De Vos, of himself and his family.

127. De Crayer: St. Anthony, with his pig and staff, and St. Paul the Hermit, in his robe of palm-leaves, fed by a raven. In the background, the Death of St. Paul; two lions dig his grave. right, below, late figure of donor, seldom so introduced at this period. Jay in the background. Good landscape.

Room IV

This room is populated largely by landscapes and still life of the later period. Left of the door, 381, Rubens: The Woman Taken in Adultery. 605. Good *family group of the Van Vilsteren household, attributed to Van Dyck.

466. Interior of a picture-gallery, Teniers.

The room also contains several pictures worthy of note, but too modern in tone to need explanation. Observe that landscape has now almost vindicated its right to be heard alone, though figures in the foreground are still considered more or less necessary.

Now enter Corridor C. which contains good pictures of the later Flemish school. right of door, 435, A. Van Utrecht: one of the favourite Dutch kitchen scenes, well painted.

Left of the door.

95. Philippe de Champaigne: Presentation in the Temple, with characteristic crude French colouring.

437. Stag Hunt by Snyders.

375. Rubens: *Martyrdom of the local Bishop, St. Lieven. His tongue is torn out and given to dogs. Very savage pagans;

rearing horse; and characteristic angels, with celestial scene. In Rubens' less pleasing "allegorical" manner. Plenty of force, but too fiercely bustling.

383. Rubens: Fine portrait of the Archduke Albert.

384. Rubens: companion portrait of the Infanta Isabella, wife of 383.

376. Rubens: *Painfully un-Christian subject: mainly by a pupil, re-touched by the master: The Saviour about to destroy the World, which is protected by St. Francis and Our Lady. A strange method by which a votary seeks to impress his devotion to his own patrons. Behind, burning towns, murder, etc.

374. Rubens: *The Way to Calvary. (Almost all these large Rubenses are from High Altars.) In the foreground, the two thieves; then Christ falling, and a very Flemish and high-born St. Veronica unconcernedly wiping his forehead. Our Lady faints close by, supported by St. John. St. Longinus mounted, and Roman soldiers. The composition somewhat sketchy, but immensely vigorous. A gorgeous pageant, it wholly lacks pathos.

377. Rubens: **Adoration of the Magi (Altar-piece of the Capuchin Church at Tournai). One of his noblest works, magnificently and opulently coloured. The subject was one he often painted. Note still the Three Kings, representing the three ages and continents, but, oh, how transfigured! In their suite are Moors and other Orientals. Behind, St. Joseph with flambeaux, representing the earlier candle. This is a painting in Rubens's best Grand Seigneur manner—vast, throbbing, concentrated. He thinks of a Nativity as taking place with all the pomp and ceremony of the courts which he frequented. Charming pages in the foreground.

382. Rubens: Venus in the Forge of Vulcan. A made-up picture. Splendid studies of the exuberant nude by Rubens; with effects of light and shade in a smithy, added in the late 17th century to make up for a lost portion.

380. Rubens (much restored): *Christ on the knees of Our Lady. A noble composition, greatly injured. In the foreground kneels the Magdalen (her hair falling ungracefully), with the nails and Crown of Thorns. Notice always her abundant locks. To the right, St. Francis, with the Stigmata, bends over in adoration (a Franciscan picture). To the left are some very fleshy angels (Antwerp models) holding the instruments of the Passion. White sheet and dead flesh in their usual strong combination. (Painted for the Franciscan Capuchins of Brussels.)

The De Crayers, close by, contrast in the comparative crudity of their colour with the splendid harmonies of the master.

507. Paul de Vos: Horse and Wolves. Full of spirit.

129. De Crayer. The Martyrdom of St. Blaise. Shows him combed with a wool-carder.

Then flowers, hunting scenes, etc., requiring no comment.

Now pass through Room VII. (with Italian pictures to be considered later) and enter Corridor D.

Left of door, 231, Janssens: Our Lady appearing to St. Bruno.

125. De Crayer: *Assumption of St. Catherine, with her wheel and sword. A fine picture, in which De Crayer approaches very near Rubens. In the foreground are St. Augustine with the flaming heart; St. Gregory, habited as Pope; St. Ambrose, and

St. Jerome,—the four Doctors of the Church, with other saints, contemplating devoutly the glory of St. Catherine.

To the right and left of the central door, 136, 137, good saints, by De Crayer. Beneath them, excellent landscapes.

The remaining pictures in this room can be inspected by the visitor without need for explanation.

It is interesting to stand by the balustrade, here, above the sculpture gallery, not only for the general outlook upon the handsome hall, but also to note how the colour of the Rubenses stands out at a distance among the other pictures.

Now, go on through Room VIII. to Corridor A. On your left will be Room V.

Room V

This room contains works of the Dutch Masters. On these, for the most part, I shall have little to say. Their landscapes, flower-pieces, and portraits are admirable, indeed, but they are of the sort which explain themselves at sight, and need rather for their appreciation critical faculty than external knowledge. Begin on the left of the door.

282. Nicolas Maes: Good portrait of a 17th century lady.

263. Leerman's Crucifixion, finely executed.

Near it, good landscape or flower-pieces, etc., by Cuyp, De Heem, and Isaac van Ostade.

448. St. Pierre at Louvain.

525. Good hunting scene by Wouwerman.

279. **Admirable figure of an old woman fallen asleep over her reading, by Nicolas Maes.

Above it, 284. *Good portrait by Nicolas Maes.

278. *Fine portrait by Luttichuys.

304. Van Mieris: Susannah and the Elders. Frankly anachronistic.

233 is a fine *landscape with cattle, by Karel du Jardin.

147. Van Delen: Excellent architectural piece, with good *portraits in the foreground, painted in later by Emmanuel Biset.

End Wall.

44. Admirable *portrait by Bol.

45. Bol: *Portrait of a lady, probably wife of the last. On either side 310, 311, characteristic tavern scenes by Molinaer.

Right Wall.

398. One of Jacob Ruysdael's finest landscapes, with ruined tower.

399. Excellent *sea piece by Jacob Ruysdael, representing the Lake of Haarlem in a storm. Good foam.

I pass by, on the same wall, many meritorious Dutch works which cannot fail to strike the observer.

141. Albert Cuyp: *Cows. Excellent.

232. *Delicately luminous piece by Karel du Jardin, "L'Avant-garde du Convoi."

153. Gerard Dou: **The artist drawing a Cupid by lamplight. One of his finest studies in light and shade. It should be looked at long and carefully.

On either side of it, delicate small pieces by Steen, A. van Ostade and Dietrich.

47. *Good portrait by Bol.

281. *Portrait by Maes. Fine and audacious in colouring. Above it, 403, good Ruysdael.

Do not imagine because I give little space to the pictures in this room that they are not therefore important. As works of art, many of them are of the first value; but they do not require that kind of explanation which it is the particular province of these Guides to afford.

Now, pass through the small passage to Room VI.

Room VI

This room mostly contains works by the Dutch masters, the finest of which are here exhibited.

Left of the door.

364. Van Ravestein, capital portrait.

280. Maes: **Old woman reading.

206. Fruit piece by De Heem. One of his finest.

490. Van der Velde, junior: Shipping on the Zuyder Zee. The Dutch interest in the sea begins to make itself felt.

345. Portraits by Palamedes, arranged as a musical party.

352 (old number, no new number given). Molyn the Elder: Town fête by night. Good effect of light.

333. Admirable *portrait by Nicolas Maes.

251 and 250. De Keyser: Two fine portraits of women.

46. Bol: **Excellent portrait of Saskia, wife of Rembrandt.

463. **Exquisite miniature portrait by Ter Burg, which should be inspected closely.

328. Van der Neer: The Burning of Dordrecht. A lurid small piece.

501. A. de Voys: The Jolly Drinker. Highly characteristic of Dutch sentiment.

528. Landscape by Wynants.

The other still life and fruit or flower pieces on this wall need no comment.

End wall.

616. Weenix: Dutch lady dressing, with good effects of light and colour.

203. Frans Hals: **Portrait of W. van Heythuysen. One of his finest works. Broadly executed, and full of dash and bravado.

496. Excellent still life by Jan Weenix.

522. De Witte: Fine architectural church interior.

222. Above it, *peacock and other birds by Hondecoeter, who painted almost exclusively similar subjects. The solitary feather in the foreground recalls his famous masterpiece at the Hague.

On each side of this, tolerable portraits by Van der Helst.

36. Fruit and still life by Van Beyeren.

444. *One of Jan Steen's most characteristic pieces of Batavian humour. A Dutch lover offering affection's gift, in the shape of a herring and two leeks, to a lady no longer in her first youth. Behind, her unconscious husband. The painting of every detail is full of the best Dutch merits, and the tone of the whole frankly repulsive.

Right wall.

221. Hobbema: *The Wood at Haarlem. Characteristic Dutch landscape.

202. Frans Hals: **Splendid portrait of Professor Hoornebeck of Leyden. Extremely vivacious and rapidly handled.

220. *One of Hobbema's most famous mills.

Above this, 19, Storm at Sea, by Backhuysen.

368. Excellent **portrait by Rembrandt.

216. Portrait by Van der Helst. Not in his best manner.

445. A very characteristic and excellent Jan Steen, known as *The Rhetoricians—that is to say, members of a Literary Club or Debating Society, one of whom is engaged in reading his prize verses to a not too appreciative audience outside. Even here, however, Jan cannot omit his favourite touch of coarse Dutch love-making, with a tavern-girl introduced out of pure perversity.

357. Paul Potter: *Pigs. Admirably piggy.

End wall.

223. More of Hondecoeter's unimpeachable *poultry.

48. Bol: *Portrait of a Mathematician and Anatomist. One of the painter's masterpieces.

367. **Splendid portrait by Rembrandt ("L'Homme au grand chapeau"). An excellent and characteristic example of his art. The light and shade, the painting of the hair, and the masterly handling of the robe are all in the great painter's noblest manner.

402. Capital *water scene by S. van Ruysdael: a ferry on the Meuse.

224. Hondecoeter. More poultry, this time dead, with realistic nails, and other little tricks to catch the great public.

Left wall (Right of the door).

88. Van der Capelle: Calm sea, with excellent fishing boats.

Now, return through Corridors A. and D. to Room VII.

Room VII

In this room reside a multitude of early Italian pictures. Few of these are of much value, and as they are not connected with Flanders or Brabant, I will not enlarge upon them. Right of door,

631. An early Italian Adoration of the Magi, where you may compare the Three Kings, Joseph with the gift, the ox and ass, etc., with Flemish examples.

631 (left) is a characteristic example of St. Francis receiving the stigmata. Study it for comparison with the Rubens at Ghent, and others.

628. Above is a set of panels containing events in the History of Our Lady. I give the subjects, running along the top row first, with necessary brevity: Joachim expelled from the Temple: Warned by the Angel: Anna warned by the Angel: Meeting of Joachim and Anna at the Golden Gate: Birth of the Virgin: Presentation of the Virgin in the Temple: The Nativity: Adoration of the Magi: Christ found in the Temple: Miracle at Cana: Raising of Lazarus: Death of the Virgin, with Christ receiving her soul as a new-born baby. All these may be studied as early examples of the subjects they represent. Above them, 629 and 630: two Crucifixions of various ages.

140. Good characteristic Carlo Crivelli of *St. Francis with the stigmata.

3. Adam and Eve. Albani.

Above it, a tolerable Veronese of *Juno scattering wealth into the lap of Venice, St. Mark's lion beside her.

140. Beautiful Carlo Crivelli of *Our Lady and Child. This picture and the corresponding one opposite are parts of a large altar-piece, the main portion of which, a Pietà, is in the National Gallery in London.

415. Vannuchi (not Perugino): Leda and the Swan.

412 is a good portrait of Mary of Austria.

634. A tolerable Marriage of the Virgin.

473. Tintoretto: Portrait of a Venetian gentleman.

474. Another by the same.

Room VIII

This room, located just opposite, contains later Italian pictures, with a few French works too.

472 is a Martyrdom of St. Mark, by Tintoretto.

497 is a Holy Family by Paolo Veronese, with St. Theresa and St. Catherine.

The other works in the room do not call for notice.

Near to the passage leading into Room VI.

Skied. 477. Perugino: Madonna and Child, with the infant St. John of Florence, in a frame of Delia Robbia work. This is one of the best Italian pictures in this Gallery, but not a good example. Near it, School of Mantegna, Christ and St. Thomas with St. John the Baptist.

If you want further information about the pictures in the Brussels Gallery, you will find it in Lafenestre and Richtenberger's La Belgique, in the series of La Peinture en Europe.

This concludes our examination of works permanently housed within the Royal Museums of Fine Arts of Belgium. Altogether in the modern day the gallery boasts a total of 10,000 *objets d'art* – here, in the preceding pages most of the notables have received coverage. Be advised that exhibitions are frequent,

Cathedral of St. Michael and St. Gudula

The Cathedral of Brussels is dedicated to St. Gudula or Ste. Gudule, and to St. Michael the Archangel. St. Gudule is a holy person who takes us back to the earlier ages of Christianity among the Middle Franks.

St. Michael and St. Gudula Cathedral front - Image: Donaldytong

St. Gudula was a member of the family of Pepin d'Heristal, the kinsman of Charlemagne, and she died about 712. She became a nun at Nivelles under her aunt, St. Gertrude. The only fact of importance known as to her life is that she used to rise early, in order to pay her devotions at a distant church, whither she guided her steps by the aid of a lantern. Satan frequently extinguished this light, desiring to lead her feet astray, but the prayers of the saint as often rekindled it. Hence she is usually represented carrying a lantern, with the devil beside her, who endeavours to blow it out.

In the 10th century, the body of Ste. Gudule was brought to Brussels from Morseel; and in the 11th (1047), Lambert, Count of Louvain, built a church on this site above it: but the existing building, still containing the body of the saint, was not begun till 1220.

More important, however, than Ste. Gudule, in the later history of Brussels Cathedral, is the painful mediæval incident of the Stolen Hosts. The Jew-baiting of the 14th century led to a story that on Good Friday, 1370, certain impious Jews had stolen 16 consecrated Hosts from the Cathedral, and sacrilegiously transfixed them with knives in their synagogue. The Hosts miraculously bled, which so alarmed the Jews that they restored them to the altar. Their sacrilege was discovered by the aid of an accomplice, and on this evidence several Jews were burned alive, and the rest banished from Brabant forever.

A chapel on the site of the synagogue still commemorates the event, and the Miracle of the Hosts (as it is called) gives rise to several works of art now remaining in the Cathedral. An annual ceremony (on the Sunday after the 15th of July) keeps green the memory of the miraculous bleeding: the identical wafers are then exhibited. You will then be able to inspect the whole place peaceably at your leisure.

Approach the Cathedral, if possible, from the direction of the Grand Place, it is built so as to be first seen from this side, and naturally turns its main West Front towards the older city. Go to it, therefore, by the street known as the Rue de la Montagne and the short (modern) Rue Ste. Gudule, which lead straight up to the handsome (recent) staircase and platform. The building loses much by being approached sideways, as is usually the case, from the Upper Town, which did not exist at all in this direction when the Cathedral was built. Consider it in relation to the nucleus in the valley.

First examine the exterior. The accompanying rough plan will sufficiently explain its various portions.

The façade has two tall towers, and a rather low gable-end, with large West Window. In style, it approaches rather to German than to French Gothic. Over the Principal Entrance are (restored) figures of the Trinity, surrounded by angels, with the Twelve Apostles, each bearing his symbol or the instruments of his martyrdom. Below, on the central pillar, the Three Magi, the middle one a Moor. High up on the gable-end is the figure of Ste. Gudule, the human patron, with the Devil endeavouring to extinguish her lantern. Above her is the other and angelic patron, St. Michael. (These two figures also occur on the middle of the carved wooden doors.) At the sides, two bishops, probably St. Géry and St. Amand. Though the sculpture is modern, it is of interest from the point of view of symbolism. The left portal has St. Joachim, St. Anne, and the education of the Virgin. The right portal has St. Joseph and Our Lady with the Divine Infant.

Now, go round the building to the right, to observe its arrangement. You pass first the chapels or bays of the S. Aisle, with weather-beaten sculpture, and then reach the slightly projecting South Transept. Beyond the South Portal, the Choir is hidden by the addition of a large projecting chapel (that of Notre-Dame-de-Délivrance), whose architecture will be better understood from the interior. At the East End, you get a good view of the Gothic Choir and Apse, with its external chapels and flying buttresses. The extreme East point is occupied by the ugly little hexagonal rococo Chapel of the Magdalen, a hideous addition of the 18th century. Still passing round in the same direction, you arrive at a second projecting Chapel (du Saint Sacrement), which balances the first. The best general view is obtained from the North Side, taking in the beautiful porch of the North Transept. (The handsome Louis XVI. building opposite is the Banque Nationale.)

Image: Donaldytong

The Cathedral as an interior is disappointing. It contains no pictures of any importance, and its architecture is less striking within than without. The stained glass, indeed, is famous; none of it, however, is medieval. The best windows date only from the High Renaissance; the remainder is 17th century or modern.

Walk first into the centre of the Church, where you can gain a good idea of the high Choir, with its Apse and Triforium of graceful Early Gothic architecture, as well as of the short Transepts, the two additional chapels, on the right and left respectively are the Nave and single Aisles, and the great west window.

A closeup of the same stained glass - Image: Pbrundel

Now, begin the tour of the church with the South Aisle, to the left as you enter. The glass here is modern. It represents the story of the Stolen Hosts, some of the subjects being difficult to decipher. We see the Jew bribing a Christian, who removes the Hosts in a monstrance: then the Christian departing from the Jewish Synagogue with his ill-gotten gains. The third window I do not understand. After that, we see the Jews betrayed by one of their number; the Miracle of the Blood, with their horror and astonishment; the Recovery of the Hosts; and in the North Aisle, their Return to the Church in procession, and the various miracles afterward wrought by them. I cannot pretend to have deciphered all these accurately. The Nave has the usual Flemish figures of the Twelve Apostles set against the piers, most of them of the 17th century. The great west window has the Last Judgment, by Floris, a poor composition, overcrowded with indistinguishable figures.

Image: Steve Cadman

The pulpit, by Verbruggen, is a quintessential seventeenth century wood-carving. Below are Adam and Eve driven from Paradise: above, on the canopy, the Virgin and Infant Saviour wound the serpent's head with the cross: the Tree of Life, supporting the actual platform, gives shelter to incredible birds and animals. This ugly object was made for the Jesuits' Church at Louvain, and given to the Cathedral by Maria Theresa on the suppression of the Society of Jesus.

Return to the Transepts. The window in the North Transept represents Charles V., kneeling, attended by his patron, Charlemagne, who was a canonized saint, but who bears the sword and orb of empire. Behind him, Charles's wife Isabella, with her patroness, St. Elizabeth of Hungary, holding the crown. This window, erected in 1538, from designs by Bernard van Orley, was the gift of the Emperor. That in the South Transept represents the Holy Trinity, with King Louis of Hungary kneeling in adoration, attended by his patron, St. Louis of France. Behind him is his Queen, Marie (sister of Charles V.), with her patron, the Blessed Virgin. This window also is by Van Orley.

Image: Donaldytong

Now, enter the Chapel by the north Transept, that of the Holy Sacrament, erected in 1535-39, in honour of the Miraculous (Stolen) Hosts, which are still preserved here, and which are carried in procession annually on the Sunday following the 15th of July. The windows in this chapel, each of which bears its date above, were placed in it immediately after its erection, and are the best in the Cathedral. They exhibit the style of the Transitional Renaissance. Each window shows, above, the story of the Stolen Hosts, with, below, the various donors and their patrons. First window as you enter: Above, the Bribery: below, King John III. of Portugal with his patron, St. John-Baptist; and Queen Catherine, his wife (sister of Charles V.), with her patron, St. Catherine, holding her sword of martyrdom and trampling on the tyrant Maximin: (all by Michael Coxcie).

Charles with Isabella of Portugal

Second window: above, the Hosts insulted in the Synagogue: below, Louis of Hungary, with his patron, St. Louis; and Marie, his wife (sister of Charles V.), with her patroness, Our Lady (Coxcie). Third window: above, same subject as in the 3rd of the S. Aisle—perhaps the attack on the Jews: below, Francis I. of France, with his patron, St. Francis, receiving the Stigmata;

behind him, Eleonora, his wife (sister of Charles V.), with her patroness, St. Helena (Bernard van Orley). Fourth window: above, Denunciation of the Jews: below, Ferdinand, brother of Charles V., with his patron, St. Ferdinand; and his wife, Anne, with her patron, St. Anna (Bernard van Orley). The end window represents the Adoration of the Holy Sacrament, and of the Lamb that was slain, in a composition suggested by the Van Eyck at Ghent. Below, to the left are an Emperor and Empress (Charles V. and Isabella), a king and queen, and other representatives of the world secular: to the right are a pope, a cardinal, bishops, prophets, and other representatives of the church or the world ecclesiastical.

Altar - Image: Viktorhauk

Now, proceed to the opposite chapel, by the S. Transept, that of Our Lady of Deliverance (Notre-Dame de Délivrance). This chapel was erected in 1649-53, to balance that in the N. Transept. Its windows, made after designs by Van Thulden, in 1656, represent the continued decadence of the art of glass-painting. The subjects are taken from the History of Our Lady, above, with the donors and their patrons, princes of the House of Austria, below. Unlike the last, the subjects here begin at the inner end, near the altar.

First window: the Presentation of Our Lady in the Temple. She mounts the steps to the High Priest: below are St. Joachim and St. Anna. Second window: The Marriage of the Virgin. Third window: The Annunciation, with the Angel Gabriel and the Dove descending in a glory. Fourth window: The Visitation of Mary to Elizabeth: the figure of Mary, in its odd hat, taken from the Rubens in Antwerp Cathedral. The Austrian Princes and Princesses below, in the insipid taste of the 17th century, have commemorated their own names so legibly on the bases that I need not enumerate them.

The St Gudule statue - Image: Viktorhauk

Now, return to the north Transept, to make the tour of the Ambulatory. At the entrance to the Apse, On the left is a colossal statue of the patroness, Ste. Gudule, with the Devil under her feet. The stained glass of the Apse is good modern. Notice the fine pillars to your right. The hexagonal rococo Chapel of St. Mary Magdalen, at the end of the Apse, has modern windows where on the left and right are the two patrons, St. Michael and Ste. Gudule, the latter with the lantern and Devil: and, Centre, the Trinity. Exit from the Apse: on the left is a gilded statue of the other patron, St. Michael, to balance the Ste. Gudule. Beside it, curious wooden Easter Sepulchre, with Nicodemus, Joseph of Arimathea, the Mater Dolorosa, and the Maries. Above it, the Risen Christ, with Roman soldiers on the pediment. Fine view from near this point of the Choir and Transepts.

The high Choir has in its Apse stained-glass windows (use your opera-glass), representing Our Lady, and the patron saints, with various kings and queens in adoration (middle of the 16th century). The portraits are (1) Maximilian and Mary of Burgundy: (2) Philippe le Beau, their son, with his wife, Johanna the Mad, of Castille: (3) Charles V. and his brother Ferdinand, sons of Philippe: (4) Philip II. of Spain, son of Charles V., with his second wife. The architecture here is Early Gothic and interesting.

The Upper Town and Churches

From the Grand Place, two main lines of streets lead towards the Upper Town. The first, which we have already followed, runs straight to the Cathedral; the second, known as the Rue de la Madeleine and then as the Montagne de la Cour, mounts the hill to the Place Royale.

Saint Jacques sur Coudenberg

The city of the merchants lay about the Hôtel-de-Ville, the Senne, and the old navigation. The town and court of the Counts of Louvain and Dukes of Brabant clustered about the Castle on the high ground overlooking the Lower City. On this hill, the Coudenberg, the Counts of Louvain built their first palace, close to what is now the Place Royale. Their castle was burnt down in 1731, but the neighbourhood has ever since been the seat of the Belgian court for the time being—Burgundian, Austrian, Dutch, or Coburger. All this quarter, however, has been so greatly altered by modern "improvements" that scarcely a relic of antiquity is now left in it, with the exception of a few mediæval churches.

In spite of the competition of the Central or Inner Boulevards, the Montagne de la Cour, which mounts directly from the Grand' Place to the Cour (the residence of the Dukes or afterwards of the Emperors and the Austrian Viceroys), still remains the principal street for shopping in Brussels. It takes one straight into the Place Royale, one of the finest modern squares in Europe, occupying in part the site of the old Castle. Its centre is filled by the famous *statue of Godfrey de Bouillon by Simonis: the great Crusader is represented on horseback, waving his banner, and crying his celebrated cry of "Dieu le veut!" The unimpressive Church, with Corinthian pillars, a crude fresco in the pediment, and a green cupola, which faces you as you enter, is St. Jacques sur Coudenberg. To right and left you open up vistas of the Rue de la Régence and the Rue Royale. The former is closed by the huge mass of the new Palais de Justice. The latter ends in the great domed church of Ste. Marie de Schaerbeck.

In order to gain a proper conception of the Upper Town, one of the best-arranged in Europe, you must take the Place Royale and the Ancienne Cour (just below it) as your starting-point. The Place, the Park, and the streets about them were all laid out, under Austrian rule, at the end of the 18th century (1774) by the architect Guimard, who thus made Brussels into the handsome town we now see it. Turning to the right from the Place Royale, towards the Rue de la Régence, you come first to the gateway of a courtyard, guarded by sentinels which you may pass.

The quadrangle you have entered is the site of the old Palace of the Dukes of Brabant, for which the present building, known as the Ancienne Cour, was substituted by the Austrian Stadtholders in 1731 after the great fire. The first building to your left is occupied by the Royal Museum and Library. In this gallery are collected the chief works of the modern Belgian School of Painters, which the tourist should not omit to study, but a full description of which lies wholly outside the scope of these Guide Books.

This modern Belgian School was started in Antwerp, after the Revolution of 1830. It answered at first to the romantic movement in France (headed by Delaroche, Géricault, and others:) but the Belgian painters dealt mainly in historical pictures drawn from the struggles for liberty in their own country. The most distinguished of these "romantic" Belgian artists were Louis Gallait and Edouard de Bièfve, whose chief national works are to be seen in this gallery. Though they belong to a type which now strikes us as mannered and artificial, not to say insipid, they may help to impress historical facts on the spectator's memory. A very different side of the national movement will meet us at Antwerp. The later Belgian School has been gradually swamped by Parisian tendencies.

Royal Parliament Building - partly modern, partly neoclassical

Returning to the Place Royale, and continuing along the Rue de la Régence, the first building on the left is closed with a grille, is the Palace of the Comté de Flandre. Nearly opposite it (with four granite pillars) is the Palais des Beaux-Arts, containing the Ancient Pictures (already noticed). Further on to the right we arrive at the church of Notre-Dame-des-Victoires ("Église du Sablon"), to be described in detail hereafter. The pretty and coquettish little garden on the left is the Square or Place du Petit Sablon. It contains a modern monument to Counts Egmont and Hoorn, the martyrs of Belgian freedom, by Fraikin, and is worth a visit. The little statuettes on the parapet of the square represent artisans of the old Guilds of Brussels.

The building at the back of the Place is the Palace of the Duke d'Arenberg: its central part was Count Egmont's mansion erected in 1548. Today, it forms part of the Belgian Ministry of Foreign Affairs. Further on, to your left, comes the handsome building of the Conservatoire de Musique and then the Jewish Synagogue. The end of the street is blocked by the gigantic and massive façade of the new Palais de Justice, one of the hugest buildings of our period, imposing by its mere colossal size and its almost Egyptian solidity, but not architecturally pleasing. The interior need not trouble you.

The Belgian Foreign Ministry, formerly Count Egmont's Mansion - Image: Zinneke

Northward from the Place Royale, again, stretches the Rue Royale, along which, as we walk, we have ever before us the immense gilt dome of Ste. Marie de Schaerbeck. This fine street was admirably laid out in 1774 by the architect Guimard, who was the founder of the modern plan of Brussels. It is a fine promenade, along the very edge of the hill, beautifully varied, and affording several attractive glimpses over the earlier town by means of breaks in the line of houses, left on purpose by Guimard, some of which have, however, been unfortunately built up. Starting from the Place Royale, we have first, on our right, the Hôtel Bellevue; beyond which, round the corner, facing the Park, extends the unprepossessing white façade of the King's Palace (18th century, rebuilt). Then, again on the right, we arrive at the pretty little Park, laid out by Guimard in 1774, on the site of the old garden of the Dukes of Brabant. This is a pleasant lounging-place, animated in the afternoon, when the band plays. It contains ponds, sculpture, nursemaids, children, and one of the principal theatres.

Statue of Count Belliard - in the Koningstraat, Brussels - Image: Ad Meskens

Continuing still northward, we pass the Statue of Belliard, in the first break, and then the Montagne du Parc to the left, leading direct to the Lower Town. At the end of the Park, the Rue de la Loi runs right, eastward, towards the Exhibition Buildings. The great block of public offices in this street, facing the Park, includes the Chamber of Representatives (Palais de la Nation) and the principal Ministries. Beyond these we get, on the left, a glimpse of the Cathedral, and on the right a number of radiating streets which open out towards the fashionable Quartier Léopold. Then, on the left, we arrive at the Place du Congrès with its Doric column, commemorating the Congress which ratified the Independence in 1831. It can be ascended (193 steps, spiral) for the sake of its admirable *view, the best general outlook to be obtained over Brussels. (A few sous should be given to the guardian.) The prospect from the summit (morning light best) will enable you to identify every principal building in the city (good map by Kiessling, 72, Montagne de la Cour).

Place de la Liberté - Image: Zinneke

Continuing our route, the street to the right leads to the little and very verdant Place de la Liberté. Beyond this, the Rue Royale goes on to the Outer Boulevards, and finally ends at Ste. Marie de Schaerbeck, a gigantic modern Byzantine church, more splendid than beautiful, but a good termination for an afternoon ramble.

The Outer Boulevards of Brussels, which ring round the original 14th century city, have now been converted into magnificent promenades, planted with trees, and supplied with special lanes for riders. These Boulevards, perhaps the handsomest in the world, replace the ancient walls, erected in 1357-1379, when the town had already reached such considerable limits. Most of what is interesting or important in Brussels is still to be found within the irregular pentagonal ring of the Boulevards. A pleasant way of seeing the whole round is to take the electric tram, from the Gare du Nord, by the Upper Boulevards, to the Gare du Midi. You first mount the steep hill, with the Botanical Gardens on your left, backed by the extensive hot-houses. The line then crosses the Rue Royale, looking left towards Ste. Marie de Schaerbeck, and right towards the Place Royale.

Place des Barricades - Image: Ben2

As you turn the corner, you have on your left a small triangular garden, and on your right the circular Place des Barricades, with a statue of the great anatomist Vesalius, physician to Charles V., and an indirect victim of the Inquisition. The rail then bends round the Boulevard du Régent, with glimpses (to the right) of the Park, and (to the left) of the Squares in the Quartier Léopold. You next pass, right, the Palais des Académies, in its neatly kept garden, beyond which you arrive at the private gardens of the Royal Palace and the Place du Trône. Hence you continue to the Place de Namur and the Fontaine de Brouckere, and continue on to the Place Louise, at which point the open Avenue Louise leads direct to the pleasant Bois de la Cambre.

Boulevard du Midi - Image: Raf24

The Boulevard de Waterloo carries you on to the Porte de Hal, the only one of the old gateways still standing. This is a massive fortress of irregular shape, built in 1381, and it was used by the Spanish authorities in the time of Alva as the Bastille of Brussels.

The interior contains a fine winding staircase and a small collection of arms and armour which is worth a ten minute visit in passing. Hence, the Boulevard du Midi conducts you straight to the Gare du Midi, from which point you can return, on foot or by tram, through the Inner Boulevards or diagonally through the old town, to your hôtel.

The remainder of the Outer Boulevards, leading from the Gare du Midi to the Gare du Nord by the western half of the town, is commonly known as the Lower Boulevards, (Note the distinction of Upper, Lower, and Inner.) It passes through a comparatively poor quarter, and is much less interesting than the other half. The only objects of note on its circuit are the slaughter houses and the basins of the canal. Nevertheless, a complete tour of the Boulevards, Upper, Lower, and Inner, will serve to give you a better general conception of Brussels within the old walls than you can otherwise obtain.

I cannot pretend in this Guide to point out all the objects of interest in modern Brussels, within this great ring. Speaking generally, the reader will find pleasant walks for spare moments in the quarter between the Rue Royale or the Rue de la Régence and the Upper Boulevards. This district is high, healthy, and airy, and is chiefly given over to official buildings. On the other hand, the quarter between these two streets and the Inner Boulevards, especially southward about the Place St. Jean and the Rue de l'Étuve, leads through some interesting portions of 17th century and 18th century Brussels, with occasional good domestic architecture. The district lying west of the Inner Boulevards is of little interest, save in its central portion already indicated. It is the quarter of docks, entrepôts, and the more squalid side of wholesale business.

The immense area of Brussels outside the Outer Boulevards I cannot pretend to deal with. Pleasant walks may be taken at the eastern end of the town about the Chaussée de Louvain, the Square Marie-Louise, the Exhibition Grounds, the Parc Léopold (near which is the too famous Musée Wiertz), and the elevated land in the eastern quarter generally. The Bois de la Cambre, the true park of Brussels, makes a delightful place to walk or drive in the afternoon, especially on Sundays. It somewhat resembles the Bois de Boulogne, but is wilder and prettier. Perhaps the most satisfactory way of visiting it is to take the tram to the gate of the wood, and then walk through it.

Art Deco structure at the Chaussée du Louvain - Image: Michel Wal

There are three other churches, beside the Cathedral, in the neighbourhood of the Place Royale, which you may go to see, if you have plenty of time left, but which you need not otherwise trouble about. The three can be easily combined in a single short round.

Go down the Montagne du Parc, and take the first turning to the left, Rue des Douze Apôtres, which will bring you direct to the little Chapelle de l'Expiation, erected in 1436, on the site of the synagogue where the Stolen Hosts were profaned, and in expiation of the supposed crime. The exterior of the building has been modernized, and indeed the whole is of little interest, save in connection with the Cathedral and the Stolen Hosts; but a glance inside is not undesirable. The interior, flamboyant Gothic, is thoroughly well decorated throughout, in modern polychrome, with scenes from the Gospel History. The Apse has good modern stained-glass windows, and frescoes of angels holding the instruments of the Passion. It is separated from the Nave by a high Rood-Loft, without a screen. Modern taste has here almost entirely ignored the painful and malicious story of the Stolen Wafers.

Now, continue down the Rue des Sols as far as the Rue de l'Impératrice (where a slight détour to the right takes you in front of the Université Libre, a large and somewhat imposing, but uninteresting building). Continue rather to the left down the Rue de l'Impératrice, crossing the Montagne de la Cour, into the Rue de l'Empereur and the Rue d'Or, till you arrive at the Place de la Chapelle, containing the church of Notre-Dame de la Chapelle—after the Cathedral, the finest mediæval church of Brussels. The exterior has lately (alas!) been quite too much restored. It shows a fine Nave and Aisles of the 15th century, and a much lower and very beautiful Choir of the 13th century, with some Romanesque details of an earlier building (10th century?) Walk once round the church, to observe the exterior architecture. The West Front is massive rather than beautiful. The sculpture over the door (the Trinity with angels, and Our Lady) is modern. Over the southern portal is a modern relief, in a Romanesque tympanum, representing the Coronation of Our Lady by God the Father and the Son. The Romanesque and transitional work of the beautiful low Choir and Apse has unfortunately been over-restored.

The Chapel of Notre Dame - Image: Morburre

The interior, with its fine Nave and Aisles, is impressive, especially as you look from the centre down towards the West end. The round pillars of the Nave are handsome, and have the usual figures of the Twelve Apostles. The pulpit is one of the familiar 17th century monstrosities, with palms, and Elijah in the Wilderness. The interior of the pretty little Apse has been so completely modernized as to leave it little interest. There are a few good pictures of the School of Rubens (De Crayer, Van Thulden, etc.).

On emerging from the church, follow the tramway line up the hill to the market-place of the Grand Sablon. Good views in every direction as you enter the Place. The square is animated on Fridays and Sundays, when markets are held here. Pass through the market-place, which contains an absurd 18th century monument, erected by a Marquis of Ailesbury of the period, in gratitude for the hospitality he had received from the citizens of Brussels, and continue on to the Rue de la Régence, passing on your right the beautiful Apse of the church of Notre-Dame-des-Victoires, now unhappily in course of restoration. The entrance is in the Rue de la Régence, and the church is not oriented.

Notre-Dame-des-Victoires, or Notre-Dame du Sablon, was founded in 1304 by the Guild of Crossbowmen; but the existing late-Gothic building is almost entirely of the 15th and 16th centuries. It has been over-restored in parts, and the beautiful crumbling exterior of the Apse has come precariously close to disfigurement.

The interior is pleasing. Over the Main Entrance, within, is a curious ex voto of a ship, in commemoration of the arrival of a sacred image, said to have floated miraculously by sea.

The first chapel to your left as you enter has a *tomb of Count Flaminio Gamier, secretary to the Duke of Parma, partly restored, but with fine original alabaster reliefs of the early Renaissance, representing the History of the Virgin. The series begins below: (1) Meeting of Joachim and Anna at the Golden Gate; (2) The Birth of the Virgin; (3) The Presentation of the Virgin in the Temple. Then, above: (4) Annunciation; note the relative positions of the angel and Our Lady, the lily, the prie-dieu, and the loggia in the background; (5) the Visitation, with the usual arch; and (6) the Presentation of Christ in the Temple.

The Apse has restored figures of saints (named) in imitation of those which were discovered in ruined fresco during the restoration. They are a good typical collection of the saints most venerated in the Low Countries in the Middle Ages.

The Nave has the usual figures of Apostles, named, and a small open Triforium just below the Clerestory. The Pulpit has on its face a medallion of Our Lady; right and left, Moses and St. Augustine. Below, the four beasts of the Evangelists.

You need not trouble about any other special building in Brussels; but you may occupy yourself pleasantly with many walks through all parts of the city.

Palais de Justice during its dome and frontage renovations - Image: Martin Mycielski

You are now in a position to understand the growth and spread of Brussels. From the very beginning, the merchant town occupied the valley, while the capital of the Counts, Dukes, or Sovereigns spread over the hill, in the neighbourhood of what are still significantly called the Montagne de la Cour and the Place Royale.

To this day the two contrasted parts of the city are broadly distinct. The valley speaks Flemish; the mountain, French. In the valley stand all the municipal and mercantile buildings—the Hôtel-de-Ville, the Bourse, the Post-Office, the markets, and the principal places of wholesale business. On the hill stand the Royal Palace, the Government Offices, the Legislative Body, the Ministries, the Palais de Justice, and the whole of the National Museums and collections. From this point of view again, in our own day, the valley is municipal, and the hill national. The contrasted aspects of the Inner Boulevards and the Rue de la Régence well mark the difference. In the valley, you will find, once more, the hotels of commerce and of the passing traveller; on the hill, those frequented by ambassadors and the wealthier class of foreign tourists. Near the Place Royale were situated the houses of the old Brabant nobility, the Egmonts and the Cuylenburgs; as at the present day are situated those of the Arenbergs and the De Chimays.

Historically, the spread of the town from its centre began towards the Castle of the Counts of Louvain and Dukes of Brabant, in the Ancienne Cour, now occupied by the Royal Library and the Modern Picture Gallery, as well as towards the ecclesiastical quarter of the Cathedral and the Chancellerie. The antiquity of this portion of the Upper Town is well marked by the continued existence of the mediæval churches of Notre-Dame de la Chapelle, Notre-Dame-des-Victoires, and the Chapelle de l'Expiation. Under the Burgundian princes, Brussels ranked second to Ghent and Bruges; but after the Hapsburgs obtained possession of the Low Countries, it was made the principal residence of the sovereigns in their western domains.

Charles V. inhabited it as one of his chief capitals. Under Philip II. of Spain, it became the official residence of the Stadtholder of the Netherlands; and Margaret of Parma, who bore that office, held her court in the old Palace. From that time forth Brussels was recognised as the common capital of the southern Low Countries. The Austrian Stadtholders habitually lived here; and when, after the Napoleonic upheaval, Belgium and Holland were united into a single kingdom, Brussels was made the alternative capital with Amsterdam. By the time that Belgium asserted her independence in 1830, Brussels had thus obtained the prescriptive right to become the seat of government of the new nation.

The present day Royal Palace of Brussels - Image: Alvesgaspar

The old Palace had been burnt down in 1731, and the outer wings of the existing Palace were built by the Austrians shortly after. It was they, too, who laid out the Rue Royale and Place Royale, with the Park and its surroundings, as we still see them at the present day. To the Austrian rulers are also due the Parliamentary Buildings: but the Palais des Académies was built under Dutch rule in 1829.

Since 1830 the town has been greatly beautified and improved. The Inner Boulevards have been opened through the labyrinth of streets in the old centre: the Palais de Justice has been built, the Quartier Léopold has grown up, and great edifices have been erected at Schaerbeck and elsewhere on the outskirts. At the present day, of Brussels within the Boulevards, the Hill District is governmental and fashionable; the Central District, municipal and commercial: the Western District contains the markets, basins, canals, and wholesale business side of the city. Without the Boulevards, Fashion has spread eastward towards the Bois de la Cambre and the Parc Léopold.

The poorer districts run southward and westward. But every part of the city is amply provided with wide thoroughfares and open breathing-spaces. The modern tramways, bus routes and easy access via train further enhance the open navigability which the visitor values so highly in terms of seeing all there is to see. In this respect, Brussels is one of the best-arranged cities in Europe.

Places of Interest near Brussels

Close to Brussels, there are several small towns and landmarks significant enough to merit a visit.

Laeken

The only excursion of interest in the immediate neighbourhood of Brussels is a recommended journey to Laeken, which may be taken by tram from the Inner Boulevards, the Gare du Nord, the Gare du Midi, Bourse, and so on. Departures occur roughly every 10 minutes.

Royal Palace of Laeken - Image: Jean-Pol Grandmont

The 19th century Church of St. Mary at Laeken is a handsome building. A little to the right lie the Park and the Royal Château, inaccessible and unimportant. The road behind the church ascends the Montagne du Tonnerre, a little hill with a Monument to Léopold I., not unlike the Albert Memorial in London. A good *view of Brussels is obtained from the summit of the monument, ascended by a winding staircase. (No fee.) The easiest way to make this excursion is by carriage in the afternoon.

Unless you are a military man or a student of tactics, I do not advise you to undertake the dull and wearisome excursion to Waterloo. The battlefield is hot and shade-less in summer, cold and draughty in spring and autumn. The points of interest, such as they are, lie at considerable distances. Waterloo is country, and ugly country—no more. The general traveller who desires to be conducted round the various strategic landmarks of the field will find his wants amply catered for by Baedeker. But I advise him to forego that foregone disappointment.

The time saved by not visiting Waterloo may, however, be well devoted to a morning excursion to Louvain.

Leuven / Louvain

This ancient and important town, which should be visited both on account of its magnificent Hôtel-de-Ville, and in order to make a better acquaintance with Dierick Bouts, the town painter, can be conveniently reached by train from the Gare du Nord.

Louvain Town Hall / Hotel de Ville - Image: Nk

The best trains take little more than half an hour to do the journey. A single morning is sufficient for the excursion, especially if you start early. Wednesday is the most convenient day, as you can catch a . There are many varied and quality eateries all around Louvain centre, particularly infront of the left-hand side of the Hôtel-de-Ville. (It is a private club, but contains a public restaurant, on the right, within, to which, push through boldly.) If you have Conway, take him with you on this excursion, to compare the doubtful Roger van der Weyden at St. Pierre with the woodcut he gives of its supposed original at Madrid. Read before you start (or on the way) his admirable accounts of Roger van der Weyden and Dierick Bouts.

Louvain is, in a certain sense, the mother city of Brussels. Standing on its own little navigable river, the Dyle, it was, till the end of the 14th century, the capital of the Counts and of the

Duchy of Brabant. It had a large population of weavers, engaged in the cloth trade. Here, as elsewhere, the weavers formed the chief bulwark of freedom in the population. In 1378, however, after a popular rising, Duke Wenseslaus besieged and conquered the city; and the tyrannical sway of the nobles, whom he re-introduced, aided by the rise of Ghent or, later, of Antwerp, drove away trade from the city. Many of the weavers emigrated to Holland and England, where they helped to establish the woollen industry.

During the early Middle Ages, Louvain was also celebrated for its University, founded in 1426, and suppressed by the French in 1797. It was re-established by the Dutch in 1817, but abandoned by the Belgian Government in 1834, and then started afresh in the next year as a free private Roman Catholic University. Charles V. was educated here.

The modern town has shrunk far away within its ancient ramparts, whose site is now for the most part occupied by empty Boulevards. It remains still the stronghold of Roman Catholic theology in Belgium.

As you emerge from the station, you come upon a small Place, adorned with a statue (by Geefs) of Sylvain van de Weyer, a revolutionary of 1830, and long Belgian Minister in England. Take the long straight street up which the statue looks. This leads direct to the Grand' Place, the centre of the town, whence the chief streets radiate in every direction, the ground-plan recalling that of a Roman city.

The principal building in the Grand' Place is the Hôtel-de-Ville, standing out with three sides visible from the Place, and probably the finest civic building in Belgium. It is of very florid late-Gothic architecture, between 1448 and 1463. Begin first with the left façade, exhibiting three main storeys, with handsome Gothic windows. Above come a gallery and then a gable-end, flanked by octagonal turrets, and bearing a similar turret on its summit. In the centre of the gable is a little projecting balcony of the kind so common on Belgian civic buildings.

The architecture of the niches and turrets is of very fine florid Gothic, in better taste than that at Ghent of nearly the same period. The statues which fill the niches are modern. Those of the first storey represent personages of importance in the local history of the city: those of the second, the various medieval guilds or trades: those of the third, the Counts of Louvain and Dukes of Brabant of all ages. The bosses or corbels which support the statues are carved with scriptural scenes in high relief. I give the subjects of a few (beginning left): the reader must decipher the remainder for himself. The Court of Heaven: The Fall of the Angels into the visible Jaws of Hell: Adam and Eve in the Garden: The Expulsion from Paradise: The Death of Abel, with quaint rabbits escaping: The Drunkenness of Noah: Abraham and Lot: etc.

The main façade has an entrance staircase and two portals in the centre, above which are figures of St. Peter, and on the left is Our Lady and Child, right, the former in compliment to the patron of the church opposite. This façade has three storeys, decorated with Gothic windows, and capped by a gallery parapet, above which rises the high-pitched roof, broken by several quaint small windows. At either end are the turrets of the gable, with steps to ascend them. The rows of statues represent as before (in 4 tiers) persons of local distinction, medieval guilds, and the Princes who have ruled Brabant and Louvain. Here again the sculptures beneath the bosses should be closely inspected. Among the most conspicuous are the Golden Calf, the Institution of Sacrifices in the Tabernacle, Balaam's Ass, Susannah and the Elders, etc.

The gable-end to the right, ill seen from the narrow street, resembles in its features the one opposite it, but this façade, which was even finer than the others, is at present in course of wholesale restoration.

The best general view is obtained from the door of St. Pierre, or near either corner of the Place, diagonally opposite.

Do not trouble about the interior.

The church of St. Pierre - Image: Jeanhousen

Opposite the Hôtel-de-Ville stands the Church of St. Pierre, originally erected in 1040, but entirely rebuilt in 1430, to which date the whole existing edifice belongs. It is a handsome late-Gothic building, with a fine West Front, never completed, and a truncated tower. The central West Window is imposing, but the ruined portal has a depressing effect. Once you are outside, walk around the church to observe its exterior architecture, obscured towards the Grand' Place by the usual agglomeration of small Renaissance houses. The main entrance is in the South Transept; above it stands a poor modern statue of the patron, St. Peter. The High Choir, with its flying buttresses, would form a fine element if the houses were cleared away, so as to afford a view of the chapels below.

St Peter's Church interior - Image: Mattana

Now view the interior. Go at once into the body of the church. The general effect is handsome, but the walls are cold and white-washed. The church has a fine Nave, with single Aisles, short Transepts, high Choir, and Ambulatory. The Nave, Transepts, and Choir, have all an exactly similar clerestory, with an unusual Triforium of open latticework, and tracery in the same style in the spandrils of the arches.

Go down to the W. end of the Nave. The entrance doors at this end have good but not beautiful carved woodwork of the Renaissance.

Left Aisle. First chapel. Late Gothic copper font, with large crane, to support a heavy iron cover, now removed. The other chapels on this side contain nothing of interest.

Right Aisle. First chapel (of San Carlo Borromeo), has an altar-piece, copied from one by De Crayer, carried off by the French and now at Nancy. It represents San Carlo ministering to the plague-stricken at Milan. Also, a triptych, by Van de Baeren, 1594. Centre, St. Dorothea beheaded. Her head praising God. And on the left is her trial before the governor, Fabricius. To the right witness, her torture in enduring the sight of her sister's martyrdom. Statue of San Carlo by Geefs.

Second chapel, of the Armourers, has a railing with arms and cannon, and contains an old blackened crucifix, much venerated because it is said to have caught a thief who had entered the church to steal the treasures.

The pulpit is a carved wooden specimen of the 18th century, representing, behind, the Repentance of Peter, with the cock crowing, a maladroit subject for a church dedicated to the saint. In front, the Conversion of St. Paul, with his horse overthrown. Above are two palm trees.

The Choir is separated from the Transepts and Nave by a very handsome and elaborate *Rood-Loft, in the finest flamboyant late-Gothic style (1450), one of the best still remaining examples in Europe. It supports a Crucifixion, with St. John and Our Lady. Its arcade of three handsome arches is surmounted by a sculptured balustrade, containing figures of saints (the Saviour, Our Lady and Child, the Twelve Apostles with the instruments of their martyrdom, the Doctors of the Church, and a few others). Examine carefully.

Now, pass behind the Choir, into the Ambulatory, beginning on the N., or left side. The first recess has a fine mediæval tomb of Mathilde de Flandre. On your right in the Choir a little further on, is a beautiful late-Gothic tabernacle or canopy of 1450, gilded, and containing scenes from the Passion. Just behind the High Altar is a curious little 15th century relief: Centre, the Crucifixion with St. John and Our Lady: on the right is, The Resurrection, with sleeping Roman soldiers: to the left is The donor, with his patron St. John the Baptist.

The first chapel beyond the High Altar contains **The Last Supper, by Dierick Bouts. This picture forms the central piece of a triptych, painted for the Confraternity of the Holy Sacrament. The left wing of it is now at Munich, and the right at Berlin. It represented, when entire, the same mystical series of the Institution of the Eucharist which we have already seen in the Pourbus of the Cathedral at Bruges. The central panel represented the Institution of the Eucharist; the left (Munich) has Melchizedeck offering bread and wine to Abraham; the right (Berlin) Elijah fed by ravens in the wilderness. On the outer sides of the panels are two similar typical subjects: to the left (Munich), the Gathering of the Manna or food from Heaven; and to the right (Berlin), the Feast of the Passover, the Paschal

Lamb being regarded as a type of the Christian sacrifice. The picture as it stands in this chapel has of course lost its mystical significance. It closely resembles the smaller Last Supper in the Brussels Gallery; but the architecture here is Gothic, not Renaissance. Study well, especially the figures of the donor (by the door) and the servant. The floor is characteristic.

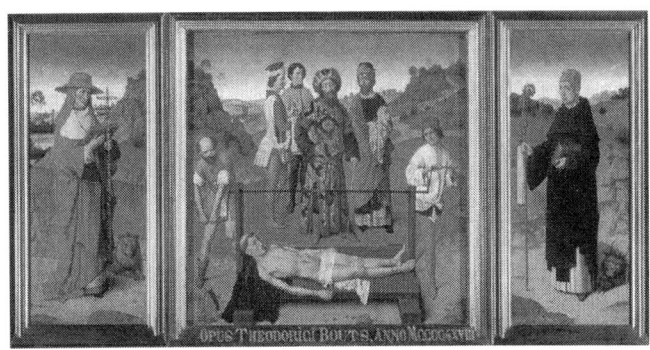

Also a **triptych, by Dierick Bouts, the Martyrdom of St. Erasmus, patron against intestinal diseases: a bishop, martyred at Formia in the persecution of Diocletian. It represents the hideous episode of the unwinding of the saint's bowels. The executioner on the left is a good specimen of Dierick Bouts's rude artisan figures; he looks like a cobbler. In the background is the Emperor Diocletian, richly attired, with a courtier, whose attitude recalls more than one of those in the Justice of Otho. The landscape is characteristic of Bouts's manner. This is a good, hard, dry picture. The left hand panel has St. Jerome, robed as cardinal, with his lion; the right has St. Anthony, accompanied by a vanquished demon. This, however, is a St. Anthony as the abbot, not as the hermit in the desert.

On the roof of the fourth chapel have recently been discovered some frescoes, from which the plaster and whitewash is now being removed.

In the chapel next it to the right is a triptych, the Descent from the Cross; usually attributed to Roger van der Weyden, but much disputed. It is probably a smaller (altered) copy of the famous composition in the Escurial at Madrid (see Conway). The central picture has Christ supported by Joseph of Arimathea and Nicodemus, with the fainting Madonna, St. John, and the other Maries. The singularly unpleasing fat cook-like Magdalen, in a rich robe, is a constant feature in the group of Descents from the Cross by Roger and his pupils. Study this picture. The left hand panel has a good portrait of the donor, with his two sons, accompanied by his patron St. James the Greater (or St. William?). The right panel has his wife, with her two daughters and her patroness, St. Adelaide (or St. Elizabeth of Hungary, holding the crown which she gave up for the Franciscan profession?).

In the sixth chapel is a fine Renaissance tomb, representing Adolf van Baussede in adoration before the Trinity, introduced by his patron St. Adolphus, with allegorical figures of Faith, Hope, and Charity. The work is almost Italian in character.

Over the High Altar is a modern figure of the patron, St. Peter, enthroned as pope, and with papal symbols behind him. Left of it is the fine canopy we have already observed from the outside, with scenes from the Passion. The architecture here is striking.

The great Quentin Matsys of the Family of St. Anne in the Brussels Picture Gallery was formerly an altar-piece in this church.

There is nothing else at Louvain that need detain you. If you like, you can stroll a little way down the Rue de Namur, just to the right of the Hôtel-de-Ville. It contains some good old houses. The desolate building on your right was originally the

Halles, but is now the University. It was built for the Guild of Clothmakers in 1317, and has been wholly modernised; but there are some good Gothic arches on the basement floor within (approach down the side street to the right). Further on is the Collège du St. Esprit on the right, and the Church of St. Michel (uninteresting) on the left is The street which here runs off obliquely conducts to the Collège Marie-Thérèse, and the Collège Adrien VI., uninteresting, and all used as hostelries for the students.

St. Gertrude Church in Leuven - Image: Flamenc

The only other objects to look at in Louvain are the choir-stalls in carved wood, early Renaissance, at the Church of St. Gertrude, dedicated to the Abbess of Nivelles and aunt of St. Gudula. It lies down the Rue de Malines, in the opposite direction from the Rue de Namur. You have then seen Louvain.

Antwerp

Panorama of Antwerp's *Grote Mark* - Image: 3BRBS

The city of Antwerp successfully marries together the attributes of art and culture in a sublime combination which splendidly impresses many who visit. Centuries of artistic and architectural heritage are displayed, with the legacy of its Baroque school of painting evident in the galleries we examine.

Today Antwerp shines splendidly in modernity, choosing to place emphasis on its fashionable boutiques and tasteful blend of the old and the modern. Through hard work during the past few decades, the city has attained a reputation in gems and jewellery, becoming a favourite of the connoisseur. Its fashion shows and flamboyancy are afforded reputation by the Royal Academy, the frequent catwalk shows acting in distinct contrast of form and beauty to the ancient art and architecture examined in this guide.

Transport links by air, train and tram are consistent with visitor numbers consistently high in particular during the summer season. A visit by train is particularly satisfactory, given that the Central Station is itself offers up impressive example of symmetric archways well worth stopping a few minutes to admire and observe.

Interior of Antwerp central station - Image: Alan Stanton

Traditionally the most populous and prosperous city in Flanders, it is undoubtedly true that Antwerp offers much to do and see before we even reach the cultural and artistic legacy Antwerp boasts. Our mission however is to trace, through the civic history, the wellspring of artistic talent and religious faith which led the city to become as it is today. To equip visitors inclined to the appreciation of art and architecture with the insight required to profit most during perusals of Antwerp's greatest heritage buildings.

The Origins of Antwerp

Antwerp, the seaport of the Schelde estuary, is practically the youngest of the great Belgian towns. It should therefore be visited last by the historically-minded tourist. A small town, known in Flemish as Antwerpen ("at the Wharf"),—a name altered in French and English into Anvers and Antwerp,—existed here, it is true, as early as the 7th century, and suffered heavily in the 9th from the ubiquitous Northmen.

Karl Kaufmann - Antwerp port, 1890

But its situation at the open mouth of the great estuary of the Schelde, exposed to every passing piratical invader, rendered it unfit for the purposes of early commerce. The trade of Flanders, in its first beginnings, accordingly concentrated itself in the more protected inland ports like Bruges and Ghent; while that of Brabant, of which province Antwerp itself formed a part, found a safer home in Brussels or Louvain, far up some minor internal river. Hence the rise of Antwerp dates no further back than the end of the 15th and beginning of the 16th century.

Its rise, that is to say, as a great commercial port, for from an early period it was the capital of a petty margrave, under the Duke of Brabant. As northern Europe grew gradually quieter during the 11th and 12th centuries, Antwerp rose somewhat in importance; and the magnificence of its cathedral, the earliest part of which dates from 1352, sufficiently shows that the town was increasing in wealth and population during the palmy period when Bruges and Ghent governed the trade of the Continent.

But when, in the 15th century and the beginning of the 16th, Bruges began to decline (partly from political causes, but more still from changes in navigation and trade routes), Antwerp rose suddenly to the first position in the Low Countries and perhaps in Europe. Its large, deep, and open port was better adapted to the increasing shipping of the new epoch than were the shallow and narrow canals or rivers of Ghent, Bruges, and Brussels. The discovery of America, and of the route to India by the Cape of Good Hope, had revolutionized both commerce and navigation; vessels were built larger and of deeper draught; and the Schelde became for a time what the Thames, the Clyde, and the Mersey have become in our own period. Antwerp under Charles V. was probably even more prosperous and wealthier than Venice.

The centre of traffic was shifting from the Mediterranean to the Atlantic seaboard. The city reached its highest point of prosperity about 1568, when it is said that thousands of vessels lay at anchor in the Schelde, and that more than a hundred craft sailed and arrived daily. Even allowing for the smaller burden of those days, however, this is probably an exaggeration. The great fairs of Antwerp, of which those of Leipzig and Nijni Novgorod are now the only modern representatives, also drew thousands of merchants from all parts of the world. The chief imports were wool and other agricultural produce from England, grain from the Baltic, wines from France and Germany, spices and sugar from Portuguese territory, and silks and Oriental luxuries from Venice and other parts of Italy. The exports were the manufactured goods of Flanders and Brabant, countries which still took the lead in textile fabrics, tapestries, carpets, and many other important industries.

Samuel Prout - Market Day in Antwerp

It is to this late period of wealth and prosperity that Antwerp owes most of the great buildings and works of art which still adorn it. Its cathedral, indeed, varies in date in different parts from the middle of the 14th to the beginning of the 16th century, and some portions were not quite completed till the 17th; but the general aspect of the core of the town is of the Renaissance epoch. It contains in its modern gallery not a few Flemish paintings of the earlier period, produced by the artists of Ghent, Bruges, and Brussels; but its own native art dates no further back than Quentin Matsys (1466-1531), the last of the painters of the Netherlands who adhered to the national type of art; while it reached its highest point in Rubens (1577-1640), who introduced into the Low Countries the developed style of the Italian Renaissance, adapted and strained through an essentially robust Flemish nature. It is only at Antwerp that these two great masters can be studied to the highest advantage; they illustrate, one the rise, the other the culmination and after-glow, of the greatness of their native city. I say native advisedly, for though Rubens most probably was born at Siegen (in Nassau), he was an Antwerper by descent, by blood, by nature, and by residence.

The decline of the city in later times was due to a variety of concurrent causes, some of them strangely artificial, which long distracted trade from one of its most natural outlets in Europe. The Spanish troops began the devastation, during the abortive attempt of the southern provinces to shake off the yoke of Spain; in 1576, the Town Hall and nearly a thousand noble buildings were burnt, while 8,000 people were ruthlessly massacred. In 1585, the Duke of Parma completed the destruction of the local prosperity: the population was largely scattered, and the trade of Antwerp completely ruined. The long and unsuccessful rebellion, the division which it unhappily caused between Holland and Belgium, and the rapid commercial rise, first of Amsterdam and then of England, all contributed to annihilate the mercantile importance of Antwerp.

Photochrome of Antwerp - 1890-1900

The Dutch erected forts on their own territory at the mouth of the Schelde, and refused to allow shipping to proceed up the river. Finally by the Treaty of Munster in 1648 it was agreed that no sea-going vessel should be allowed to ascend the estuary to Antwerp, but that all ships should unload at a Dutch port, goods being forwarded by river craft to the former capital of European commerce. From that date forward to the French occupation in 1794, Antwerp sank to the position of a mere local centre, while Rotterdam and Amsterdam took its place as commercial cities. In the latter year, however, the French reopened the navigation of the Schelde, and destroyed the iniquitous Dutch forts at the entrance to the river. Napoleon, in whose empire the town was included, constructed a harbour and built new quays; but after his fall, Antwerp was made over to Holland, and began to trade as a Dutch seaport.

The erection of Belgium into a separate kingdom in 1830 again told against it, as the Dutch maintained their unjust power of levying tolls on the shipping; in addition to which drawback, Antwerp had suffered heavily from siege during the War of Independence. In 1863, however, the Dutch extortionists were bought off by a heavy money payment, and Antwerp, the natural outlet of the Schelde, and to a great extent of the German empire, once more regained its natural place as a main commercial port of Europe.

Since that date, its rise has been extraordinarily rapid, in correspondence with the large development of Belgian manufactures and still more with the new position of Germany as a world-trading power. Indeed, nothing but the artificial restrictions placed upon its commerce by the selfishness and injustice of the Dutch could ever have prevented the seaport of the Schelde from ranking as one of the chief harbours of the world, as soon as ocean-going ships demanded ports of that size, and as commerce had no longer anything to fear from marauding pirates.

As a consequence of these conditions, we have to expect in Antwerp mainly a central town of the 15th and 16th centuries, with an immense modern outgrowth of very recent origin. Save its fine Cathedral, and its imported pictures, it has little or nothing of medieval interest.

The population of Antwerp is almost entirely Flemish, though French is the language of the higher commerce; and the town is the stronghold of the old Flemish feeling in Belgium, as opposed to the Parisian tone of Brussels.

Concurrently with the rise of its renewed commercial importance, Antwerp has become once more a centre of Belgian art, and especially of the pure Flemish school of archaists, who have chosen their subjects from Flemish history, and followed to some extent the precedents of the early Flemish painters. Examples of these will meet us later.

The flag covered Antwerp Stadhuis - Image Klaus with a K

Choose a hotel close to City Hall (Stadhuis) if possible or at least very near it. You cannot gain a first impression of Antwerp in less than four or five days. Antwerp is a confused town, a maze without a plan: till you have learnt your way about, I advise you to follow the tramlines: you will thus attain a good knowledge and command of the most important districts.

Cathedral of Our Lady

The first thing to see at Antwerp is the High Church of Our Lady, once simply named the Cathedral.

Cathedral of our Lady exterior - Image: Ad Meskens

[For general information, see the Cathedral's official English language webpage: http://www.dekathedraal.be/en/

The building is open Mondays to Fridays from 10am to 5pm. On Saturdays it is open from 10am to 3pm, while on Sundays it is open only from 1pm to 4pm.

Individual visitors can enter the church for 6 euros, while groups of twenty or more, plus students and those aged over 60 receive a discount of 4 euro. Children under the age of 12 are admitted freely.]

It is a fine early and middle Gothic church, with a late Gothic or flamboyant tower; but, relatively to its fame, it is externally disappointing. This is partly because mean houses have been allowed to gather round it, but partly also because its somewhat meretricious spire has been unduly praised by earlier generations. Modern taste, which admires the simpler and severer early forms of Gothic, tends to find it fantastic and overelaborate.

The plaza near the Cathedral (once the churchyard), is planted with trees, and has its centre occupied by a modern statue of Rubens. This is one of the few points from which you can view (more or less) the exterior of the Cathedral, the greater part of which is obstructed by shabby shops clustered round its base. The only really good views, however, are obtained from the second-floor windows of the houses on the E. side of the Square, such as the Hôtel de l'Europe. Nevertheless, it will be well to walk round the building outside, in order to inspect as much of it as is visible.

The famed statue of Rubens, with the cathedral in the backdrop. - Image: Ad Meskens

The chief portal (practically), recently restored, and the S. Transept are seen from the Place Verte. There is little sculpture on them, save a small late figure of the patroness, Our Lady, with the Child, high up between the angels of the gable-end.

Now, go round to the left, into the little triangular Place known as the Marché aux Gants, to view the main West Front, best seen from the apex of the triangle opposite. It has a fine central Portal and West Window, flanked by two great towers, the southern incomplete. Its niches have statues of six only out of the Twelve Apostles. The northern tower, up to the first gallery, is middle Gothic of 1352-1449. The upper portion, with the octagonal lantern of very open work, flanked by projecting pinnacles, tied by small buttresses, is in later flamboyant Gothic, and was erected in 1502-1518, by Dominic de Waghamakere, the architect of the Gothic portion of the Town Hall at Ghent. This florid spire has been excessively praised above its merits, but will hardly satisfy a modern taste. It can be ascended but is dark and steep: the view, though fine, hardly repays the trouble.

Sculptures by Joseph Lambeaux on the exterior of the Cathedral - Image: Piotr Kuczyński

The well in the Handschoenmarkt near the front of the Cathedral, has a beautiful wrought-iron canopy, to support its lid, said to have been made by Quentin Matsys when he was a blacksmith, or rather a metal-worker, before he took to painting. (But the legend is doubtful.) It consists of a trellis of vine, supporting wild men and women with clubs, and capped by a figure of Brabo, the eponymous hero of Brabant, flinging the hand of the giant Antigonus (see later, under the Hôtel-de-Ville).

Now, continue on round the north Side of the Cathedral. A few glimpses of the N. Transept and Aisles, as well as of the Nave and Choir, may be obtained as we proceed, much of it unfortunately now marred by excessive restoration. The beautiful Choir and Apse, with their flying buttresses, are almost entirely concealed by neighbouring houses. If these were cleared away, a fine view would be obtained of a noble piece of architecture, now only visible by occasional glimpses from the upper floors of surrounding houses.

This portion of the church is further disfigured by the abrupt terminations to the roofs of the Transepts, and by the pepper-caster top which replaces the central spire or flèche of the original conception. Continue on through the narrow streets till you have made a complete tour of the Cathedral and returned to the Place Verte and the door of the south Transept. The best general view, however, is not obtainable from any of these points, but from the Grand' Place, and especially the upper windows of the Hôtel-de-Ville, to be visited later.

Cathedral of our Lady, main nave - Image: Alvesgaspar

Now, enter the Cathedral, by the door in the S. Transept. Services in the church are regular, but if you wish really to inspect the works of art it contains you should view them at your leisure when there are no services in progress and the place is enveloped in a tranquil quietude. If choral and instrumental worship is to your liking, the fine music at High Mass at 10 on Sundays is of great appeal.

The interior is impressive and solemn, with its high Nave, Transepts, and Choir, of good simple Gothic, and its three rows of Aisles, the perspective of which, with their many pillars, is extremely striking. The Aisles, however, are unusually low in proportion to the height of the central cruciform building. First walk down the Nave to the West End, to form a general conception of the fine and impressive interior, grand in its colossal simplicity, and commendably free from 18th century disfigurements.

Now, begin at the right hand or southern Aisle, which contains admirable modern Stations of the Cross by Vinck and Hendrickx, excellently painted in the archaic spirit. I do not describe these, as they need no explanation, but each is worthy of individual attention. Do not hurry.

The Chapel of the Sacrament, at the end of this Aisle, has good polychrome decoration, and fine stained glass windows (Last Supper, 1503: St. Amand converting Antwerp; St. Norbert preaching against the heresy of Tanquelin at Antwerp, etc.): also, a reliquary of St. Roch, and an interesting modern statue of that great plague-saint.

The south Transept has a good modern stained glass window, and affords fine views of the central Dome and Aisles.

On the right wall are the Marriage at Cana in Galilee, appropriately painted for the Altar of the Wine-merchants, by M. de Vos (excellent for comparison with others of the same subject), and a Last Supper by Otto van Veen, the master of Rubens, formerly the Altar-piece of the Chapel of the Sacrament.

The left hand wall of the south Transept is occupied by Rubens's great triptych of St. Christopher, commonly called (from its central portion) **The Descent from the Cross. This is a splendid work, conceived (as to idea) in the mystical spirit of old Flemish art, though carried out, of course, in the utterly different and incongruous style of Rubens. In order to understand it we must remember that triptychs were usually kept closed on the altar, and that the picture which first met the eye was that which occupies the outer shutters. It struck the key-note. Now, the outer shutters of this work (seldom seen, unless you ask the Sacristan to close it) are occupied by a figure of St. Christopher, with the hermit who directed him to Christ, accompanied by his lantern and owl, as in the earlier St. Christopher triptych by Memling in the Academy at Bruges.

This painting was ordered from Rubens by the Guild of Arquebusiers, whose patron is St. Christopher. On the outside, therefore, Rubens painted the saint himself, whose name (of course) means the Christ-Bearer. But on the inner portion he painted three other symbolical or allusive scenes of the Bearing of Christ: to the left is The Visitation; the unborn Christ borne by His mother: on the right, The Presentation in the Temple; the living Christ borne by Simeon: Centre, The Descent from the Cross; the dead Christ borne by Joseph of Arimathea and the Disciples.

The left wing shows us Our Lady, in a big Flemish hat, approaching St. Elizabeth. Behind, Joseph and Zacharias, the two husbands, shake hands. (This composition has been copied in the stained glass window of the Cathedral at Antwerp.) In order to impress the mystical meaning of the picture, the fact of Our Lady's pregnancy has been strongly insisted upon.

The central panel shows us the Descent from the Cross. Nicodemus holds the body by one shoulder, while St. John, below, receives it in his arms, and the Magdalen at the feet expresses her tenderness. Joseph of Arimathea descends the ladder.

The actual corpse forms the salient point in the picture. It is usual to say that the contrast of the dead body and white sheet is borrowed from the famous treatment of the same subject by Daniele da Volterra in Santa Trinità de' Monti at Rome; and indeed, the composition in this work has probably been suggested by the Italian example; but a similar white sheet, with the dead body seen against it, is found in all early Flemish art, and especially in works of the School of Roger van der Weyden. (It is known as the Holy Sudarium.) In this splendid and gorgeous conception, Rubens has given the greatest importance to the body of the Saviour; but he is so intensely occupied with the mechanical difficulties of its support, the strain and stress of the dead weight, that he forgets feeling; in spite of the agonised attitude of the Mater Dolorosa, the picture is sadly lacking in pathos. He realizes the scene as to its material facts; he fails to realize its spiritual significance. (For an opposite opinion, see M. Max Rooses, who speaks of "the profound expression of a tender and respectful love.") To my mind, the man who holds the Sudarium in his teeth is a fault of taste of the most flagrant character. We think of the whole work rather as a wonderful piece of art than as the fitting delineation of a sacred subject. But as art it is triumphant. The faces of the St. John and the Magdalen are also charming.

Rubens - Assumption of the Virgin

The right wing, with the Presentation, and the aged Simeon receiving Christ in his arms, is of less interest.

Next, enter the Ambulatory, behind the Choir.

1st Chapel. Good modern stained glass window of the Pietà.

2nd Chapel. Tomb of John Moretus, the son-in-law of Plantin, the famous printer (see after, under Musée Plantin-Moretus) erected by Martina Plantin, his widow, and with pictures by Rubens. Above, in an oval, portrait of John Moretus (by a pupil, re-touched by Rubens). Below, triptych; centre, *The Resurrection, emblematic of hope for his glorious future. On the left wing is his patron, St. John-Baptist; the right wing, his widow's patroness, St. Martina. This triptych, too, loses by not being first seen closed: on the outside are two angels, about to open a door; as the wings unfold, you behold the luminous figure of the risen Christ, grasping the red Resurrection banner. This figure is celebrated. The dismay of the Roman soldiers is conceived in the thorough Rubens spirit. Observe the arrangement of this triptych on the tomb: it will help you to understand others in the Museum.

Opposite this, Tomb of a Premonstratensian Friar, with St. Norbert, founder of the Order, in adoration, by Pepyn.

This chapel is also one of the best points of view for Rubens's famous **Assumption, above the High Altar. We here see one of these great altar-pieces (of which we shall meet many examples in the Museum) placed in the situation for which it was originally designed. This Assumption ranks as one of Rubens's masterpieces. Above, Our Lady is caught up into the air by a circle of little cherubs, dimly recalling the earlier Italian mandorla. Below, stand the Apostles, looking into the empty tomb, with the youthful figure of St. Thomas stretching out his hands in an attitude derived from the Italian subject of the Sacra Cintola. In the centre of the foreground, the Holy Women, about to pick roses from the empty tomb. (See a similar work in the Brussels Museum. This composition can only be understood by the light of earlier Italian examples.)

On the pier between this and the next chapel, Crucifixion, with Scenes from the Passion.

3rd Chapel. Master of the School of Cologne, 14th century. A Glory of the Angels. In the centre, St. Michael the Archangel slaying a dragon, whose double tongue divides into many heads of kings. Right and left depict the insignificant donor and donatrix. On either side, choirs of angels in hierarchies.

Above, Christ enthroned in a mandorla (almond-shaped halo) worshipped by angels. Beneath, in the predella, St. Stephen with his stone; St. Ursula with bow and arrow; St. Peter (keys); a Pietà; St. John the Evangelist; St. Agnes with her ruby ring; and St. Anthony the Abbot with his staff and bell. A good picture of the school from which Van Eyck was a reaction. Opposite it, Tomb of Bishop Ambrosio Capello, by Arthus Quellin, the only one remaining tomb of a bishop in the Cathedral.

4th Chapel. Good 16th century figure of Our Lady and Child. Tomb of Plantin, with Last Judgment by De Backer.

5th Chapel. Beautiful modern archaic altar-piece of St. Barbara.

6th Chapel. Nothing of special interest, though in all these chapels the stained-glass windows and polychromatic decorations are worthy of notice.

Opposite it, on the back of the High Altar, painted imitations of reliefs by Van Bree: an extraordinary illusion; Annunciation, Marriage of the Virgin, Visitation. In front of these, Tomb of

Isabella of Bourbon, wife of Charles the Bold, and mother of Mary of Burgundy. Altar-back, Death of the Virgin, 17th cent.

7th Chapel. Good modern archaic altar-piece, with a miracle of St. John Berchman. The saints are named on it.

8th Chapel. Tolerable modern archaic altar-piece of Our Lady and Child, with donors and saints.

On the pier, between this and the next chapel, School of Roger van der Weyden, Selection of Joseph as the husband of the Virgin, and Marriage of the Virgin; a good picture.

9th Chapel, of St. Joseph, patron saint of Belgium, and therefore honoured with this larger shrine. On the Altar, modern carved and gilt altar-piece, St. Joseph bearing the Infant Christ. Around it, Scenes from his Life. On the left (beginning below), Marriage of the Virgin and Joseph, Nativity, Presentation in the Temple; on the right (beginning above), Flight into Egypt, Finding of Christ in the Temple, the Holy Carpenter's Shop. Centre, Death of St. Joseph. On the right hand wings, Philip IV. dedicating Belgium to St. Joseph; to the left is Pius IX., accompanied by St. Peter, appointing Joseph patron saint of Belgium.

Now enter the north Transept.

The right hand wall features Rubens's famous *Elevation of the Cross. In form a triptych, but with the same subject continued through its three members. Centre, The Elevation: on the left is St. John, the Mater Dolorosa, and the Holy Women: to the right, Longinus and the soldiers, with the two thieves. This is one of Rubens's most bustling pictures, where the mere muscular effort almost wholly chokes the sense of pathos. The dog in the foreground is an exceptionally unhappy later addition by the master. The tone of colour is brown and cold; the work is mainly painted for light and shade. It was formerly the altar-piece in the Church of St. Walburga, who appears with other saints on the outer shutters.

Rubens - Elevation of the Cross

This Transept also contains stained glass of the 17th century.

On the left wall is a triptych by Francken: Centre, Christ among the Doctors, said to be portraits of the Reformers. On the left wing, St. Ambrose baptizing Augustine, with the donor, kneeling. On the right wing, Elijah causing the widow's cruse of oil to be replenished.

The Chapel in the N. Transept has nothing of interest.

Now, enter the Choir, with good modern carved stalls, and a different but less impressive view of Rubens's Assumption.

The N. Aisle has little of interest, save its stained-glass windows, and a Head of Christ, painted on marble, ascribed to Leonardo, but really of Flemish origin. This is affixed to the first pillar of the Lady Chapel. Further on in the Aisle, confessionals with tolerable wood-carvings.

The Nave has the usual overloaded 17th century pulpit, with Europe, Asia, Africa, and America.

I have only briefly enumerated the principal contents; but you will find much more that is interesting for yourself if you spend an hour or two longer in examining the Cathedral.

Royal Museum of Fine Arts - Antwerp

[Renovations to the Royal Museum in Antwerp proceed through to the end of 2018.

Should you wish to view the latest roster and layout of the artworks within Antwerp's Royal Museum, visit their official, English language website: http://www.kmska.be/en]

The chief object of interest at Antwerp, even more important than the Cathedral itself, is the Royal Museum of Fine Arts, regally housed in a magnificent structure at the south end of the town.

The building alone might make Trafalgar Square blush, if Trafalgar Square had a blush left in it. To this collection you should devote at least two or three mornings.

In addition to a historic appraisal, most of the ancient works present in the museum are noted here. Given that works are frequently toured between galleries today, please do not expect to see all I mention.

The Antwerp Gallery contains in its palatial rooms a large number of Flemish pictures, many of them collected from the suppressed Churches and Monasteries of the city. (Remember that they were painted for such situations, not to be seen in Museums.) You will here have an opportunity of observing a few good pictures of the early Flemish School, and especially of improving your slight acquaintance with Roger van der Weyden, one of whose loveliest works is preserved in the gallery. You will also see at least one admirable example of Quentin Matsys, as well as several fine works of the Transitional School between the early and the later Flemish periods.

But the special glory of the Antwerp Museum is its great collection of Rubenses. It is at Antwerp alone, indeed, that you can begin to grasp the greatness of Rubens, as you may grasp it afterwards at Munich and Vienna. I do not say you will love him: I will not pretend to love him myself: but you may at least understand him. This, then, is the proper place in which to consider briefly the position of Rubens in Flemish Art.

From the days of the Van Eycks to those of Gerard David, painting in the Low Countries had followed a strictly national line of development. Its growth was organic and internal. With Quentin Matsys, and still more with Bernard van Orley, Pourbus, and the rest, the influence of the Italian Renaissance had begun to interfere with the native current of art in the Low Countries. It was Rubens who finally transformed Flemish painting by adopting to a certain extent the grandiose style of the later Italian and especially the Venetian Masters, at the same time that he transfused it with local feeling and with the private mark of his own superabundant and vigorous individuality.

Rubens was an Antwerp man, by descent and education, though accidentally born at Siegen in Nassau. His father was an Antwerp justice of an important family, exiled for supposed Calvinistic leanings, and disgraced for an intrigue with a royal lady, Anna of Saxony, the eccentric wife of William of Orange. A gentleman by birth and breeding, Peter Paul Rubens painted throughout life in the spirit of a generous, luxurious aristocrat. His master was Otto van Veen, Court Painter to the Dukes of Parma, and himself an Italianised Flemish artist, whose work is amply represented in the Museum.

Early in life, Rubens travelled in Italy, where he imbibed to a great extent the prevailing tone of Italian art, as represented by Titian, Veronese, and to a less extent, Tintoretto, as well as by Domenichino and the later Roman School of painters. To these influences we must add the subtler effect of the general spirit of the late 16th and early 17th centuries, the age when voyages to America and to India, and the sudden opening of the Atlantic seaboard, had caused in men's minds a great ferment of opinion and given rise to a new outburst of activity and struggle. Romance was rife. The world was turned upside down. It was the day of Spanish supremacy, the day when the gold and silver of the Indies poured in vast sums into Madrid and the Low Countries. The Mediterranean had given way to the Atlantic, Venice to Antwerp. In England, this age gave us the rich and varied Elizabethan literature; in the Low Countries, it gave us the highly analogous and profusely lavish art of the School of Rubens.

Rubens lived his life throughout on a big scale. He travelled much. He was statesman and diplomatist as well as painter. He moved from Paris to London, from Madrid to Mantua. All these things give a tone to his art. He is large, spacious, airy, and voluptuous. He has a bold self-confidence, a prodigal freedom, an easy opulence. He delights in colossal figures, in regal costume, in court dresses and feathers,—the romance and pageantry of the royal world he lived in. Space seems to swell and soar on his canvas. Vast marble halls with huge pillars and lofty steps are the architectural background in which his soul delights.

Peter Paul Rubens - Self-portrait with a Big Hat

His outlines are too flowing to be curbed into stiff correctness. His sturdy Flemish nature, again, comes out in the full and fleshy figures, the florid cheeks, and the abundant fair hair of his female characters. All scenes alike, however sacred, are for him just opportunities for the display of sensuous personal charm, enlivened by rich costume or wealthy accessories. Yet in his large romantic way he is doing for cosmopolitan mercantile Antwerp in the 17th century what Van Eyck and Memling did for cosmopolitan Ghent and Bruges in the 15th.

One more peculiarity of his art must be mentioned. The early painters, as we saw in the St. Ursula casket, had little sense of real dramatic life and movement. Rubens had learned to admire this quality in his Venetian masters, and he bettered their instruction with Flemish force and with the stir and bustle of a big seaport town in an epoch of development. His pictures are full, not merely of life, but of strain, stress, turmoil. It is more than animation—it is noise, it is tumult. He often forgets the sacredness of a scene by emphasizing too much the muscular action and the violent movement of those who participate in it. This is particularly noticeable in the Descent from the Cross in the Cathedral, and still more in the famous Coup de Lance at the Museum.

The astonishing number of pictures which Rubens has left may be accounted for in part by his incredible rapidity of execution—he dashed off a huge picture in a fortnight,—but in part also by the fact that he was largely assisted by a numerous body of pupils. Of these, Van Dyck was by far the most individual, the tenderest, the most refined: and not a few of his stately and touching masterpieces may here be studied.

The Dutch School is also represented by several excellent small pictures.

Of alien art, there are a few fine pieces by Early Italian artists.

The entrance door is under the great portico on the west front, facing the river. It is open daily during ordinary working hours.

You pass from the Vestibule into a Hall and Staircase of palatial dimensions, admirably decorated with fine modern paintings by N. De Keyser, of Antwerp, representing the Arts and Artists of the city, the influence upon them of Italian masters, and the recognition extended to their work in London, Paris, Rome, Bologna, Amsterdam, and Vienna. I do not describe these excellent pictures, as the inscriptions upon them sufficiently indicate their meaning, but they are well worth your careful attention.

The rooms are lettered (A. B. C. etc.) over the doorways. On reaching the top of the staircase, pass at once through Rooms J. and I., and go straight into Room C, otherwise called the Hall of the Ancient Masters.

Room C - Hall of the Ancient Masters

By far the grandest of the rooms, the artworks within are by far the most important in the Antwerp Museum. Should you find yourself pressed for time, an intense perusal of this room alone will provide sufficient artistic succour on your journey.

Right of the door:

224. Justus of Ghent: a bland old pope, probably St. Gregory, holding a monstrance, between two angels. In the background,

a curious altar-piece, with the Annunciation, Nativity, Adoration of the Magi, Flight into Egypt, Presentation in the Temple, and Finding of Christ in the Temple. Above it, two female saints (or figures of Our Lady?). A good work, in an early dry manner.

Above it, 463. Madonna and Child, by Van Orley: the landscape by Patinier. From a tomb in the Cathedral.

383. Van der Meire. Triptych from an altar; Centre, Way to Calvary, with St. Veronica offering her napkin, and brutal, stolid Flemish soldiers bearing the hammer, etc. In the background, the Flight into Egypt. The wings have been transposed. On the left (should be right), is the Finding of Christ in the Temple. On the right (should be left), the Presentation in the Temple.

Above it, 380. Van den Broeck (1530-1601): a Last Judgment. Interesting for comparison with previous examples. Renaissance nude.

557. Unknown. Dutch School of the early 16th century. The Tiburtine Sibyl showing the Emperor Augustus the apparition of the Virgin and Child on the Aventine. A page, his robe embroidered with his master's initial A., holds the Emperor's crown. Very Dutch architecture. (The Catalogue, I think erroneously, makes it the Madonna appearing to Constantine.)

560. Good hard early Dutch portrait.

527. Unknown. Resurrection, the Saviour, bearing the white pennant, with red cross, and sleeping Roman soldiers.

42. An Adam and Eve, attributed to Cranach the Elder. Harsh northern nude.

341. Good portrait by Susterman, alias Lambert Lombard.

Above these, Madonna, in the Byzantine style, with the usual Greek inscriptions.

521. School of Albert Dürer: Mater Dolorosa, with the Seven Sorrows around her.

549. Good Flemish portrait of William I., Prince of Orange.

Above, 387, Van der Meire: an Entombment, with the usual figures, Nicodemus and Joseph of Arimathea; the Magdalen in the foreground with the box of ointment; the Mater Dolorosa supported by St. John (in red); and, behind, the two Maries. In the background, a Pietà—that is to say, the same group mourning over the Dead Saviour.

425. Van Hemessen: The Calling of Matthew from the receipt of custom. Harsh and uninteresting.

568. School of Quentin Matsys: Christ and St. Veronica. Probably part only of a Way to Calvary. The spiked club is frequent.

241. Quentin Matsys: a fine and celebrated *Head of the Saviour Blessing, with more expression than is usual in the Flemish type of this subject. Notice even here, however, close adhesion to the original typical features.

242. Quentin Matsys: Companion *Head of Our Lady, as Queen of Heaven. Full of charm and simplicity.

Between these, 4, *Antonello da Messina (an Italian profoundly influenced by the School of Van Eyck, and the first to introduce the Flemish improvements in oil-painting into Italy). Crucifixion, with St. John and Our Lady. This work should be carefully studied, as a connecting link between the art of Flanders and

Italy. It is painted with the greatest precision and care, and bears marks everywhere of its double origin—Flemish minuteness, Italian nobility.

254. Memling: **admirable cold-toned portrait of a member of the De Croy family. The hands, face, and robe, are all exquisitely painted.

Centre of the wall, 412, good early copy of Jan van Eyck's altar-piece for Canon George van der Paelen, in the Academy at Bruges. If you have not been there, see page 59 for particulars. Better preserved than the original: perhaps a replica by the master himself.

519. Crucifixion, with Our Lady and St. John, on a gold background. Interesting only as a specimen of the very wooden Dutch painting of the 14th century. Contrast it with the Van Eyck beneath it, if you wish to see the strides which that great painter took in his art.

397. Good hard *portrait of Philippe le Bon of Burgundy, an uninteresting, narrow-souled personage, wearing the collar of the Golden Fleece, by Roger van der Weyden.

43. Cranach the Elder: Charity. A study of the nude, somewhat more graceful than is the wont of this painter.

264. Mostaert (Jan, the Dutchman), tolerable hard portrait: same person reappears in 262.

179. Gossaert: *a beautiful panel representing the Return from Calvary. The Mater Dolorosa is supported by St. John. On the left is the Magdalen with her pot of ointment; On the right, the other Maries. Very touching. Notice the Flemish love for these scenes of the Passion and Entombment.

198. Hans Holbein the Younger: **admirable portrait of Erasmus. It lives. Full of vivacity and scholarly keenness, with the quick face of a bright intelligence, and the expressive hands of a thinker. The fur is masterly.

180. Gossaert: group of figures somewhat strangely known as "The Just Judges." Probably a single surviving panel from an extensive work of the same character as the Adoration of the Lamb at Ghent.

263. Jan Mostaert: *very fine portrait of a man in a large black hat and yellow doublet. Pendant to 264.

558. Holy Family. Dutch School. Early 16th century.

202. Lucas van Leyden: *portraits. Characteristic, and well thrown out against the background.

566. School of Quentin Matsys: a genre piece; an unpleasant representation of a young girl attempting to cut the purse strings of an old man. Probably a companion picture to one now in the possession of the Countess of Pourtalés, Paris.

Above these, 168, Triptych by Fyol, German School. Centre, the Adoration of the Magi. The Old King has removed his crown, as usual, and presented his gift. He is evidently a portrait: he wears a collar of the Golden Fleece, and is probably Philippe le Bon. Behind him, the Middle-aged King, kneeling; then the Young King, a Moor, with his offering. (The story of the Three Kings—Gaspar, Melchior, Balthasar—was largely evolved in the Cologne district, where their relics formed the main object of pious pilgrimage.) To the right, an undignified Joseph, with his staff, and the peculiar robe with which you are now, I hope, familiar. In the background, the family of the donor, looking in through a window. The wings have, I think, been misplaced. On the left is The Circumcision; On the right, the Nativity: notice the ox and ass, and the costume of Joseph.

325. Schoreel: Crucifixion, with Our Lady, St. John, the Magdalen, and angels catching the Holy Blood. (A frequent episode.)

Above it, 570, School of Gossaert: Our Lady.

262. Jan Mostaert: The Prophecies of Our Lady. Above, she is represented as Queen of Heaven, in an oval glory of angels, recalling the Italian mandorla. Below, those who have prophesied of her: in the centre, Isaiah, with scroll, "Behold, a Virgin shall conceive," etc.: respectively on the right and left are Micah and Zechariah. Further on the right and left are two Sibyls. The one to the right is the same person as 264.

567. School of Quentin Matsys: Favourite subject of the Miser.

25. More monstrosities by Bosch.

Beyond the door:

534. Unknown: Flemish School: Assumption of Our Lady. Above, the Trinity waiting to crown her.

123. Dunwege: German School. The Family of St. Anne, resembling in subject the Quentin Matsys at Brussels. Centre, St. Anne enthroned. Below her, Our Lady and the Divine Child. (Often Our Lady sits on St. Anne's lap.) on the left, Joachim offers St. Anne and Our Lady cherries. (See Legends of the Madonna.) On the right is St. Joseph with his staff and robe. On either side, the Maries, with their children, here legibly named, and their husbands. (From a church at Calcar.)

Above this, 523. Triptych: Madonna and Child, with donors and patron saints (Sebastian and Mary Magdalen). Note their symbols. On either side,

Van der Meire: 388: Mater Dolorosa; her breast pierced with a sword: and on the other side of the triptych 389 (attribution doubtful, according to Lafenestre), a donatrix with St. Catherine, holding the sword of her martyrdom.

569. School of Gossaert, Way to Calvary, with the usual brutal soldiers.

47. Herri Met de Bles: Repose on the Flight into Egypt. Notice the sleeping St. Joseph, and the staff, basket, and gourd, which mark this subject.

539. Good unknown Flemish portrait.

Beyond this, a frame containing five excellent small pictures.

243. Quentin Matsys: *St. Mary Magdalen with her alabaster box. Sweet and simple. In reality, portrait of an amiable round-faced Flemish young lady, in the character of her patron saint. Her home forms the background.

526 and 538. Fine unknown portraits.

199. *Exquisite and delicate miniature by Hans Holbein the Younger. (Lafenestre doubts the attribution.)

132. Fouquet, the old French painter, 1415-1485. Hard old French picture of a Madonna and Child, of the regal French type, with solid-looking red and blue cherubs. Said to be a portrait of Agnes Sorel, mistress of Charles VII. From the Cathedral of Melun.

Then, another case, containing six delicate works of the first importance.

396. *Roger van der Weyden (more probably, School of Van Eyck): Annunciation. The angel Gabriel, in an exquisitely painted bluish-white robe, has just entered. Our Lady kneels at her prie-dieu with her book. In the foreground, the Annunciation lily; behind, the bed-chamber. The Dove descends upon her head. This is one of the loveliest works in the collection.

253. Memling: **Exquisite portrait of a Premonstratensian Canon.

28. Dierick Bouts: The Madonna and Child. An excellent specimen of his hard, careful manner.

203. Lucas of Leyden: David playing before Saul.

30. Bril, 1556-1626. Fine miniature specimen of later Flemish landscape, with the Prodigal Son in the foreground.

559. Unknown but admirable portrait of a man.

223. Justus van Ghent: Nativity, with Adoration of the Shepherds. A good picture, full of interesting episodes.

Beyond these, another case, containing fine small works. A beautiful little *Madonna with the Fountain of Life (411) by Jan van Eyck, closely resembling a large one by Meister Wilhelm, in the Museum at Cologne. Two good unknown portraits. A splendid **portrait of a medallist (5) by Antonello da Messina (sometimes attributed to Memling). A portrait (33) of François II. of France as a child, by Clouet, of the old French School. A characteristic *Albert Dürer (124), portrait of Frederick III. of Saxony: and a good Gossaert (182). These do not need description, but should be closely studied.

The place of honour on this wall is occupied by 393, a magnificent **Seven Sacraments, usually attributed to Roger van der Weyden, though believed by some to be a work of his master, Robert Campin of Tournai. At any rate, it is a work full of Roger's mystic spirit. In form, it is a triptych, but the main subjects are continued through on to the wings. The central panel represents the Sacrament of the Mass, typified in the foreground by a Crucifixion, taking place in the nave of an unknown Gothic church. At the foot of the cross are the fainting Madonna, supported by St. John (in red as usual) and a touching group of the three Maries. The robe of one to the left overflows into the next panel. In the background, the actual Mass is represented as being celebrated at the High Altar. The architecture of the church (with its triforium, clerestory, and apse, and its fine reredos and screen) is well worth notice.

So are the figures of Our Lady, St. Peter and St. John, on the decorative work of the screen and reredos. I believe the kneeling figure behind the officiating priest to be a portrait of the donor. The side panels represent the other sacraments, taking place in the aisles and lateral chapels of the same church. To the left is, Baptism, Confirmation, Confession: in the Confirmation, the children go away wearing the sacred bandage. On the right are the Holy Orders, Matrimony, Extreme Unction. Each of these groups should be carefully noted. The colours of the angels above are all symbolical:—white (innocence) for Baptism: yellow (initiation) for Confirmation: red (love or sin) for confession and absolution: green (hope) for the Eucharist: purple (self-sacrifice) for Holy Orders: blue (fidelity) for Marriage: violet, almost black, (death) for Extreme Unction. The picture is full of other episodes and mystical touches. In all this beautiful and touching composition, the Mary to the right of the Cross is perhaps the most lovely portion. For a fine criticism, see Conway.

Beyond this, another frame with exquisite small works.

250. Quentin Matsys: Head of Christ, with the Crown of Thorns and Holy Blood; painful.

540. Admirable unknown miniature portrait.

544. Excellent little St. Helena.

542. A little donor, with his patron, St. John.

204, 205, 206. Good Lucas of Leyden, of the Four Evangelists (John missing). Luke, with the bull, painting; Matthew, with the angel, and Mark, with the lion, writing.

537. Admirable unknown portrait. These little works again need no description, but close study.

Above them, 244. Quentin Matsys (?). The Misers, one of the best known of this favourite subject.

Then, another frame of miniatures.

517, 518. Unknown Flemish 14th century Madonna and Child, with donor and wife.

541, 522. Tolerable portraits.

545. Fine portrait, of the Spanish period.

410. **Van Eyck's celebrated unfinished St. Barbara, holding her palm of martyrdom, and with her tower in the background. It should be closely studied, both as an indication of the master's method, and as a contemporary drawing illustrating the modes of mediæval building. For a careful criticism, see Conway.

Above these, Engelbrechtsen, 130. St. Hubert, attired as bishop, bearing his crozier and hunting horn, and with the stag beside him, with the crucifix between its horns.

127. The same. St. Leonard releasing prisoners.

Then, another case of good small pictures.

3. A Fra Angelico. Interesting in the midst of these Flemish pictures. St. Romuald reproaching the Emperor Otho III. for the murder of Crescentius.

32. Petrus Christus (?). A donor and his patron, St. Jerome.

64. A landscape by Patinir.

536. A Baptism of Christ, where note the conventional arrangement and the angel with the robe.

561. Triptych. Madonna and Child. St. Christopher, and St. George. Harsh and angular.

548. Mater Dolorosa, transpierced by the sword.

535. Good Flemish Madonna with angels.

207. Lucas of Leyden: Adoration of the Magi. You can now note for yourself the ox, ass, Joseph, position, age, and complexion of Kings, etc.

29. Attributed (doubtfully) to Dierick Bouts: St. Christopher wading, with the Infant Christ. In the background, the hermit and lantern. (See Mrs. Jameson.)

176. Giotto: A St. Paul with the sword. Characteristic of early Florentine work.

257, 258, 259, 260. Simone Martini of Siena: Four panels. Extreme ends, **Annunciation, closely resembling the figures in the Ufizzi at Florence: Annunciations are often thus divided into two portions. Centre, Crucifixion and Descent from the Cross. These exquisitely finished little works are full of the tender and delicate spirit of the early Sienese School. In the Crucifixion, notice particularly the Magdalen, and St. Longinus piercing the side of Christ. Our Lady in the Annunciation has the fretful down-drawn mouth inherited by early Italian art from its Byzantine teachers.

177. Giotto: St. Nicolas of Myra with the three golden balls, protecting a donor.

Above are three good portraits by Van Orley, and other works which need no description.

On easels at the end, 255. Attributed to Memling: **Exquisite Madonna and Child in a church. Our Lady, arrayed as Queen of Heaven, with a pot of lilies before her, stands in the nave of a lovely early Gothic cathedral, with a later Decorated apse, and admirable rood-screen. Every detail of the tiles, the crown, the screen, and the robe, as well as Our Lady's hair and hands, should be closely looked into. This is one of the loveliest pictures here. It is a very reduced copy from one by Jan van Eyck at Berlin: the church is that of the Abbey of the Dunes near Furnes. Its attribution to Memling has been disputed: Conway believes it to be by a follower. In any case, it is lovely.

256. **Companion panel, of the donor, a Cistercian Abbot of the Dunes, in a sumptuous room, half bed-chamber, half study, with a beautiful fireplace and fire. He kneels at his prayers, having deposited his mitre on a cushion beside him, and laid his crozier comfortably by the fireplace. Creature comforts are not neglected on the side-board. Here also every decorative detail should be closely examined. These are two of the very finest works of the School of Memling. Probably the Abbot admired Jan van Eyck's Madonna, painted for a predecessor, and asked for a copy, with himself in adoration on the other wing of the diptych.

At the back, on a revolving pivot, 530, 531. Christ blessing, and a Cistercian Canon in adoration. As usual, the outer panels are less brilliant in colouring than the inner. Notice the Alpha and Omega and the P. and F. (for Pater and Filius) on the curtain behind the Saviour. These works are by an inferior hand.

The other easel has a fine (208, 209, 210) *Lucas van Leyden: Adoration of the Magi, with fantastic elongated figures. Note the ruined temple. The other features will now be familiar. Lucas's treatment is peculiar. On the left is St. George and the Dragon. The saint has broken his lance and attacks the fearsome beast with his sword. In the background, the Princess Cleodolind and landscape. On the right is The donor, in a rich furred robe, and behind him, St. Margaret with her dragon. At the back, 181, wings, by the same, with a peculiar Annunciation (the wings being open, reversed in order). Between them has been unwisely inserted an Ecce Homo by Gossaert.

Now, go straight through Rooms H, F, and E, to three rooms en suite, the last of which is Room A.

Room A

Within this room are the Transitional Pictures. (It is usual to skip these insipid works of the intermediate age, and to jump at once from the School of Van Eyck to the School of Rubens—I think unwisely—for Rubens himself can only properly be appreciated as the product of an evolution, by the light of the two main influences which affected him—his Flemish masters, and his Italian models, Veronese and Giulio Romano.) Begin at the far end, near the lettered doorway, and note throughout the effort to imitate Italian art; the endeavour at classical knowledge; and the curious jumble of Flemish and Tuscan ideas. But the Flemish skill in portraiture still continues.

698. Good portrait of Giles van Schoonbeke, by P. Pourbus.

Next to it, 103, Martin De Vos, the Elder: St. Anthony the Abbot, accompanied by his pig and bell, and his usual tempters, burying the body of St. Paul the Hermit, whose grave two lions are digging. To the right are hideous Flemish devils, grotesquely horrible. Above, phases of the Temptation of St. Anthony.

372. Michael Coxcie: Martyrdom of St. George—one of his tortures. Good transitional work, inspired by Italian feeling.

72. M. De Vos: Triptych, painted for the altar of the Guild of Crossbowmen in the Cathedral. Centre, Triumph of the risen Christ. In the foreground, St. Peter (keys), and St. Paul (sword), with open pages of their writings. On the left is St. George, patron of the Crossbowmen, with his banner and armour; On the right is, St. Agnes with her lamb. Left panel, Baptism of Constantine by St. Sylvester. Right panel, Constantine ordering the erection of the Church of St. George at Constantinople. In the sky, the apparition of Our Lady to the Emperor. A gigantic work, recalling the later Italian Renaissance, especially the Schools of Bronzino and Giulio Romano.

374. Michael Coxcie: Martyrdom of St. George; the other wing of the same triptych in honour of St. George as 372; central portion lost.

89. M. De Vos: St. Conrad of Ascoli, a Franciscan friar, in devout contemplation of the founder of his Order, St. Francis, receiving the Stigmata. Around it, small scenes from the life of St. Conrad, unimportant. Below, Devotion at the tomb of St. Conrad: royal

personages praying, offerings of rich images, and the sick healed by his relics. A curious picture of frank corpse-worship.

699. Good portrait by Pourbus.

576. Triptych, unknown. St. Eligius of Noyon (St. Éloy), one of the apostles of Brabant, preaching to a congregation really composed of good local portraits. (A pious way of having oneself painted.) On the right and left respectively we see St. Eligius feeding prisoners, and St. Eligius healing the sick.

741. Another of Bernard van Orley's General Resurrections, the type of which will now be familiar to you. In the centre, strangely introduced group of portraits of the donors, engaged in burying a friend, whose memory this triptych was doubtless intended to commemorate. On either wing, the six works of Mercy (the seventh, burial, is in the main picture).

77. Good transitional triptych, by M. De Vos, for the Guild of Leather-dressers. Centre, The Incredulity of St. Thomas. On the wings, Scenes from the life of the Baptist. On the left is the Baptism of Christ; where note the persistence of the little symbolical Jordan, with angels almost inconspicuous. To the right is The Decollation of St. John. Salome receiving his head in a charger. In the background, Herodias.

371. Coxcie the Younger: Martyrdom of St. Sebastian, patron saint of Bowmen, from their altar in the Cathedral. An attempt to be very Italian. The wings of this triptych are by Francken. On the left, St. Sebastian is exhorting Marcus and Marcellinus to go to martyrdom. R., St. Sebastian miraculously healing the dumb woman, with portrait spectators, in dress of the period, deeply interested.

Now with your examination of these greats concluded, proceed into Room B.

Room B

This room is unlettered, the centre of the three). It contains works of an earlier period.

The left wall is entirely occupied by three large panels of a fine old Flemish 15th century picture, attributed to Memling (and apparently accepted as his by Lafenestre), representing *Christ Enthroned, with orb and cross, surrounded by choirs of angels; those in the central panel singing; the others, playing various musical instruments. This is a beautiful work, but less pleasing than those of the same school on a smaller scale. It has been recently bought from the monastery of Najera in Spain. It was intended, I think, to be seen at a height, probably on an organ-loft, and loses by being placed so near the eye of the spectator.

The opposite wall to the right is occupied by 245, Quentin Matsys's masterpiece, the triptych of **the Entombment, painted for the altar of the Guild of Cabinet-makers. The colouring is much more pleasing than in the Family of St. Anne at Brussels. Central panel, The Entombment. Nicodemus supports the emaciated body of the dead Saviour, while Joseph of Arimathea wipes the marks of the crown of thorns from his head. The worn body itself, with a face of pathetic suffering, lies on the usual white sheet in the foreground. At the foot, Mary Magdalen, with her pot of ointment and long fair hair, strokes the body tenderly. In the centre is the fainting Madonna, supported, as always, by St. John, in his red robe. Behind are the three Maries. The usual attendant (a ruffianly Fleming, in a queer turban-like cap) holds the crown of thorns. At the back, preparations for the actual placing in the sepulchre. In the background, Calvary.

The wings have scenes from the lives of the two St. Johns. On the left is the daughter of Herodias, a very mincing young lady, in a gorgeous dress, brings the head of St. John the Baptist on a charger to her mother and a fiercely-bearded Herod. The queen appears to be about to carve it. Above, a gallery of minstrels. Admirable drapery and accessories. The right wing has the so-called Martyrdom of St. John the Evangelist, in the cauldron of boiling oil, with a delightful boy spectator looking on in a tree. The Emperor Domitian (older than history), on a white horse, behind. Flemish varlets stir the fire lustily. This noble work originally decorated the altar in the Chapel of the Menuisiers of Antwerp in the Cathedral.

On easels, 649, Claeissens: Triptych of the Crucifixion, with the Way to Calvary and the Resurrection. Elongated, attenuated figures.

680. Giles Mostaert (the elder): Singular complex picture, painted for the Hospital of Antwerp; representing, above, The General Resurrection: Christ enthroned between Our Lady and St. John-Baptist. Beneath, naked souls rising from the tomb. To the left, St. Peter welcomes the just at the gate of the Celestial City. To the right are devils driving the wicked into the gaping jaws of Hell. Beneath, the courses that lead to either end: the Seven Works of Mercy, inspired by the Redeemer, and the Seven Deadly Sins, suggested by devils. I will leave you to identify them as it is rather easy.

Go on into Room D.

Room D

This area contains more works of the Transition. These large altar-pieces of the early 17th century, the period of the greatest wealth in Antwerp, though often frigid, as works of art, are at least interesting as showing the opulence and the tastes of the Antwerp guilds during the epoch of the Spanish domination. They are adapted to the huge Renaissance churches then erected, as the smaller triptychs of the 15th century were adapted to the smaller Gothic altars.

529. Feast of Archers, with the King of the Archers enthroned in the background.

696, 697. Tolerable portraits by Pourbus.

183. A Madonna by Gossaert.

114. Frans Floris: St. Luke painting, with his bull most realistically assisting, and his workman grinding his colours. From the old Academy of Painters, whose patron was St. Luke. Italian influence.

135. Ambrose Francken: Loaves and fishes.

148. The same. Decollation of St. Cosmo and St. Damian: painted for the Guild of Physicians, of whom these were the patron saints.

357. A splendid and luminous Titian, in the curious courtly ceremonial manner of the Venetian painters. **Pope Alexander VI. (Borgia), in a beautiful green dalmatic, introducing to the enthroned St. Peter his friend, Giovanni Sforza da Pesaro, Bishop of Paphos, and admiral of the Pope's fleet. At the

bishop's feet lies his helmet, to show his double character as priest and warrior. He grasps the banner of the Borgias and of the Holy Church. In the background (to show who he is), the sea and fleet. St. Peter's red robe is splendid. The Venetians frequently paint similar subjects,—"Allow me to introduce to your Sainthood," etc. This is a fine work in Titian's early harder manner, still somewhat reminiscent of the School of Bellini. Its glorious but delicate colour comes out all the better for the crudity of the works around it.

146. Ambrose Francken: St. Cosmo and St. Damian, the Doctor Saints, amputating an injured leg, and replacing it by the leg of a dead Moor. In the background, other episodes of their profession. (Wing of the triptych for the Guild of Physicians.)

83. M. De Vos: Triptych, painted for the Guild of the Mint, and allusive to their functions. Centre, The Tribute Money. "Render unto Cæsar," etc., with tempting Pharisees and Sadducees, and Roman soldiers. In the foreground, St. Peter in blue and yellow, with his daughter Petronilla. Left wing: Peter, similarly habited, finds the tribute money in the fish's mouth. Right wing: The Widow's Mite. (The French titles, "Le Denier de César," "Le Denier du Tribut," "Le Denier de la Veuve," bring out the allusion better.)

88. M. De Vos: St. Luke painting Our Lady, with his bull, as ever, in attendance. The wings by others – the left sees St. Luke preaching. To the right meanwhile is St. Paul before Felix. From the altar of the (painters') Confraternity of St. Luke in the Cathedral.

113. Frans Floris: Adoration of the Shepherds. Note persistence of formal elements from old School, with complete transformation of spirit.

663. Floris: Judgement of Solomon.

112. Frans Floris's horrible St. Michael conquering the devils; the most repulsive picture by this repulsive and exaggerated master.

Right and left of it, good late Flemish portraits of donors.

483. Portrait by Van Veen, Rubens's master.

Room E

This entire room is chiefly occupied by works of the school of Rubens, most of which can now be satisfactorily comprehended by the reader without much explanation. I will therefore treat them briefly.

Left of the door,

82. A Nativity, by De Vos. Can be instructively compared with earlier examples.

57. Good 17th century landscape.

646. Attributed to Brueghel: Paying tithes.

644. P. Brueghel the Younger: A village merry-making ("Kermesse Flamande"). With more than the usual vulgarity of episode.

722 and 724. Capital portraits. Good Still life, etc.

Room F

This room contains no artistic works which the reader cannot adequately understand for himself.

Omit Room G for the present (it contains the Dutch Masters), and turn instead into

Room H

This room is mostly devoted to works of the School of Rubens.

End Wall, 305. Rubens: *The Last Communion of the dying St. Francis of Assisi. A famous work, in unusually low tones of colour—scarcely more than chiaroscuro. St. Francis, almost nude, is supported by his friars. Above, angels, now reduced to cherubs, wait to convey his soul to Heaven. Painted for the altar of St. Francis in the Franciscan Church of the Récollets. See it from the far end of the room, where it becomes much more luminous.

On either side, 662, good portrait by S. De Vos (himself, dashing and vigorous: every inch an artist): and

104. C. De Vos: Admirable and life-like **portrait of the messenger or porter of the Guild of St. Luke, the Society of Painters of Antwerp, exhibiting the plate belonging to his confraternity. He is covered with medals, which are the property of the Society, and has the air of a shrewd and faithful servant. This living presentment of a real man is deservedly popular.

661. Tolerable portrait by C. De Vos.

403. Van Dyck's *Entombment (or Pietà), often called Descent from the Cross. This is one of his noblest pictures, but badly restored.

335. Angry swans disturbed by dogs. Snyders.

215. Jordaens: Last Supper. The effect of gloom somewhat foreshadows Rembrandt.

401. Van Dyck: **A Dominican picture (Guiffrey calls it "cold and empty"), painted at his father's dying wish for the Dominican Nunnery at Antwerp. The two great saints of the Order, St. Dominic, the founder, and St. Catherine of Assisi, the originator of the female branch, stand at the foot of the Cross, which is itself a secondary object in the picture. St. Dominic looks up in adoration; St. Catherine, wearing the crown of thorns, fervently embraces the feet of the Saviour. On the base, a child angel, in a high unearthly light, with a half extinguished torch, points with hope to the figure of the crucified Lord. The whole is emblematic of belief in a glorious Resurrection, through the aid of the Dominican prayers. Interesting inscription on the rock: "Lest earth should weigh too heavily on his father's soul, A. van Dyck rolled this stone to the foot of the Cross, and placed it in this spot."

381. Van Hoeck: Madonna and Child, with St. Francis, from the Franciscan Church of the Récollets.

660. Tolerable portrait by C. De Vos.

406. Van Dyck's noble **Crucifixion, with the sun and moon darkened. One of his most admirable pictures.

677. Jordaens: **Charming family scene, known by the title of "As sing the Old, so pipe the Young." Three generations—

grandparents, parents, and children—engaged in music together. Very catching: a most popular picture.

734. Good *portrait of a priest, by Van Dyck.

402. Fine *portrait of a bishop of Antwerp, by Van Dyck.

404. Van Dyck: **Pietà, altar-piece for a chapel of Our Lady of the Seven Sorrows. Our Lady holds on her lap the dead Christ, while St. John points out with his finger the wound in His hand to pitying angels. All the formal elements in this scene—Our Lady, St. John, the angels, etc.—belong to the earlier conception of the Pietà, but all have been entirely transfigured by Van Dyck in accordance partly with the conceptions of the School of Rubens, though still more with his own peculiar imagination. It is interesting, however, to note in this touching and beautiful picture, full of deep feeling, how far the type of the St. John has been inherited, remotely, from the School of Van der Weyden. Even the red robe and long hair persist. The features, too, are those with which we are familiar. This is one of the gems of the collection. It shows the direct influence of Italian travel modifying Van Dyck's style, acquired from Rubens.

This room also contains several other excellent works of the School of Rubens or his more or less remote followers, which I need not particularize.

Now continue into Room I.

Room I

This room contains what are considered to be the gems among the Rubenses and the later pictures.

Right of the door, Rubens and Brueghel, 319: Small copy of the Dead Christ. Schut, 327: The Beheading of St. George. A pagan priest, behind, endeavours to make him worship an image of Apollo. Above, angels wait to convey his soul to Heaven. This is a somewhat confused picture, with a spacious composition and a fine luminous foreground: it is considered its painter's masterpiece. Intended for the altar of the Archers (whose patron was St. George), in Antwerp Cathedral.

673. Good still life by Gysels.

669. F. Francken: Portraits of a wealthy family in their own picture gallery.

107. C. De Vos: *Portraits of the Snoek family, in devotion to St. Norbert. This picture requires a little explanation. St. Norbert was the Catholic antagonist of the heretic Tankelin at Antwerp in the 12th century. In this frankly anachronistic picture the Snoek family of the 17th century, portly, well-fed burghers, are represented restoring to the mediæval saint the monstrance and other church vessels removed from his church during the Calvinist troubles. The Snoeks are living personages; the Saint is envisaged as a heavenly character. It is, in short, a highly allegorical picture of the family showing their devotion to true Catholicism, and their detestation of current heresy. In the background stands the town of Antwerp, with the Cathedral and St. Michael. (From the burial chapel of the Snoek family at St. Michael.) There is a Brueghel in Brussels Museum, representing St. Norbert preaching against Tankelin.

307. Beyond the door, Rubens: **Triptych, to adorn a tomb, for the funerary chapel of his friend Rockox. Compare, for size and purpose, the Moretus tomb in the Cathedral. It shows the painter's early careful manner, and represents in its central

piece the Incredulity of St. Thomas. On the wings, the Burgomaster Nicolas Rockox, and his wife, for whose tomb it was painted. The wings are finer than the central portion. This early work, still recalling Van Veen's academic tone, should be compared with the Van Veens and also with Rubens's fine portrait of himself and his brother, with Lipsius and Grotius, in the Pitti at Florence. It marks the earliest age, when he was still content with comparatively small sizes, and gave greater elaboration to his work, but without his later dash and vigour. M. Rooses thinks ill of it.

781. *Fine farmyard scene by Rubens, with the story of the Prodigal Son in the foreground. One of the many signs of his extraordinary versatility.

Beyond, on either side of the great Rubens, to be noticed presently, are two pictures by his master, Otto van Veen: 480, The Calling of Matthew, and 479, Zacchæus in the Fig-Tree. These two careful works recall the later Italian Schools, more particularly Titian, and are good examples of that careful academic transitional Flemish art which Rubens was to transform and revivify by the strength of his own exuberant and powerful personality. They are admirably placed here for comparison.

297. Rubens's famous altar-piece of the Crucifixion, for the Church of the Franciscans, commonly known as the **Coup de Lance. In this splendid work Rubens is seen in one of his finest embodiments. The figure of Christ has fine virility. St. Longinus, to the left, on a white horse, is in the very act of piercing his side. The Magdalen, embracing the foot of the Cross, as ever, throws up her arms with supplicating gesture. To the right is the Madonna. Behind, a soldier is engaged in breaking the limbs of the Impenitent Thief (always on Christ's left) who writhes in torture. The whole work is full of Rubens's life and bustle, well contrasted with the academic calm of the Van Veens beside it. Even those who do not love Rubens (and I confess I am of them) must see in such a work as this how his great powers succeeded

in effects at which his contemporaries aimed ineffectually. Boldly dramatic, but not sacred.

300. **Triptych by Rubens, commonly known as the Christ à la Paille, painted for a tomb in the Cathedral (compare the Moretus one). In the centre is a Pietà: Joseph of Arimathea supporting the dead body of the Christ on the edge of a stone covered with straw. Behind, Our Lady and another Mary, with the face of St. John just appearing in the background. This "too famous" work is rather a study of the dead nude than a really sacred picture. Some of its details overstep the justifiable limits of horror. The wings are occupied by, left, a so-called Madonna and Child, really a portrait of a lady and boy—(his wife and son?): on the right, St. John the Evangelist (patron of the person for whose tomb it was painted), accompanied by his eagle.

706. Admirable *portrait by Rubens of Gaspard Groaerts, town secretary. The bust is Marcus Aurelius.

171. J. Fyt: Excellent screaming eagles, with a dead duck. One of the earliest and best presentations of wild life at home.

315. Rubens: Small copy (with variations) of the Descent from the Cross in the Cathedral (by a pupil).

708. One of the best *portraits by Rubens in the Gallery, subject unknown: lacks personal dignity, but Rubens has made the most of him.

The rest of this wall is occupied by some tolerable gigantic altar-pieces and other good works of the School of Rubens. Most of them derive their chief interest from their evident inferiority in design and colour to the handicraft of the Master. They are the very same thing—with the genius omitted.

End wall, 314, Rubens: called the *Holy Trinity. The Almighty supports on His knees the figure of the dead Christ. Behind, hovers the Holy Ghost. On either side, boy angels hold the crown of thorns, the three nails, and the other implements of the Passion. This is really a study in the science of foreshortening, and in the painting of the dead nude, largely suggested, I believe, by a still more unpleasing Mantegna in the Brera at Milan.

719. Above. Excellent fishmongery by Snyders.

212. Janssens: The Schelde bringing wealth to Antwerp, in the allegorical taste of the period.

712. Rubens: St. Dominic.

172. Fyt: Excellent dogs and game.

299. Rubens: An **allegorical picture to enforce the efficacy of the prayers of St. Theresa. The foundress of the Scalzi, dressed in the sober robe of her Carmelite Order, is interceding with Christ for the soul of Bernardino de Mendoza, the founder of a Carmelite convent at Valladolid. Below, souls in Purgatory. In the left-hand corner stands Bernardino, whom, at St. Theresa's prayer, angels are helping to escape from torment. A fine luminous picture of a most unpleasing subject. Painted for the altar of St. Theresa in the church of her own barefooted Carmelites.

405. Van Dyck: Magnificent portrait of Cesare Alessandro Scaglia, in black ecclesiastical robes, with lace cuffs and collar, and the almost womanish delicate hands of a diplomatic, astute, courtier-like ecclesiastic. The thoughtful eyes and resolute face might belong to a Richelieu.

306. Rubens: **The Education of the Virgin, painted for a chapel of St. Anne. A charming domestic picture of a wealthy young lady of Flanders, pretending to be Our Lady, in a beautifully painted white silk gown. Beside her, her mother, a well-preserved St. Anne, of aristocratic matronly dignity. Behind is St. Joachim, and above, two light little baby angels. The feeling of the whole is graceful courtly-domestic.

481, 482. Two scenes from the life of St. Nicholas, by Van Veen, the master of Rubens. On the right, he throws through a window three purses of gold as dowries for the three starving daughters of a poor nobleman. (This ornate treatment contrasts wonderfully with the simpler early Italian pictures of the same subject.) To the left he brings corn for the starving poor of Myra. Both pictures represent the bourgeois saint in his favourite character of the benefactor of the poor. They are here well placed for contrast with

298. Rubens: **Adoration of the Magi, considered to be his finest embodiment of this favourite subject, and one of his masterpieces. To the right is Our Lady and Child, with the ox in the foreground, and St. Joseph behind her. On the left two kings make their offerings. Behind them, the third, a Moor, in an Algerian costume, leering horribly. Above, the ruined temple, the shed, and the camels. M. Max Rooses calls this work "the chef d'œuvre by which Rubens inaugurated his third manner," and other critics praise loudly its gorgeous colouring, its audacious composition, its marvellous certainty. To me, the

great canvas, with its hideous ogling Moor, is simply unendurable; but I give the gist of authoritative opinion.

312. Rubens: *The Holy Family, known as La Vierge au Perroquet. It is chiefly remarkable as a rich and gorgeous piece of colouring, with a charming nude boy of delicious innocence.

313. Rubens: *Crucifixion. One of his best embodiments of this subject.

Opposite wall.

709. Rubens, partly made-up: Jupiter and Antiope. A mythological subject, treated in a somewhat Italian style, with a quaint little huddling Cupid in the foreground.

Beyond this, three designs by Rubens for Triumphal Cars and Arches, on the occasion of the entry of Ferdinand of Austria in 1635.

The whole of this room contains several other excellent altar-pieces, many of which are Franciscan.

Room J

Within this room are a variety of Flemish and Dutch works.

To the right and left of the door we see 105, C. De Vos: Portraits of a husband and wife, with their sons and daughters.

370. Van Cortbemde: The Good Samaritan, pouring in oil and wine in a most literal sense. In the background, the priest and the Levite.

109. Fine portrait of a well-fed Flemish merchant, William Van Meerbeck, by C. De Vos. Behind him his patron, St. William.

748. Van Thulden: Continence of Scipio.

265. Murillo (Spanish School). St. Francis. A reminiscence of the older subject of his receiving the Stigmata. It has the showy and affected pietism of the Spaniards. A mere study.

214. Jordaens: Pharaoh in the Red Sea.

Room N contains several good portraits and views of the town and other places, of the 17th and 18th centuries, many of them excellent as studies of Old Antwerp, enabling us to appreciate the greatness of the architectural losses which the city has sustained. These, however, are essentially works for the visitor to inspect at his leisure. They need little or no explanation. Notice especially 728, 348, 726.

775. Good unknown Flemish portrait.

22. Portraits by Boeyermans.

Room O, beyond, is filled for the most part with canvases of the school of Rubens, mainly interesting for comparison with the works of the master, and needing little comment.

Now, turn around and revisit Room G.

Room G

This room contains the Dutch Pictures. Many of these are masterpieces of their sort, but need here little save enumeration. The Reformation turned Dutch art entirely upon portraiture, landscape, and domestic scenes. Dutch art is frankly modern.

338. Jan Steen: Samson and the Philistines, as Jan Steen imaged it.

767. Admirable calm sea-piece, by Van der Capelle.

752. Weenix poaching on Hondecoeter's preserves.

502. A beautiful little Wynants.

399. W. van de Velde the younger: Calm sea, with ships.

398. Admirable cows, by A. van de Velde.

293. Rembrandt: **Admirable portrait of his wife, Saskia; almost a replica of the one at Cassel, perhaps either painted by a pupil, or else from memory after her death, and badly restored. It breathes Dutch modesty.

349. Terburg: *Girl playing a mandoline.

705. Excellent *portrait of a Burgomaster, by Rembrandt.

324. A charming Schalken.

628. Unknown: perhaps Frans Hals: Excellent portrait of a calm old lady.

668. Karel du Jardin: Admirable landscape, with cows.

188. Celebrated and vigorous **Fisher-boy of Haarlem, with a basket, by Frans Hals, rapidly touched with the hand of a master.

339. One of Jan Steen's village merry-makings.

26. Delicate soft landscape, by J. and A. Both.

675. A mill, by Hobbema.

768. Van der Velde: Fine landscape, with cows.

427. Flowers by Van Huysum.

674. Admirable *portrait, by Frans Hals, of a round-faced, full-blooded, sensuous Dutch gentleman. Full of dash and vigour.

738. Venus and Cupid, by W. van Mieris.

437. Excellent fishmonger, by W. van Mieris.

466. *The Smoker, by A. van Ostade.

682. Arch and charming portrait, by Mytens.

773. A fine Wynants.

382. B. van der Helst: Child with a dog.

679. Some of Molenaer's peasant folk.

713. Ruysdael: *Waterfall in Norway.

The room is full of other fine and delicately-finished pictures of the Dutch School, of which I say nothing, only because they are of the kinds which are to be appreciated by careful examination, and which do not need explanation or description.

Room K

This room contains Flemish works of the later School of Rubens and the beginning of the decadence.

The remaining rooms of the Gallery have modern pictures, belonging to the historical and to the archaic Schools of Antwerp. These works lie without the scope of the present

Guides, but many of them are of the highest order of merit, and they well deserve attention both for their own intrinsic excellence and for comparison with the works of the 15th and early 16th centuries on which they are based. The paintings of Leys and his followers, mainly in Room T, are especially worth consideration in this connection. These painters have faithfully endeavoured to revert to the principles and methods of the great early Flemish Masters, and though their work has often the almost inevitable faults and failings of a revival, it cannot fail to interest those who have drunk in the spirit of Van Eyck and Memling.

On the ground floor, a good copy, 413, etc., of the Adoration of the Lamb at Ghent, useful for filling up the gaps in your knowledge, and more readily inspected at leisure and from a nearer point of view than the original. The portraits and battle scenes on the remaining walls need little comment.

The Town of Antwerp

Medieval Antwerp, now no more, lay within a narrow ring of walls in the neighbourhood of the Cathedral. Its circumference formed a rough semi-circle, whose base-line was the Schelde, while its outer walls may still be traced on a good map about the Rempart Ste. Catherine and the Rempart du Lombard.

This oldest district still remains on the whole an intricate tangle of narrow and tortuous streets, with a few ancient buildings. Later Renaissance Antwerp stretched to the limit of the existing Avenues in their northern part, though the southern portion (from the Place Léopold on) extends beyond the boundary of the 17th century city, and occupies the site of the huge demolished Old Citadel, built by Alva. Antwerp, however, has undergone so many changes, and so few relics of the medieval age now survive, that I can hardly apply to its growth the historical method I have employed in other Belgian towns. It will be necessary here merely to point out the principal existing objects of interest, without connecting them into definite excursions.]

The centre of medieval Antwerp was the Grand Place, which may be reached through the little triangular Marché aux Gants, in front of the main façade of the Cathedral. It was, however, so entirely modernized under the Spanish régime that it now possesses very little of interest. The west side of the square is entirely occupied by the Hôtel-de-Ville, a poor Renaissance building, which looks very weak after the magnificent Gothic Town Halls of Bruges, Ghent, Brussels, and Louvain. The façade is extremely plain, not to say domestic. The ground floor has an arcade in imitation of Italian rustica work, above which come two stories with Doric and Ionic columns (and Corinthian in the centre); the top floor being occupied by an open loggia, supporting the roof. In the centre, where we might expect a spire, rises a false gable-end, architecturally meaningless. The niche in the gable is occupied by a statue of Our Lady with the Child (1585), the patroness of the city, flanked by allegorical figures of Wisdom and Justice.

The interior has been modernized: but it contains one fine hall, the Salle Leys, decorated with noble archaistic paintings by Baron Leys. In the Burgomaster's Room is also a good Renaissance chimney-piece, from the Abbey of Tongerloo, with reliefs of the Marriage at Cana, the Brazen Serpent, and Abraham's Sacrifice.

Grand Place market area - Image: G Lanting

The square contains a few Guild Houses of the 17th century, the best of which is the Hall of the Archers, to the right of the Hôtel-de-Ville, a handsome and conspicuous building, lately surmounted by a gilt figure of St. George slaying the Dragon, in honour of the patron saint of the Archers. The older Guild Houses, however, were mostly destroyed by the Spaniards. The square, as it stands, being Renaissance or modern, cannot compare with the Grand' Place in most other Belgian cities.

The centre of the Place is occupied by a bronze fountain, with a statue of Silvius Brabo, a mythical hero of medieval invention, intended to account for the name Brabant. He is said to have cut off the hand of the giant Antigonus, who exacted a toll from all vessels entering the Schelde, under penalty of cutting off the hand of the skipper,—a myth equally suggested by a false etymology of Antwerp from Hand Werpen (Hand throwing).

The Hand of Antwerp, indeed, forms part of the city arms, and will meet you on the lamp-posts and elsewhere. It is, however, the ordinary Hand of Authority (Main de Justice), or of good luck, so common in the East, and recurring all over Europe, as on the shields of our own baronets. Such a hand, as an emblem of authority, was erected over the gate of many medieval Teutonic cities.

Plantin Moretus Museum exterior - Image: Manfreeed

One of the objects best worth visiting in Antwerp, after the Cathedra, is the Plantin-Moretus Museum containing many memorials of a famous family of Renaissance printers, whose monuments we have already seen in the Cathedral. To reach it you turn from the Place Verte into the Rue des Peignes, almost opposite the S. door of the Cathedral. The second turning to the right will lead you into the small Place du Vendredi, the most conspicuous building in which is the Museum.

Beyond advising a visit, it is difficult to say much about this interesting old house and its contents. Those who are lovers of typography or of old engravings will find enough in it to occupy them for more than one morning. Such had better buy the admirable work, Le Musée Plantin-Moretus, by M. Max Rooses, the conservator. On the other hand, the general sight-seer will at least be pleased with the picturesque courtyard, draped in summer by the mantling foliage and abundant clusters of a magnificent old vine, as well as with the spacious rooms, the carved oak doorways, balustrades, and staircases, the delicious galleries, the tiles and fireplaces, and the many admirable portraits by Rubens or others. Were it merely as a striking example of a Flemish domestic interior of the upper class during the Spanish period, this Museum would well deserve attention. Read the following notes before starting.

Plantin Moretus Museum - library

The house of Plantin was established by Christopher Plantin of Tours (born 1514), who came to Antwerp in 1549, and established himself as a printer in 1555. He was made Archetypographer to the King by Philip II., and the business was carried on in this building by himself, his son-in-law, Moretus, and his descendants, from 1579 till 1875. It was Plantin's daughter, Martina, who married John Moretus (see the Cathedral), and under the name of Plantin-Moretus the business was continued through many generations to our own day.

The firm was essentially comprised of learned printers, setting up works in Latin, Greek, and Hebrew, or even in Oriental types, and issuing editions of many important classical authors. I will not describe the various rooms, about which the reader can wander for himself at his own sweet will, but will merely mention that they contain admirable portraits of the Plantin and Moretus families, and of their famous editor, Justus Lipsius, by Rubens, and others. (The Lipsius is particularly interesting for comparison with the one at Florence in the Pitti.) The dwelling-rooms and reception-rooms, of the family, with their fine early furniture, are now open to the visitor. So is the quaint little shop, facing the street, the composing room and proof-readers' room, the study occupied by Lipsius, and the library, with examples of many of the books printed by the firm. The original blocks of their woodcuts and of their capital letters, with the plates of their engravings, are likewise shown, together with old and modern impressions. Do not suppose from this, however, that the place is only interesting to book-hunters or lovers of engravings. The pictures and decorations alone,—nay, the house itself—will amply repay a visit.

A walk should be taken from the Place Verte, by the Vieux Marché au Blé, or through the Marché aux Gants, to the river front and Port of the Schelde. (Follow the tram-line.) Here two handsome raised promenoirs or esplanades, open to the public, afford an excellent *view over the river, the old town, and the shipping in the harbour.

The southernmost (and pleasantest) of these promenoirs ends (S.) near the Porte de l'Escaut, a somewhat insignificant gateway, designed by Rubens, and adorned with feeble sculpture by Arthus Quellin. It stood originally a little lower down the river, but has been removed, stone by stone, to its present situation. The quaint red building, with hexagonal turrets at the angles, visible from both esplanades, is the Vieille Boucherie, or Butchers' Guild Hall, of 1503. It stands in a squalid quarter, but was once a fine edifice. Near the N. end of this promenoir, a ferry-boat runs at frequent intervals to the Tête-de-Flandre on the opposite shore of the river. Here there is a Kursaal and a strong fort. It is worth while crossing on a fine day in order to gain a general view of the quays and the town.

The northernmost promenoir is approached by an archway under the castellated building known as the Steen. This is a portion of the old Castle of Antwerp, originally belonging to the Margraves and the Dukes of Brabant, but made over by Charles V. to the burghers of Antwerp. The Inquisition held its sittings in this castle. It is now, though much restored and quite modern-looking (except the portal), almost the only remaining relic of Mediæval Antwerp, outside the Cathedral. It contains a small Museum of Antiquities. Unless you have plenty of time you need not visit it.

A little way beyond the north end of the northern promenoir a tangled street leads to the Church of St. Paul, which will be described hereafter. Continuing along the Quays in this direction you arrive at last at the Docks. The large modern castellated building in front of you is the Pilotage, round which sea-captains congregate in clusters. Turning along the dirty quay to the right, you reach shortly on the left hand side the site of the Maison Hanséatique, which was the entrepôt in Antwerp of the Hanseatic League. But it was burnt down a few years since, and its place is now occupied by mean sheds and warehouses. All this quarter is given over to the most unsightly and malodorous realities of modern seafaring life and commerce.

Antwerp is somewhat ill provided with drives or country walks. The prettiest of its public gardens is the little Park, which may be reached from the Avenue des Arts by either of the three main Avenues eastward, adorned respectively with statues of Quentin Matsys, Leys, and Jordaens. The Park is a small but ingeniously laid out triangular area, occupying the site of an old bastion, with a pleasing sheet of ornamental water (originally the moat), crossed by a bridge, and backed up by the twin spires of the modern Church of St. Joseph. Around it lies the chief residential quarter of 19th century Antwerp. This is a cool stroll in the afternoon, for one tired of sight-seeing. (Ask your hotel porter when and where the band plays daily.) Further on in the same direction is the pretty little public garden known as the Pépinière, and lying in a pleasant open quarter. (Band here also.)

Antwerp Zoo gardens entrance - Image: ScaraMcDuck

The Zoological Garden – or ZOO Antwerpen - is just behind the Gare de l'Est, is well worth a visit if you are making a stay. It is particularly well stocked with birds and animals, and has a rather pretty alpine rock-garden. On Sunday afternoons. Music and other performances are frequent, to the point where crowds of enthusiastic families and onlookers from all over Antwerp are common.

A round of the Avenues may best be made in an open tram. The northern portion, leading from the Entrepôt and the Goods Station as far as the Place de la Commune, has few objects of interest. In the Place de la Commune you pass on the right, the handsome and ornate Flemish Theatre; while, left, the Rue Carnot leads to the Zoological Garden, and to the uninteresting industrial suburb of Borgerhout.

Beyond this comes a Covered Market, left, and then the Place Teniers, with a statue of Teniers. Here the Avenue de Keyser leads, left, to the main Railway Station (Gare de l'Est). Further on, left, the Avenue Marie-Thérèse, with a statue of Matsys, runs to the Park. So, a little later, do the Avenue Louise-Marie, with a statue of Leys, and the Avenue Marie-Henriette, with a statue of Jordaens.

The handsome building, with domed and rounded turrets, on your right, just beyond the last-named Avenue, is the Banque Nationale, intended to contain the public treasure of Belgium in case of war. Here the Chaussée de Malines leads off, S.E., to the uninteresting suburb of Berchem. The heavy new building on the left, a little further S., looking like a French mediæval château, is the Palais de Justice. From this point the Avenue du Sud runs through an unfinished district, occupying the site of the old Citadel (Alva's) past the Museum and the Palais de l'Industrie, to the desolate Place du Sud, with the South Railway Station. You can return by tram along the Quays to the Hôtel-de-Ville and the Cathedral.

If you have plenty of time to spare, you may devote a day to The Rococo Churches.

Most of the Antwerp churches, other than the Cathedral, are late Gothic or Renaissance buildings, disfigured by all the flyaway marble decorations so strangely admired during the 17th and 18th centuries. Few of them deserve a visit, save for a picture or two of Rubens still preserved on their altars. There are one or two, however, usually gone through by tourists, and of these I shall give some brief account, for the benefit of those who care for such things, though I do not think you need trouble about them, unless you have plenty of time, and are specially attracted by the later School of Antwerp.

St. James Church

The most important of these rococo churches is St. James, the principal doorway of which opens into the Longue Rue Neuve. The pleasantest way to reach it, however, is to go from the

Place Verte through the Marché aux Souliers, following the tramway to the Place de Meir.

This broad street (one of the few open ones in Antwerp), lined by baroque Renaissance mansions of some pretensions, has been formed by filling up an old canal. The most imposing building on your right is marked by two angels holding an oval with the letter L. (the king's initial), is the Royal Palace. A little further on, upon the same side of the street, is the House of Rubens's Parents, with his bust above, and an inscription on its pediment signifying the fact in the Latin tongue.

To reach St. James you need not go quite as far down the street as these two buildings. Turn to your left at the Bourse, a handsome modern edifice, standing at the end of what looks like a blind alley. The road runs through it, and it is practically used as a public thoroughfare. The building itself is recent—1869-72—but it occupies the site of a late-Gothic Exchange of 1531, erected by Dominic van Waghemakere.

Image: Parsifall

The present Bourse resembles its predecessor somewhat in style, but is much larger, has an incongruous Moorish tinge, and is provided with a nondescript glass-and-iron roof. Turn to the right at the end of the lane, and continue down the Longue Rue Neuve, which leads you towards St. Jacques, a late-Gothic church, never quite completed. The entrance is not by the façade, but on the S. side, in the Longue Rue Neuve.

The interior is of good late-Gothic architecture, terribly overloaded with Renaissance tombs and sprawling baroque marble decorations. The church was used as the Pantheon (or

Westminster Abbey) for burials of distinguished Antwerp families under the Spanish domination; and they have left in every part of it their ugly and tasteless memorials.

Begin in the south Aisle.

1st chapel. Van Dyck: St. George and the Dragon: mediocre. Above, statue of St. George, to whom angels offer crowns of martyrdom. Good modern marble reliefs of Scenes from the Passion, continued in subsequent chapels.

At the end, Baptistery, with good font.

2nd chapel, of St. Antony. Temptation of St. Antony, by M. De Vos. Italian 17th century Madonna.

3rd chapel, of St. Roch, the great plague-saint. It contains an altar-piece by E. Quellin, angels tending St. Roch when stricken with the plague. Above, the saint with his staff and gourd, in marble, accompanied by the angel who visited him in the desert. On the window wall, relics of St. Roch, patron against the plague. Round this chapel and the succeeding ones are a series of pictures from the Life of St. Roch, by an unknown Flemish master, dated 1517. They represent St. Roch in prison; relieved by the dog; resting in the forest; visited by the angel; etc. (See Mrs. Jameson.) A tomb here has a good Virgin and Child.

4th chapel. Fine old tomb; also, continuation of the History of St. Roch.

5th chapel. More History of St. Roch. On the wall, relics of St. Catherine, who stands on the altar-piece with her sword and wheel; balanced, as usual, by St. Barbara. The chapel is dedicated to St. Anna, who is seen above the altar, with Our Lady and the Infant.

6th chapel. Baptism of Christ, by Michael Coxcie, on the altar. Window wall, M. De Vos: Triptych: Centre, Martyrdom of St. James; to the left, the daughter of the Canaanite; on the right is the daughter of Jairus. (The wings are by Francken.)

The S. Transept has Renaissance figures of the Apostles (continued in the N. transept).

The Choir is separated from the Nave and Transepts by an ugly Renaissance rood-screen.

The Chapel of the Host, in the S. transept, is full of twisting and twirling Renaissance marble-work, well seconded by equally obtrusive modern works in the same spirit.

The Ambulatory has a marble screen, separating it from the Choir, in the worst taste of the Renaissance, with many rococo tombs and sculptures of that period plastered against it.

1st chapel, of the Trinity, has a Holy Trinity for altar-piece, by Van Balen.

The door to the left gives access to the Choir, with an atrocious sculptured High Altar, and carved choir-stalls.

The 2nd and 3rd chapels are uninteresting.

St. James Church Antwerp high altar - Image: Parsifall

The end chapel, behind the High Altar, is the burial chapel of the Rubens family. The altar-piece, painted by Rubens for his family chapel, represents the Madonna and Child adored by St. Bonaventura; close by stands the Magdalen; to the left is a hurrying St. George (reminiscent of the St. Sebastian by Veronese at Venice), and to the right a very brown St. Jerome. The calm of the central picture, with its group of women, is interfered with by these two incongruous male figures. It is like parts of two compositions, joined meaninglessly together. Above are infant cherubs scattering flowers. One would say, Rubens had here thrown together a number of separate studies for which he had no particular use elsewhere. But the colour is most mellow.

5th chapel, of San Carlo Borromeo (who practically replaced St. Roch in later cosmopolitan Catholicism as the chief plague-saint). The altar-piece, by Jordaens, represents the saint invoking the protection of Christ and Our Lady for the plague-stricken in the foreground. Painted for the town almoner.

6th chapel. Three good portraits.

7th chapel. Visitation, by Victor Wolfvoet.

The N. Transept has the continuation of the Twelve Apostles, with two of the four Latin Fathers by the portal (the other two being at the opposite doorway). The Chapel (of Our Lady) resembles that in the S. Transept, and is equally terrible.

North aisle: The 2nd chapel has a fine triptych by M. De Vos, of the Glory of Our Lady. Centre, the Court of Heaven, where the prominent position of Our Lady is unusual, and marks an advanced phase of her cult. In the assemblage of saints below, St. Peter, St. John-Baptist, and many others, may be recognised by their symbols. The left wing has the Calling of Matthew; the right wing features St. Hubert, with the apparition of the crucifix between the horns of the stag. Beneath are good portraits of donors. The fine stained glass window of this chapel is noteworthy. It represents the Last Supper, with donors (1538).

The 3rd chapel, of the Rockox family, has a good triptych, by Van Orley, of the Last Judgment. On the wings are portraits of the donor and family. On the left is Adrian Rockox and sons, with his patron St. Adrian (sword, anvil). On the right is his wife, Catherine with her daughters, and her patroness, St. Catherine.

4th chapel. Good triptych by Balen. Centre, Adoration of the Magi; on the right and left, Annunciation and Visitation. On a tomb opposite, good portraits by Ryckaert.

5th chapel. Triptych, by M. De Vos: Presentation of Our Lady in the Temple. On the left is the The Pagans attempt in vain to burn the body of St. Mark; while on the right is the Martyrdom of St. Lucy.

St. Paul's Church

Another church frequently visited by tourists is St. Paul, formerly belonging to a Dominican Monastery by its side, and situated in a quaint and green district. Do not attempt to go to it direct. Reach it by the Quays, turning to the right near the end of the Northern Promenoir. Over the outer doorway of the court is a rococo relief of St. Dominic receiving the rosary from Our Lady. To the right, as you enter, is an astonishing and tawdry Calvary, built up with rock and slag against the wall of the Transept.

St Paul's church exterior - Image: Bert76

It has, above, a Crucifixion; below, Entombment and Holy Sepulchre. All round are subsidiary scenes: St. Peter, with the crowing cock; Christ and the Magdalen in the Garden; Angels to lead the way, etc. The church itself is an imposing late-Gothic building, made ugly by unspeakable rococo additions.

In the northern Transept is Rubens's *Scourging of Christ, covered: the only thing here really worth seeing. In the N. Aisle, one of his weakest Adorations of the Magi. On the altar of the Sacrament, a so-called "Dispute on the Sacrament," by Rubens: really, the Fathers and Doctors of the Church, especially the Dominicans, represented by St. Thomas Aquinas, in devout contemplation of the Mystery of the Eucharist. The other pictures in the church are relatively uninteresting works of the School of Rubens; the best is a Way to Calvary by Van Dyck.

If you want more Rubenses, you will find a Madonna, with a great group of Augustinian and primitive saints, in the Church of St. Augustine (Rue des Peignes), where there is also a good Ecstasy of St. Augustine by Van Dyck; and in the Church of St. Anthony of Padua (Marché aux Chevaux), a picture, partly by Rubens, representing St. Anthony receiving the Child Jesus from the hands of the Virgin: but I do not recommend either excursion.

Antwerp is strongly fortified, and a moat, filled with water, runs round its existing enceinte. The Old Citadel to the S. has been demolished (its site being now occupied by the Museum and the unfinished quarter in that direction), and a New Citadel erected in the N. The defensive works are among the finest in Europe.

If you wish to see whither Flemish art went, you must go on to Holland. But if you wish to know whence Flemish art came, you must visit the Rhine Towns.

Tournai Cathedral - Image: Stephane Martin

If you are returning to England, via Calais or the Eurostar, before making your journey home stop on the way to see the noble Romanesque and Transitional Cathedral at Tournai. You can easily do this without loss of time by taking the first boat train from Brussels in the morning, stopping an hour or two at Tournai (break permitted with through tickets), and going on by the second train. You can register your luggage through to London, and have no more bother with it. You will then have seen everything of the first importance in Belgium, with the exception of Ypres.

Historical Notes on Belgium

Within this guidebook, the separate Introductions to the various towns deal rather with their origins than offer a blow by blow historical account. I have laid stress chiefly on the industrial and municipal facts, which in Belgium are all-important. I add here, however, a few general notes on the political history of the country as a whole, with a chiefly dynastic bent. These may serve for reference, or at least as reminders; and in particular they should be useful as giving some information about the originals of portraits in the various galleries.

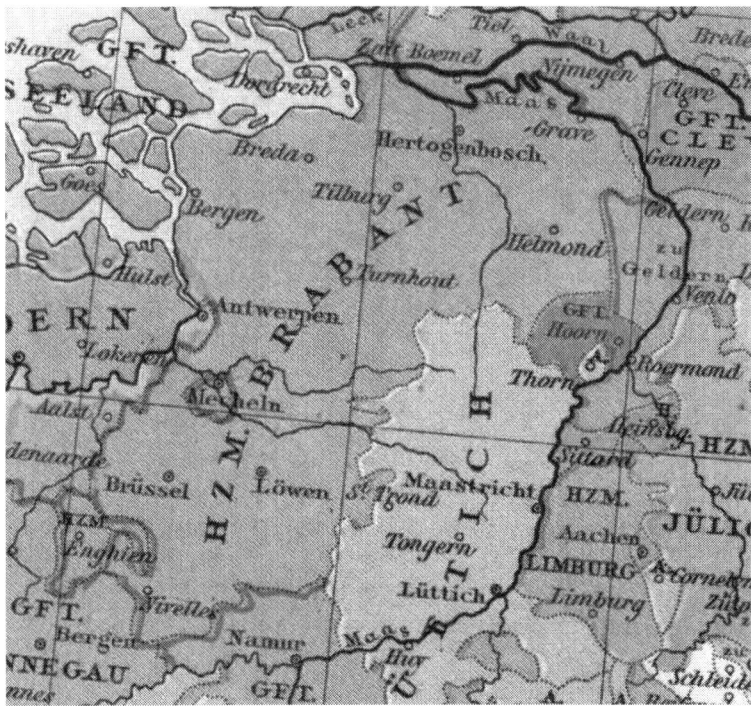

The two portions of the modern kingdom of Belgium with which we are most concerned in this Guide are the County of Flanders and the Duchy of Brabant. The first was originally a fief of France; the second, a component member of the Empire. They were commercially wealthier than the other portions of the Gallo-German borderland which is now Belgium; they were also the parts most affected by the Burgundian princes; on both which accounts, they are still by far the richest in works of art, alike in architecture, in painting, and in sculpture.

The vast Frankish dominions of the Merovingians and of the descendants of Charlemagne—of the Merwings and Karlings, to be more strictly Teutonic—showed at all times a tendency to break up into two distinct realms, known as the Eastern and Western Kingdoms (Austria—not, of course, in the modern sense—and Neustria). These kingdoms were not artificial, but based on a real difference of race and speech. The Eastern Kingdom (Franken or Franconia) where the Frankish and Teutonic blood was purest, became first the Empire, in the restricted sense, and later Germany and Austria (in part). The Western Kingdom (Neustria) where Celtic or Gallic blood predominated, and where the speech was Latin, or (later) French, became in time the Kingdom of France. But between these two Francias, and especially during the period of unrest, there existed a certain number of middle provinces, sometimes even a middle kingdom, known from its first possessor, Lothar, son of Charlemagne, as Lotharingia or Lorraine. Of these middle provinces, the chief northern members were Flanders, Brabant, Hainault, and Liège.

Flanders in the early Middle Ages was a fief of France; it included not only the modern Belgian provinces of East and West Flanders, but also French Flanders, that is to say the Department of the Nord and part of the Pas de Calais. As early as the Treaty of Verdun (843), the land of Flanders was assigned to Neustria. But the county, as we know it, really grew up from the possessions of a noble family at Bruges and Sluys, the head of which was originally known as Forester or Ranger. In 862, the King of France, as suzerain, changed this title to that of Count, in the person of Baldwin Bras-de-Fer (Baldwin I.). Baldwin was also invested with the charge of the neighbouring coast of France proper, on tenure of defending it against the Norman pirates.

In 1006, his descendant, Baldwin IV., seized the Emperor's town of Valenciennes; and having shown his ability to keep his booty, he was invested by the Franconian Henry II. with this district as a fief, so that he thus became a feudatory both of France and of the Empire. He was also presented with Ghent and the Isles of Zealand. Baldwin V. (1036) added to the growing principality the districts of Alost, Tournai, and Hainault. The petty dynastic quarrels of the 11th century are far too intricate for record here; in the end, the domains of the Counts were approximately restricted to what we now know as Flanders proper. A bare list of names and dates must suffice for this epoch:—Baldwin V. (1036-1067); Baldwin VI. (1067-1070); Robert II. (1093-1111); and Baldwin VII. (1111-1119).

After this date, the native line having become extinct, the county was held by foreign elective princes, under whom the power of the towns increased greatly. Among these alien Counts, the most distinguished was Theodoric (in French, Thierry; in German, Dietrich; or in Dutch, Dierick) of Alsace, who was a distinguished Crusader, and the founder of the Chapel of the Holy Blood at Bruges (which see).

Under Baldwin of Hainault (1191-1194) Artois was ceded to France, together with St. Omer and Hesdin. Henceforth, Ghent superseded Arras as the capital. Baldwin IX. (1194-1206) became a mighty Crusader, and founded the Latin Empire of Constantinople. Indeed, the Crusades were largely manned and managed by Flemings. He was followed in Flanders by his two daughters, Johanna and Margaret, under whose rule the cities gained still greater privileges. Margaret's son, Guy de Dampierre, was the creature of Philippe IV. of France, who endeavoured to rule Flanders through his minister, Châtillon. The Flemings answered by just revolt, and fought the famous Battle of the Spurs near Courtrai, already described, against the French interlopers (see Bruges). In 1322, Louis de Nevers (Louis I.) became Count, and provoked by his Gallicising and despotic tendencies the formidable rebellion under Van Artevelde (see Ghent). The quarrel between the league of burghers and their lord continued more or less during the reigns of Count Louis II. (1346) and Louis III., who died in 1385, leaving one daughter, Margaret, married to Philip the Bold (Philippe-le-Hardi) of Burgundy.

The political revolution caused in Flanders and Brabant by the accession of the Burgundian dynasty was so deep-reaching that a few words must be devoted to the origin and rise of this powerful family, a branch of the royal Valois of France. The old Kingdom of Burgundy had of course been long extinct; but its name was inherited by two distinct principalities, the Duchy of Burgundy, which formed part of France, and the County of Burgundy (Franche Comté), which was a fief of the Empire. In the 14th century, a new middle kingdom, like the earlier Lotharingia, seemed likely to arise by the sudden growth of a practically independent power in this debatable land between France and Germany.

Anonymous portrait of John le Bon

In 1361, the Duchy of Burgundy fell in to the crown of France; and in order, as he thought, to secure its union with the central authority, John the Good of France (Jean-le-Bon), during the troublous times after the Treaty of Bretigny, conferred it as a fief upon his son, Philippe de Valois (Philip the Bold, or Philippe-le-Hardi) who married Margaret of Flanders, thus uniting two of the greatest vassal principalities of the French crown. In 1385, on the death of Louis III., Philip succeeded to the County of Flanders, now practically almost an independent state. After him reigned three other princes of his family.

John the Fearless (Jean-sans-Peur, 1404-1419) will be remembered by visitors to Paris as the builder of the Porte Rouge at Notre-Dame de Paris. Philip the Good (Philippe-le-Bon, 1419-1467) was the patron of Van Eyck and Memling. (His portrait by Roger van der Weyden is in the Antwerp Gallery.) Charles the Bold (Charles-le-Téméraire, 1467-1477) raised the power of the house to its utmost pitch, and then destroyed it. (His portrait by Memling is in the Brussels Gallery.) Contrary, however, to the belief of John the Good, the princes of the Valois dynasty in Burgundy, instead of remaining loyal to the crown of France, became some of its most dangerous and dreaded rivals.

All these Dukes, as French princes, played at the same time an important part in the affairs of France. They also won, by marriage, by purchase, by treaty, or by conquest, large territories within the Empire, including most of modern Belgium and Holland, together with much that is now part of France. They were thus, like their Flemish predecessors, vassals at once of the Emperor and the French king; but they were really more powerful than either of their nominal over-lords; for their central position between the two jealous neighbours gave them great advantages, while their possession of the wealthy cities of the Low Countries made them into the richest princes in mediæval Europe. It was at their opulent and ostentatious court that Van Eyck and Memling painted the gorgeous pictures which still preserve for us some vague memory of this old-world splendour. At the same time, the increased power of the princes, who could draw upon their other dominions to suppress risings in Flanders, told unfavourably upon the liberties of the cities. The Burgundian dominion thus sowed the seeds of the Spanish despotism.

Jean-sans-Peur was murdered by the Dauphin, afterwards Charles VII.; and this cousinly crime threw his son, Philippe-le-Bon, into the arms of the English. It was the policy of Burgundy and Flanders, indeed, to weaken the royal power by all possible means. Philip supported the English cause in France for many years; and it was his defection, after the Treaty of Arras in 1435, that destroyed the chances of Henry VI. on the Continent. The reign of Philippe-le-Bon, we saw, was the Augustan age of the Burgundian dynasty. (Fully to understand Burgundian art, however, you must visit Dijon as well as Brabant and Flanders.) Under Charles the Bold, the most ambitious prince of the Burgundian house, the power of the Dukes was raised for a time to its highest pitch, and then began to collapse suddenly. A constant rivalry existed between Charles and his nominal suzerain, Louis XI. It was Charles's dream to restore or re-create the old Burgundian kingdom by annexing Lorraine, with its capital, Nancy, and conquering the rising Swiss Confederacy.

He would thus have consolidated his dominions in the Netherlands with his discontinuous Duchy and County of Burgundy. He had even designs upon Provence, then as yet an independent county. Louis XI. met these attempts to create a rival state by a policy of stirring up enemies against his too powerful feudatory. In his war with the Swiss, Charles was signally defeated in the decisive battles at Granson and Morat, in 1476. In the succeeding year, he was routed and killed at Nancy, whither the Swiss had gone to help René, Duke of Lorraine, in his effort to win back his Duchy from Charles. The conquered Duke was buried at Nancy, but his body was afterwards brought to Bruges by his descendant, the Emperor Charles V., and now reposes in the splendid tomb which we have seen at Notre-Dame in that city.

This war had important results. It largely broke down the power of Burgundy. Charles's daughter, Mary, kept the Low Countries and the County of Burgundy (Imperial); but the Duchy (French) reverted to the crown of France, with which it was ever after associated. The scheme of a great Middle Kingdom thus came to an end; and the destinies of the Low Countries were entirely altered.

We have next to consider the dynastic events by which the Low Countries passed under the rule of the House of Hapsburg. In 1477, Mary of Burgundy succeeded her father Charles as Countess of Flanders, Duchess of Brabant, etc. In the same year she was married to Maximilian of Austria, King of the Romans, son of the Emperor Frederic III. (or IV.). Maximilian was afterwards elected Emperor on his father's death. The children of this marriage were Philip the Handsome (Philippe-le-Beau, or le-Bel; Philippus Stok), who died in 1506, and Margaret of Austria. Philip, again, married Johanna (Juana) the Mad, of Castile, and thus became King of Castile, in right of his wife. The various steps by which these different sovereignties were cumulated in the person of Philip's son, Charles V., are so important to a proper comprehension of the subject that I advise you seek out a family tree illustration in other to fully comprehend their significance and centrality.

During the lifetime of Maximilian, who was afterwards Emperor, Mary, and her son Philippe-le-Beau, ruled at first in the Low Countries (for the quarrel between Maximilian and Bruges over the tutorship of Philippe, see p. 27). After the death of Isabella of Castile, Ferdinand retired to Aragon, and Philippe ruled Castile on behalf of his insane wife, Juana. Philippe died in 1506, and his sister, Margaret of Austria, then ruled as Regent in the Netherlands (for Charles) till her death in 1530. Charles V., born at Ghent in 1500, was elected to the Empire after his grandfather, Maximilian I., and thus became at once Emperor, King of Spain, Duke of Austria, and ruler of the Low Countries.

(In 1516 he succeeded Ferdinand in the Kingdom of Spain, and in 1519 was elected Emperor.)

The same series of events carried the Netherlands, quite accidentally, under Spanish rule. For Charles was an absolutist, who governed on essentially despotic principles. His conduct towards Ghent in 1539 brought affairs to a crisis. The Emperor, in pursuance of his plans against France, had demanded an enormous subsidy from the city, which the burgesses constitutionally refused to grant, meeting the unjust extortion by open rebellion. They even entered into negotiations with François Ier; who, however, with the base instinct of a brother absolutist, betrayed their secret to his enemy the Emperor. Charles actually obtained leave from François to march a Spanish army through France to punish the Flemings, and arrived with a powerful force before the rebellious city. The Ghenters demanded pardon; but Charles, deeply incensed, entered the town under arms, and took up his abode there in triumph.

Alva, his ruthless Spanish commander (portrait in the Brussels Gallery), suggested that the town should be utterly destroyed; but the Emperor could not afford to part with his richest and most populous city, nor could even he endure to destroy his birth-place. He contented himself with a terrible vengeance, beheading the ringleaders, banishing the minor patriots, and forfeiting the goods of all suspected persons. The city was declared guilty of lèse-majesté, and the town magistrates, with the chiefs of the Guilds, were compelled to appear before Charles with halters round their necks, and to beg for pardon. The Emperor also ordered that no magistrate of Ghent should ever thenceforth appear in public without a halter, a badge which became with time a mere silken decoration. The privileges of the city were at the same time abolished, and the famous old bell, Roland, was removed from the Belfry.

Thenceforth Charles treated the Netherlands as a conquered Spanish territory. He dissolved the monastery of St. Bavon, and erected on its site the great Citadel, which he garrisoned with Spaniards, to repress the native love of liberty of the Flemings (see Ghent). In subsequent risings of the Low Countries, the Spaniards' Castle, the stronghold of the alien force, was the first point to be attacked; and on it depended the issue of freedom or slavery in the Netherlands. Charles also established the Inquisition, which is said to have put to death no fewer than 100,000 persons.

In 1555, the Emperor abdicated in favour of his son Philip, known as Philip II. of Spain. But his brother Ferdinand, to whom he had resigned his Austrian dominions, was elected Emperor (having been already King of the Romans) as Ferdinand I. From his time forth, the Empire became more exclusively German, so that its connexion with Rome was almost forgotten save as a historic myth, degenerating into the mere legal fiction of a Holy Roman Empire, with nothing Roman in it. Thus, the Netherlands alone of the earlier Burgundian heritage remained in the holding of the Austrian kings of Spain, who ruled them nominally as native sovereigns, but practically as Spaniards and aliens by means of imported military garrisons.

Philip II.—austere, narrow, domineering, fanatical—remained only four years in the Netherlands, and then retired to Spain, appointing his half-sister, Margaret of Parma (illegitimate daughter of Charles V.), regent of the Low Countries (1559-1567). She resided in the Ancienne Cour at Brussels. Her minister, Granvella, Bishop of Arras, made himself so unpopular, and the measures taken against the Protestants were so severe, that the cities, ever the strongholds of liberty, showed signs of revolution. They objected to the illegal maintenance of a Spanish standing army, and also to the Inquisition. In April, 1567, as a consequence of the discontents, the Duke of Alva was sent with 10,000 men as lieutenant-general to the Netherlands, to suppress what was known as the Beggars' League (Les Gueux), now practically headed by the Prince of Orange (William the Silent). Alva entered Brussels with his Spanish and Italian mercenaries and treacherously seized his two suspected antagonists, Count Egmont and Count Hoorn.

The patriotic noblemen were imprisoned at Ghent, in the Spaniards' Castle, were condemned to death, and finally beheaded in the Grand' Place at Brussels. (For fuller details of the great revolutionary movement thus inaugurated, see Motley's Rise of the Dutch Republic, and Juste's Le Comté d'Egmont et le Comté de Hornes.) Alva also established in Brussels his infamous "Council of Troubles," which put to death in cold blood no less than 20,000 inoffensive burghers. His cold and impassive cruelty led to the Revolt of the United Provinces in 1568—a general movement of all the Spanish Netherlands (as they now began to be called) to throw off the hateful yoke of Spain. Under the able leadership of William of Orange, the Flemings besieged and reduced the Spaniards' Castle at Ghent. In the deadly struggle for freedom which ensued, the Northern Provinces (Holland), aided by their great natural advantages for defence among the flooded marshes of the Rhine delta, succeeded in casting off their allegiance to Philip. They were then known as the United Netherlands. The long and heroic contest of the Southern Provinces (Belgium) against the Spanish oppressor was not equally successful.

A desperate struggle for liberty met with little result, and the Spanish sovereigns continued to govern their Belgian dominions like a conquered country. In 1578, Alessandro Farnese, Duke of Parma (son of Margaret), was sent as Governor to the Netherlands, where he remained in power till 1596. In the prosecution of the war against the Northern Provinces (Holland) he besieged Antwerp, and took it after fourteen months in 1585. In the "Spanish Fury" which followed, Antwerp was almost destroyed, and all its noblest buildings ruined. Nevertheless, under Parma's rule, the other cities recovered to a certain extent their municipal freedom; though the country as a whole was still treated as a vanquished province.

The next great landmark of Belgian history is the passage of the Spanish Netherlands under Austrian rule. The first indefinite steps towards this revolution were taken in 1598, when Philip II. ceded the country as a fief to his daughter the Infanta Isabella

(Clara Isabella Eugenia) on her marriage with Albert, Archduke of Austria, who held the provinces as the Spanish Governor. (Portraits of Albert and Isabella by Rubens in the Brussels Gallery.) The new rulers made the country feel to a certain extent that it was no longer treated as a mere disobedient Spanish appanage. After the troubles of the Revolt, and the cruel destruction of Antwerp by Parma, trade and manufactures began to revive.

Albert and Isabella were strongly Catholic in sentiment; and it was under their régime that the greater part of the rococo churches of Antwerp and other cities were built, in the showy but debased taste of the period, and decorated with large and brilliantly-coloured altar-pieces. They also induced Rubens to settle in the Netherlands, appointed him Court painter, and allowed him to live at Antwerp, where the trade of the Low Countries was still largely concentrated. During their vice-royalty, however, Brussels became more than ever the recognised capital of the country, and the seat of the aristocracy.

After Albert's death in 1621, the Netherlands reverted to Spain, and a dull period, without either art or real local history, supervened, though the wars of the 17th and 18th centuries were in great part fought out over these unfortunate provinces, "the cockpit of Europe."

The campaigns of Marlborough and Prince Eugene are too well-known as part of English and European history to need recapitulation here. At the end of the War of the Spanish Succession, the Peace of Rastadt, in 1714, assigned the Spanish Netherlands to Austria, thus entailing upon the unhappy country another hundred years of foreign domination.

Nevertheless, the Austrian Netherlands, as they were thenceforth called (in contradistinction to the "United Netherlands" or Holland), were on the whole tolerably well governed by the Austrian Stadtholders, who held their court at Brussels, and who were usually relations of the Imperial family. Few memorials, however, of Maria Theresa, of Joseph II., or of Léopold II. now exist in Belgium, and those few are not remarkable for beauty. It was during this relatively peaceful and law-abiding time, on the other hand, that the Upper Town of Brussels was laid out in its existing form by Guimard. As a whole, the Belgian provinces were probably better governed under Austrian rule than under any other régime up to the period of the existing independent and national monarchy.

The French Revolutionists invaded Belgium in 1794, and committed great havoc among historical buildings at Bruges and elsewhere. Indeed, they did more harm to the arts of the Netherlands than anybody else, except the Spaniards and the modern "restorers." They also divided Belgium into nine departments; and Napoleon half sneeringly, half cynically, justified the annexation on the ground that the Low Countries were the alluvial deposit of French rivers. The Belgian States formed part of Napoleon's composite empire till 1814, when these Southern Provinces were assigned by the Treaty of London to Holland. In 1815, during the Hundred Days, the Allied Armies had their headquarters at Brussels, and the decisive battle against Napoleon was fought at Waterloo. The Congress of Vienna once more affirmed the union of Belgium with Holland; they remained as one kingdom till the first revolutionary period in 1830.

The Southern Provinces then successfully seceded from the Dutch monarchy: indeed, the attempted fusion of semi-French and Catholic Belgium with purely Teutonic and Protestant Holland was one of those foredoomed failures so dear to diplomacy. A National Congress elected Léopold of Saxe-Coburg as King of the Belgians (Roi des Belges), and the crown is now held by his son, Léopold II. For nearly seventy years Belgium has thus enjoyed, for the first time in its history, an independent and relatively popular government of its own choosing. The development of its iron and coal industries during this epoch has vastly increased its wealth and importance; while the rise of Antwerp as a great European port has also done much to develop its resources. At the present day Belgium ranks as one of the most thickly populated, richest, and on the whole most liberal-minded countries of Europe. Its neutrality is assured by the Treaty of London, and its army exists only to repel invasion in case that neutrality should ever be violated.

Much of the country suffered greatly during the two World Wars of the 20th century. The First World War, which saw Belgium as a bulwark against the military offenses of the German Empire, saw great damage and bombardment upon the civic centres, with Antwerp particularly badly damaged in the conflict. Many towns, such as Ypres, would become inextricably associated with the carnage and conflict.

The famed retrieval of the Ghent altarpiece and its panels

The Second World War was, fortuitously, less damaging upon the many artistic and architectural attainments around the country. The occupied cities avoided catastrophic damage, the hardship mainly wrought by the citizenry rather than the established, physically manifest culture. Matters were both helped and hindered by the attention to art by the fascist invaders: while more fastidious with art than a typical aggressor, the Nazis would also set about hiding them. Over the course of years after the war, a large proportion of artworks were successfully restored or retrieved. Most notably of all was the retrieval of the Ghent Alterpiece from a salt mine in Altausee after the hostilities ended. Having been placed there by Axis forces under orders from Hitler, the recovered panels were displayed to great media attention at the time. The entire escapade was given a recent treatment in Hollywood, in the motion picture *The Monuments Men*.

Given the immensity and scale of the death, many soldiers and war dead were buried in Flanders. The area of Flanders Fields were particularly associated with the First World War, with the poppies growing there becoming synonymous with the bloodshed. An American cemetery bearing the name Flanders Field is where a total of 368 soldiers were buried, and has become a noted visitor destination for those interested in modern wartime history.

Across Belgian cities, comparatively faithful renovation projects ensued after the conclusion of World War 2. Accessibility to the major civic and cultural centres of Belgium became easier with the aid of modern advances in transportation, while dedicated art historians within and outside the city universities successfully brought the myriad artworks to justifiably good housing. Successive renovations, improved means of storage, and better education on the fragility of the works described – together with a general absence of conflict – mean the past seventy and more years have seen the twin Flemish treasures of art and architecture treated with relative fastidiousness. It is hoped that this happy state of affairs persists well into the 21st century and beyond, to the benefit and promulgation of fine art and culture.

Printed in Great Britain
by Amazon